# English for Business Studies

## A course for Business Studies and Economics students

**Third Edition**



**Student's Book**

Ian MacKenzie

CAMBRIDGE
UNIVERSITY PRESS

CAMBRIDGE UNIVERSITY PRESS
Cambridge, New York, Melbourne, Madrid, Cape Town,
Singapore, São Paulo, Delhi, Tokyo, Mexico City

Cambridge University Press
The Edinburgh Building, Cambridge CB2 8RU, UK

www.cambridge.org
Information on this title: www.cambridge.org/9780521743419



First published 1997
Second Edition 2002
Third Edition 2010
5th printing 2011

Printed in the United Kingdom at the University Press, Cambridge

*A catalogue record for this publication is available from the British Library*

ISBN 978-0-521-74341-9 Student's Book
ISBN 978-0-521-74342-6 Teacher's Book
ISBN 978-0-521-74343-3 Audio CD Set

# Thanks

Although only one name appears on the cover of this book, I need to thank a great many people for their help and hard work, beginning with Cambridge University Press commissioning editor Chris Capper.

Stephanie Ashford, Helen Bicknell, Anna Glinska, Joy Godwin, Graham Jones and Dominique Macabies gave helpful feedback on the previous edition. The outline of this edition was worked out with Chris Capper, Will Capel and Chris Willis.

Will Capel was the development editor, while Chris Willis also made suggestions for the first half of the book and Joy Godwin for the second. Alison Silver also provided ideas throughout, and expertly and good-humouredly prepared the manuscripts for production. Martin Crowdy's expertise was tapped for the units on accounting and finance. All of the editors will find some of their ideas in the book – though I probably scoffed at them at first before managing to convince myself they'd been my ideas all along!

Will Capel set up most of the UK interviews, and Pete Kyle expertly recorded them, with an extraordinarily large microphone on the end of a pole. One other recording was produced by James Richardson. Pete Kyle also produced and edited the CDs. My thanks go to all the interviewees, who graciously gave us their time and shared their expertise with us: John Antonakis, Olga Babakina, Richard Barker, Martin Beniston, Charles Cotton, Carlo de Stefanis, Denis Frucot, Janine George, Melissa Glass, Alan Goodfellow, Anna-Kim Hyun-Seung, Lakshmi Jaya, Michael Kitson, Teresa La Thangue, Alison Maitland, Tony Ramos, Chris Smart, Krishna Srinivasan, Saktiandi Supaat and Rory Taylor. Thanks also go to the writers whose texts I have used, and the cartoonists whose work (mostly from *The New Yorker*) brightens up the pages.

Thanks are also due to Chris Doggett for dealing with permissions, Hilary Luckcock for finding the photographs, Linda Matthews at Cambridge University Press for arranging the production schedule, Wild Apple Design who can and do turn sows' ears into silk purses (as the saying doesn't go), and Kevin Doherty for porof-raeding. Prospective thanks go out to all of Cambridge University Press's sales and marketing people.

I've dedicated previous books to my children, but this time I have to revert to the equally traditional apology-to-partner paragraph: sorry, Kirsten, for the surliness that went with many months of writing a book while also working full-time and taking on too many other commitments. (Oddly, she doesn't believe my assurances that this will never happen again!)

Ian MacKenzie

September 2009

# Contents

# Introduction to the learner

*English for Business Studies* is a reading, listening, speaking and writing course for learners with at least an upper-intermediate level of English (Common European Framework for Languages level B2) who need to understand and express the key concepts of business and economics. It covers the most important areas of management, production, marketing, finance and macroeconomics.

This course aims to:

- present you with the language and concepts of business and economics found in books, journals, newspapers and magazines, and on websites
- develop your comprehension of business and economics texts
- develop your listening skills in the fields of business and economics
- provide you with opportunities to express business concepts both verbally and in writing, by reformulating them in your own words while summarizing, analysing, criticizing and discussing ideas.

Most of the units contain four components:

1. An informative reading text giving an overview of a particular topic, introducing key concepts, and including a lot of relevant technical vocabulary, plus a variety of comprehension and vocabulary exercises and discussion activities. Some of the texts come from newspapers and books about business or economics.
2. Listening activities, mostly based on interviews with business people, economists and other experts. The listening material includes British, American, Australian and South African voices, but also speakers from several European and Asian countries. Listening to non-native speakers of English is important as much of the English you will hear in your professional life will be spoken by people who don't have English as their first language.
3. Speaking activities including discussions, case studies, role plays and presentations.
4. Writing activities including summaries, emails, memos and reports.

If you are using this book in a class with a teacher, it will give you lots of opportunities to discuss ideas and issues with other learners (in pairs or small groups), and to develop and defend your own point of view.

If you are using this course on your own, you will still be able to do the reading and listening exercises. You will find the answers to the exercises in the *English for Business Studies Teacher's Book*.

I hope you enjoy using this book.

# Map of the book

| Unit | | Reading | Listening | Speaking | Writing |
|---|---|---|---|---|---|
| **1** | Management | What is management? | MBA students: What makes a good manager? | Case study: Selecting a Chief Operating Officer | Summary; email |
| **2** | Work and motivation | Theory X and Theory Y; 'Satisfiers' and 'motivators' | MBA students: Managers and motivation | Case study: A car manufacturer | Summary; email |
| **3** | Company structure | Wikinomics and the future of companies; Company structure | MBA students: Big and small companies | Presentation: Presenting a company | Notes for a presentation |
| **4** | Managing across cultures | Managing across cultures | MBA students: Managers, authority, and cultural diversity | Role play: Welcoming American colleagues | Autobiographical text |
| **5** | Recruitment | Filling a vacancy; Job applications | John Antonakis (management professor): Job interviews | Role play: A job interview | Curriculum vitae or resume |
| **6** | Women in business | You're fired! *(The Guardian)* | Alison Maitland (writer and journalist): Women in business – a strategic issue | Role play: Do we need more women managers? | Memo or email |
| **7** | The different sectors of the economy | Another cup of tea (David Lodge: *Nice Work*); Manufacturing and services | The business news (radio) | Discussion: Your place in the economy | Business news item |
| **8** | Production | Capacity and inventory; 'The Dell Theory of Conflict Prevention' (Thomas Friedman: *The World Is Flat*) | Alan Goodfellow (IT director): Purchasing and low-cost manufacturing | Role play: Choosing suppliers | Email |
| **9** | Logistics | Pull and push strategies; Supply-chaining (Thomas Friedman: *The World Is Flat*); Supply chain work flow | Alan Goodfellow: Inventory, Kanban and MRP; Leica's supply chain | Case study: Risk analysis | Summary; report |

| Unit | | Reading | Listening | Speaking | Writing |
|---|---|---|---|---|---|
| **10** | Quality | Total Quality Management | Denis Frucot (hotel manager): Customer care and quality in a hotel | Role play: A hotel chain in trouble | Email |
| **11** | Products | Products and brands | Melissa Glass (juice bar director): Smoothies and a juice bar | Case study: Researching a product concept | Report |
| **12** | Marketing | The product life cycle; Marketing is everything (Regis McKenna: *Harvard Business Review*) | Melissa Glass: Promoting a juice bar | Case study: Promoting a new product | Description of distribution channels |
| **13** | Advertising | Advertising and viral marketing | Radio commercials | Scripting a radio commercial | Summaries; radio commercial |
| **14** | Banking | Banks and financial institutions; The subprime crisis and the credit crunch | Tony Ramos (HSBC): Commercial banking; Anna-Kim Hyun-Seung (expert on business ethics): Microfinance | Role play: Microfinance | Minutes of a meeting |
| **15** | Venture capital | A business plan | Chris Smart (venture capitalist): Investing in start-ups | Role play: Investing in start-ups | Summary |
| **16** | Bonds | Bonds; How to profit from bonds (*The Guardian* and *The Independent*) | Teresa La Thangue (Financial Services Authority): Bonds and subprime mortgages | Case study: Investing in funds | Report |
| **17** | Stocks and shares | Stocks and shares; Hedge funds (Geraint Anderson: *Cityboy*) | A financial news report (radio) | Role play: Investing a client's money | |
| **18** | Derivatives | Spread-betting (*Times Online*) | Teresa La Thangue: Hedge funds and structured products | Role play: Financial instruments | Training memo |
| **19** | Accounting and financial statements | Google Inc.'s financial statements | Richard Barker (senior lecturer in accounting): Valuing assets | Role play: Presenting a company's results | |

| Unit | | Reading | Listening | Speaking | Writing |
|---|---|---|---|---|---|
| **20** | Market structure and competition | Market structure | Charles Cotton (IT consultant): Companies and clusters | Case study: Encouraging clusters | Briefing document |
| **21** | Takeovers | Takeovers, mergers and buyouts | Rory Taylor (Competition Commission): Market investigations | Role play: Is this company restricting competition? | Summary |
| **22** | Government and taxation | The role of government (Milton and Rose Friedman: *Free to Choose*) | Michael Kitson (senior lecturer in international macroeconomics): Government intervention | Presentation: Taxation and government spending | Presentation or report |
| **23** | The business cycle | What causes the business cycle?; Keynesianism and monetarism | Michael Kitson: Consumption and the business cycle; Keynesianism | Discussion: Government intervention | |
| **24** | Corporate social responsibility | Profits and social responsibility | Anna-Kim Hyun-Seung: Socially responsible investment; Stakeholder groups | Role play: Problems at a clothes manufacturer | Report |
| **25** | Efficiency and employment | Reorganizing the postal service | Anna-Kim Hyun-Seung: Efficiency, the number of employees, training and productivity | Role play: Reorganizing the postal service | Report |
| **26** | Exchange rates | Exchange rates | Michael Kitson: Currency flows and the Tobin Tax; Developing Africa | Case study: A currency transaction tax | Summary |
| **27** | International trade | Education and protection (Ha-Joon Chang, economist) | Michael Kitson: Free trade and exceptions | Presentation: For and against free trade | Presentation or report |
| **28** | Economics and ecology | The economics of climate change (Christian Gollier, economist) | Martin Beniston (professor of climate science): Climate policy | Role play: Recommending an energy policy | Summary |

# 1 Management

## Aims

- Consider what the functions of management are
- Discuss what makes a good manager

## Lead-in

- To what extent is effective management something you are born with, as opposed to a set of skills that can be taught?
- Which business leaders do you admire for their managerial skills? What are these skills?
- Do managers have a good reputation in your country? Or are they made fun of in jokes, cartoons and television series? If so, why do you think this is?

*"Hey, this is brilliant! Where do you get my ideas?"*



- Which of the five famous managers below do you find the most interesting and impressive?

**Akio Morita** co-founded a company in Tokyo in 1946, and later changed its name to Sony. He moved to the US, where he had the original ideas for the Walkman and the video cassette recorder. Sony acquired music and film companies, and developed video games.

While **Jack Welch** was Chief Executive Officer (CEO) of General Electric in the 1980s and 1990s, its market value increased from $14 billion to more than $410 billion. He fired 10% of the company's managers each year.

**Steve Jobs** was first the co-founder and later the CEO of Apple. He was fired from his own company (!) in 1985, and co-founded Pixar Animation Studios, but rejoined Apple in 1997, and helped develop the iPod and the iPhone.

In 1998, **Meg Whitman** joined a start-up company called eBay in Silicon Valley as President and CEO. She resigned ten years later, when it was a hugely successful business, planning to run for Governor of California.

**Carlos Ghosn**, born in Brazil, but a French and Lebanese citizen, became the CEO of the Nissan car company in 2001. In 2005, he also became CEO of Renault. At Nissan, he converted huge debts into huge profits.

## Listening: What makes a good manager? 1.2 1.3

**Listen to two MBA (Master of Business Administration) students at the Judge Business School at Cambridge University talking about management.**

**Who says the things about managers in the table below – Carlo (the first speaker) or Olga (the second)?**

| | Carlo | Olga |
|---|---|---|
| **A good manager should:** | | |
| **1** follow the company's goals | | |
| **2** help subordinates to accomplish their own goals and objectives | | |
| **3** help young colleagues to develop | | |
| **4** know how to lead people | | |
| **5** know how to motivate people | | |
| **6** make a maximum profit for the owners (the shareholders) | | |
| **7** meet the targets they have been set | | |
| **8** successfully execute plans and strategies | | |

Carlo de Stefanis (from Italy)

Olga Babakina (from Russia)

## Discussion: What makes a good manager?

**What do *you* think are the three most important characteristics of a good manager? Are there any qualities or characteristics you would add to the ones mentioned by the MBA students?**

## **Reading:** What is management?

**Read the text summarizing the different functions of management. Which of the qualities mentioned in the Listening exercise do you think are particularly necessary for the five tasks described by Peter Drucker?**

Management is *important*. The success or failure of companies, public sector institutions and services, not-for-profit organizations, sports teams, and so on, often depends on the quality of their managers. But what do managers *do*? One well-known classification of the tasks of a manager comes from Peter Drucker. Drucker was an American business professor and consultant who is often called things like 'The Father of Modern Management'.

Drucker suggested that the work of a manager can be divided into five tasks: *planning* (setting objectives), *organizing, integrating* (motivating and communicating), *measuring performance,* and *developing people.*

- First of all, senior managers and directors set objectives, and decide how their organization can achieve or accomplish them. This involves developing strategies, plans and precise tactics, and allocating resources of people and money.
- Secondly, managers organize. They analyse and classify the activities of the organization and the relations among them. They divide the work into manageable activities and then into individual tasks. They select people to perform these tasks.
- Thirdly, managers practise the social skills of motivation and communication. They also have to communicate objectives to the people responsible for attaining them. They have to make the people who are responsible for performing individual tasks form teams. They make decisions about pay and promotion. As well as organizing and supervising the work of their subordinates, they have to work with people in other areas and functions.
- Fourthly, managers have to measure the performance of their staff, to see whether the objectives or targets set for the organization as a whole and for each individual member of it are being achieved.
- Lastly, managers develop people – both their subordinates and themselves.

A company's top managers also have to consider the future, and modify or change the organization's objectives when necessary, and introduce the innovations that will allow the business to continue. Top managers also have to manage a business's relations with customers, suppliers, distributors, bankers, investors, neighbouring communities, public authorities, and so on, as well as deal with any crisis that arises.

Although the tasks of a manager can be analysed and classified in this fashion, management is not entirely scientific. There are management skills that have to be learnt, but management is also a human skill. Some people are good at it, and others are not. Some people will be unable to put management techniques into practice. Others will have lots of technique, but few good ideas. Excellent managers are quite rare.

## Writing

**Write a brief summary of each of the five tasks listed by Drucker.**

## Vocabulary

**1 Match up the following words and definitions.**

| | |
|---|---|
| **1** consultant | **A** a plan for achieving success |
| **2** crisis | **B** a new idea or method |
| **3** innovation | **C** a person with a less important position in an organization |
| **4** objective (noun) | **D** a person who provides expert advice to a company |
| **5** promotion | **E** a situation of danger or difficulty |
| **6** public sector | **F** something you plan to do or achieve |
| **7** strategy | **G** the section of the economy under government control |
| **8** subordinate | **H** when someone is raised to a higher or more important position |

**2 The text contains a number of common verb–noun combinations. Use the word combinations in the box to complete the sentences below.**

allocate resources    deal with crises    make decisions    perform tasks
measure performance    set objectives    supervise subordinates

1. After an organization has __________ __________ , it has to make sure that it achieves them.
2. Managers have to find the best way to __________ all the human, physical and capital __________ available to them.
3. Some people __________ __________ better on their own while others work better in teams.
4. Managers __________ the work of their __________ and try to develop their abilities.
5. Managers __________ the __________ of their staff to see whether they are reaching their targets.
6. Top managers have to be prepared to __________ __________ __________ if they occur and then have to __________ quick __________ .

## Case study: Selecting a Chief Operating Officer

**Three companies are looking for a senior manager – a Chief Operating Officer who will be responsible for managing the company's day-to-day operations, and making sure that all operations are efficient and effective.**

Company A is a cigarette manufacturer that has to modernize its production systems in order to become profitable, in an industry that has an increasingly bad reputation.

Company B is a software developer that employs a lot of young, creative, talented and rather undisciplined people.

Company C is a private television channel whose objective is to broadcast programmes that get as big an audience as possible, in order to maximize advertising revenue.

**Which of the following candidates might be the most suitable for the positions on page 13? Here are some extracts from their letters.**

Candidate 1

My skills involve helping businesses achieve their objectives. Throughout my career I have ensured that my subordinates successfully executed the strategies developed by senior management, delivered results and maximized revenue.

Candidate 2

I see my main skills as being able to communicate with and motivate people, to help them develop and accomplish their objectives, while also working effectively in teams.

Candidate 3

At this stage in my career, I see myself in a challenging new position that involves setting objectives and deciding how the organization can achieve them. I would then concentrate on measuring the performance of the staff.

Candidate 4

My career demonstrates an ability to analyse problems, find solutions and implement them. I also have strong communication skills and experience in explaining difficult decisions to employees, investors, journalists, and so on.

## Writing

**Imagine you work for a recruitment agency or a headhunting firm. Write an email of 50–100 words to your boss recommending your choice of candidates for the positions above and outlining the reasons.**

# 2 Work and motivation

## Aims

- Discuss the importance of motivation
- Compare and then summarize various theories of motivation
- Consider the best way to motivate people in specific situations

## Lead-in

One of the most important responsibilities of a manager is to motivate the people who report to him/her. But how? What kind of things motivate you? Which of these motivators would be important for you in your choice of a job? Classify them in order of importance.

- ☐ good remuneration (salary, commission, bonuses, perks)
- ☐ good working relations with your line manager and colleagues
- ☐ good working conditions (a large, light, quiet office; efficient secretaries)
- ☐ job security
- ☐ the possibility of promotion
- ☐ a challenging job
- ☐ responsibility
- ☐ contact with people
- ☐ a belief in what the organization does
- ☐ a job in which you can make a difference
- ☐ opportunities to travel (business class!)
- ☐ long holidays/vacations

*"We don't offer bonuses, but the size of your desk will be adjusted quarterly."*



What other important motivators would you add to this list?

## Discussion: Attitudes to work

**Which of the following statements do you agree with?**

1. People dislike work and avoid it if they can.
2. Work is necessary to people's psychological well-being.
3. People avoid responsibility and would rather be told what to do.
4. People are motivated mainly by money.
5. Most people are far more creative than their employers realize.
6. People are motivated by fear of losing their job.
7. People want to be interested in their work and, given the right conditions, they will enjoy it.
8. Under the right conditions, most people will accept responsibility and will want to realize their own potential.

## **Reading:** Theory X and Theory Y

**The statements on the previous page can be separated into two groups reflecting two very different ways in which employers can treat their employees. Douglas McGregor, an American expert on the psychology of work, summarized these two approaches and named them Theory X and Theory Y. Read the text below and classify the statements according to which theory they support.**

| Statement | 1 | 2 | 3 | 4 | 5 | 6 | 7 | 8 |
|---|---|---|---|---|---|---|---|---|
| Theory | | | | | | | | |

In *The Human Side of Enterprise*, Douglas McGregor outlined two opposing theories of work and motivation. What he calls Theory X is the rather pessimistic approach to workers and working which assumes that people are lazy and will avoid work and responsibility if they can. Consequently, workers have to be closely supervised and controlled, and told what to do. They have to be both threatened, for example with losing their job, and rewarded with incentives, probably monetary ones such as a pay rise or bonuses. Theory X assumes that most people are incapable of taking responsibility for themselves and have to be looked after. It has traditionally been applied, for example, by managers of factory workers in large-scale manufacturing.

Theory Y, on the contrary, assumes that most people have a psychological need to work, and given the right conditions – job security, financial rewards – they will be creative, ambitious and self-motivated by the satisfaction of doing a good job. Theory Y is probably more applicable to skilled professionals and what Peter Drucker called 'knowledge workers' – managers, specialists, programmers, scientists, engineers – than people in unskilled jobs.

McGregor's two theories are based on Abraham Maslow's famous 'hierarchy of needs'. Theory X relates to the basic, 'lower order' needs at the bottom of the hierarchy, such as financial security, while Theory Y relates to 'higher order' needs such as esteem (achievement, status and responsibility) and self-actualization (personal growth and fulfilment) that can be pursued if basic needs are satisfied.

McGregor is widely considered to have laid the foundations for the modern people-centred view of management. However, Maslow spent a year studying a Californian company that used Theory Y, and concluded that there are many people who are not looking for responsibility and achievement at work. There will always be people with little self-discipline, who need security and certainty and protection against the burden of responsibility, so it is impossible to simply replace the 'authoritarian' Theory X with the 'progressive' Theory Y.

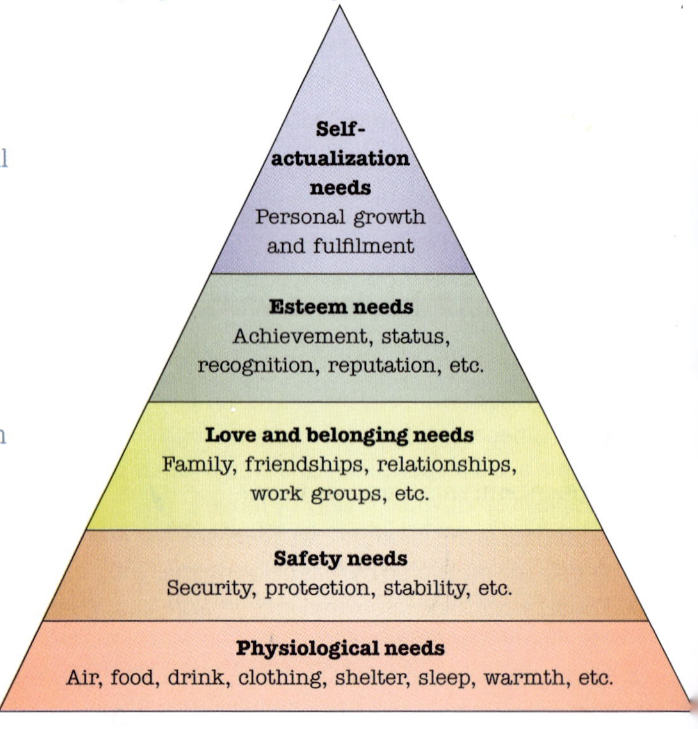


### Comprehension

**Read the text again and answer these questions.**

1 According to Theory X, why do employees have to be closely controlled?
2 According to Theory Y, why should employers give their workers responsibilities?
3 Why did Maslow criticize Theory Y?

## Writing

**Now write a summary of Theories X and Y, using no more than 50 words for each.**

## Discussion

- **In your working experience, even if it is only weekend or temporary summer holiday jobs, have your supervisors seemed to believe in Theory X or Theory Y?**
- **What would *you* do to try to motivate subordinates who did *not* want to take responsibilities at work, and who had uninteresting, repetitive jobs?**

## **Reading:** 'Satisfiers' and 'motivators'

**Another well-known theorist of the psychology of work, Frederick Herzberg, has argued that good working conditions are not sufficient to motivate people. Read the text and find out why.**

It is logical to suppose that things like good labour relations, good working conditions, job security, good wages, and benefits such as sick pay, paid holidays and a pension are incentives that motivate workers. But in *The Motivation to Work*, Frederick Herzberg argued that such conditions – or 'hygiene factors' – do not in fact motivate workers. They are merely 'satisfiers' – or, more importantly, 'dissatisfiers' where they do not exist. Workers who have them take them for granted. As Herzberg put it, 'A reward once given becomes a right.' 'Motivators', on the contrary, include things such as having a challenging and interesting job, recognition and responsibility, promotion, and so on. Unless people are motivated, and *want* to do a good job, they will not perform well.

However, there are and always will be plenty of boring, repetitive and mechanical jobs, and lots of unskilled workers who have to do them. How can managers motivate people in such jobs? One solution is to give them some responsibilities, not as individuals but as part of a team. For example, some supermarkets combine office staff, the people who fill the shelves, and the people who work on the checkout tills into a team and let them decide what product lines to stock, how to display them, and so on. Other employers encourage job rotation, as doing four different repetitive jobs a day is better than doing only one. Many people now talk about the importance of a company's shared values or corporate culture, with which all the staff can identify: for example being the best hotel chain, or hamburger restaurant chain, or airline, or making the best, safest, most user-friendly, most ecological or most reliable products in a particular field. Unfortunately, not all the competing companies in an industry can seriously claim to be the best.

## Comprehension

**Are these sentences true or false?**

1. Herzberg argued that 'hygiene factors' motivate workers.
2. Challenging jobs and responsibility are hygiene factors.
3. Some unskilled jobs will always be boring and repetitive.
4. Workers might be motivated by having responsibilities as part of a team.
5. Job rotation can make a day's work more interesting.
6. You can always motivate workers by telling them that they work for the best company in the field.

## Vocabulary

**Find the words in the text that mean the following.**

1 interactions between employers and employees, or managers and workers
2 knowing that there is little risk of losing one's employment
3 money paid (per hour or day or week) to manual workers
4 advantages that come with a job, apart from pay
5 things that encourage people to do something
6 to be raised to a higher rank or better job
7 without any particular abilities acquired by training
8 regularly switching between different tasks
9 a company's shared attitudes, beliefs, practices and work relationships

## Discussion

- **How convinced are you by Herzberg's theory of satisfiers and motivators?**

Krishna Srinivasan (from Malaysia)

Carlo de Stefanis (from Italy)

Saktiandi Supaat (from Singapore)

## Listening 1: Managers and motivation 1.4

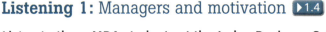

**Listen to three MBA students at the Judge Business School talking about motivation, and answer these questions.**

1 According to Krishna, what is the disadvantage of working in auditing compared to banking?
2 How did Krishna's company retain its staff?
3 According to Carlo, what is the main reason why people leave their jobs?
4 According to Carlo, does a company need a set of motivational incentives?
5 What does Carlo say a manager needs to do to engage his/her team?
6 According to Saktiandi, do the staff have to do what the organization wants, or vice versa?
7 What does Saktiandi say about the importance of influencing and convincing people?

## Discussion

- **Would you stay in a job for the reason Krishna suggests?**
- **Would you leave (or have you left) a company for the reason that Carlo says is the most common?**
- **Would working for a manager who has influence within the organization motivate you?**

Janine George
(from South Africa)

## Listening 2: Out-of-work activities 1.5

**Listen to Janine George, another MBA student at Cambridge, talking about motivation, and answer these questions.**

1. How long had some of Janine's operational team been working in their jobs?
2. What kind of company is Janine talking about?
3. How long are the working days?
4. How did she find the workers when she arrived at the company?
5. What did she do to rectify the situation?
6. What did she find out at the meetings?
7. What examples does she give of out-of-work activities that the company was able to draw on to motivate staff?
8. What was the lesson of this experience for Janine?
9. Janine talks about activities that are not 'related to the bottom line'. What does this mean?
10. Janine says managers should 'think outside of the box'. What does she mean by this and why do you think she apologizes for using this expression?

*"I'll start thinking outside the box when the box is empty."*



## Case study: A car manufacturer

**The senior managers of a car manufacturer sense an increasing level of dissatisfaction among most of the different categories of staff. The company has the following groups of employees, with different benefits:**

- senior management (high salaries, free company cars, company restaurant, 25 days annual holiday)
- designers (high salaries, free company cars, company canteen, 20 days holiday)
- production-line workers (fixed salary, company canteen, 20 days holiday)
- secretarial and administrative staff (salary according to experience, company canteen, 20 days holiday)
- sales representatives (low fixed salary plus commission on sales, 20 days holiday)
- canteen and restaurant staff (20 days holiday, free meals in canteen)
- cleaners (hourly wages, plus 8.33% extra as holiday pay, no other benefits)

**The managers meet to consider ways of increasing staff motivation. They have to decide whether any of the following suggestions would be appropriate for different groups of employees:**

- building sports facilities (e.g. a gymnasium, tennis courts)
- establishing a profit-sharing programme
- giving longer paid holidays (such as an extra day for every year worked over ten years)
- offering cars at discount prices
- offering career training
- offering early retirement
- paying a higher salary
- paying productivity bonuses
- reducing the working week (e.g. to 35 hours)
- setting up a crèche for employees' pre-school-age children
- spending some money on decorating the organization's premises (e.g. with plants, pictures)
- subsidizing the staff canteen

**In small groups, decide whether to implement any of these suggestions.**

## Writing

**Write an email of no more than 100 words to the CEO, outlining and justifying your choice of improved benefits.**

# 3 Company structure

## Aims

- Consider the different ways of organizing work
- Discuss potential conflicts between different departments in a company
- Compare the differences between large and small companies

## Lead-in

- Which department – production, finance, accounting, marketing, sales, human resources, etc. – of an organization do you think is the most interesting to work in?
- What reasons can you think of for why departments get into conflict with each other?
- Is it better to have one immediate boss or to work for more than one manager?
- Do you prefer to work alone or in a team?
- Is it more motivating to be responsible to someone for your work, or responsible for people who report to you?

## Reading: Wikinomics and the future of companies

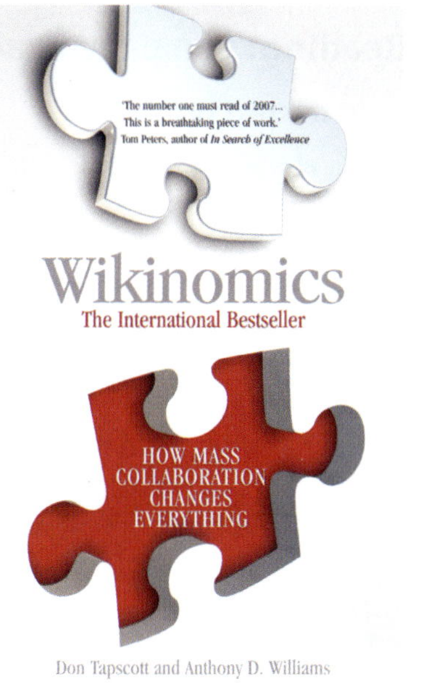


**Read the text below and answer this question.**

- How is the world of organized work changing?

Experts are forecasting that in the future companies will use the Internet and the 'wikinomics' principle (from wiki, the Hawaiian word for 'quick', and economics). This means collaborating with people outside the traditional corporate structure, letting people around the world cooperate to improve an operation or solve a problem, and paying them for their ideas. This is an extension of the trend of outsourcing: transferring some of the company's internal functions or operations or jobs to outside suppliers, rather than performing them 'in-house'. In other words, companies will no longer need to get all their knowledge from their own full-time employees.

Here are two examples from Don Tapscott and Anthony D. Williams' book *Wikinomics: How Mass Collaboration Changes Everything*:

Red Lake, a Canadian gold mine, wasn't finding enough gold and was in danger of closing down. Then its chief executive heard a talk about Linus Torvalds, the inventor of Linux, the open-source computer operating system. He decided to put the company's secret geological data on the Internet, and offered prize money to experts outside the company who could suggest where undiscovered gold might lie. People around the world recommended 110 targets, and 80% of them turned out to contain gold. The company's value has risen from $100 m to $9 bn.

If Procter & Gamble is looking for a new molecule to clean red wine off a shirt, it can use its own scientists. But there are 1.5 million other scientists around the world. The company can offer a payment for a successful solution, and see if a scientist somewhere comes up with one.

- In what ways could your organization, company or business school use the wikinomics principle?
- What do you think are the disadvantages of the wikinomics principle?

## Vocabulary

**Before reading about traditional company organization, check your understanding of some basic terms by matching up the following words and definitions.**

autonomous to delegate function hierarchy or chain of command
line authority to report to

1 hierachy ______ a system of authority with different levels, one above the other, e.g. a series of management positions, whose holders can make decisions, or give orders and instructions

2 function ______ a specific activity in a company, e.g. production, marketing, finance

3 autonomous ______ independent, able to take decisions without consulting someone at the same level or higher in the chain of command

4 line authority ______ the power to give instructions to people at the level below in the chain of command

5 to report to* ______ to be responsible to someone and to take instructions from them

6 to delegate ______ to give someone else responsibility for doing something instead of you

* „zu arbeiten"

## Reading: Company structure

**Read the text below.**

### The chain of command

Traditionally, organizations have had a hierarchical or pyramidal structure, with one person or a group of people at the top, and an increasing number of people below them at each successive level. This is sometimes called line structure. There is a clear chain of command running down the pyramid. All the people in the organization know what decisions they are able to make, who their line manager (or boss) is (to whom they report), and who their immediate subordinates are (over whom they have line authority, and can give instructions to).

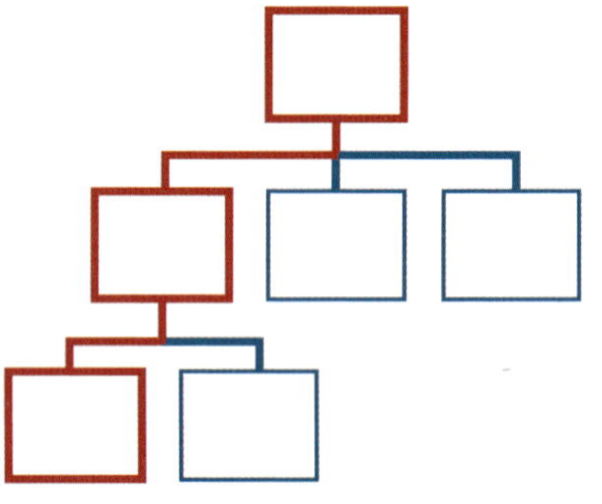

### Functional structure

Yet the activities of most organizations are too complicated to be organized in a single hierarchy. Most large manufacturing companies, for example, have a functional structure, including, among others, specialized production, finance, marketing, sales, and human resources departments. This means, for instance, that the production and marketing departments cannot take financial decisions without consulting the finance department. Large organizations making a range of products are often further divided into separate operating divisions.

A disadvantage of functional organization is that people are often more concerned with the success of their own department than that of the company as a whole, so there are permanent conflicts between, say, finance and marketing or marketing and production over what the objectives are.

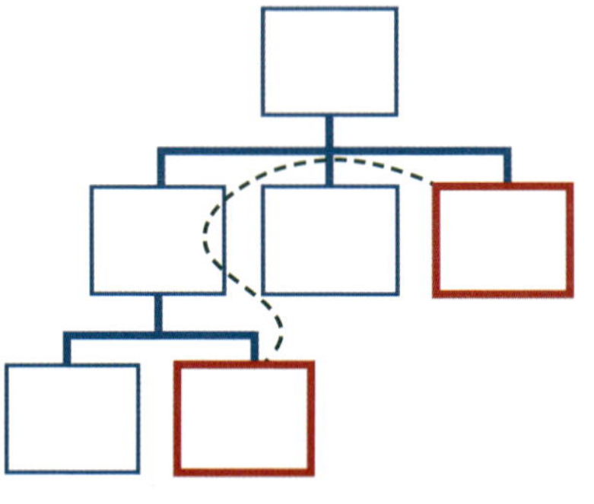

### Flattening hierarchies and delegating responsibility

A problem with very hierarchical organizations is that people at lower levels can't take important decisions, but have to pass on responsibility to their boss. However, the modern tendency is to reduce the chain of command, take out layers of management, and make the organization much flatter. Advanced IT systems have reduced the need for administrative staff and enabled companies to remove layers of workers from the structure. Many companies have also been forced to cut back and eliminate jobs in recessions. Typically, the owners of small firms want to keep as much control over their business as possible, whereas managers in larger businesses who want to motivate their staff often delegate decision making and responsibilities to other people.

### Matrix management

Another way to get round hierarchies is to use matrix management, in which people report to more than one superior. For example, a product manager with an idea could deal directly with the managers responsible for a certain market segment and for a geographical region, as well as managers in the finance, sales and production departments. Matrices involving several departments can become quite complex, so it is sometimes necessary to give one department priority in decision making.

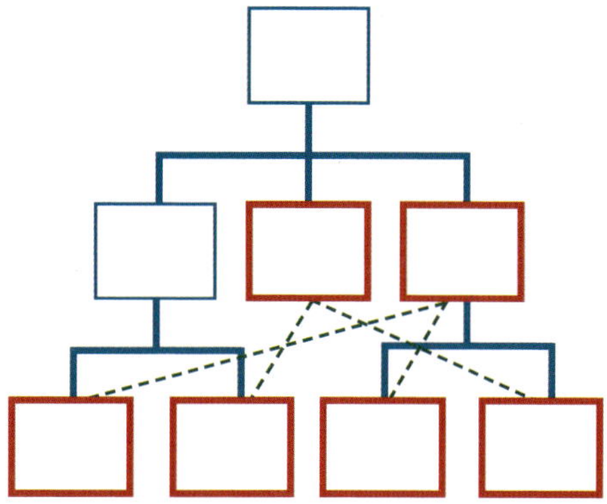

### Teams

A further possibility is to have wholly autonomous, temporary groups or teams that are responsible for an entire project, and are split up as soon as it is successfully completed. But teams are not always very good at decision making, and usually require a strong leader.

## Comprehension

1 What is the main advantage of a chain of command?
2 Why is it not usually possible to organize a large organization in a single hierarchy?
3 In what ways can dividing a business functionally cause problems?
4 What factors might lead companies to flatten their hierarchies?
5 According to the text, what kind of managers might not want to delegate decision making? small firms
6 What is the potential disadvantage of matrix management systems? complexity, long time ~~efficient~~ make decision
7 Under what circumstances might teams not be effective? if no strong leader

## Vocabulary

**Match up the verbs and nouns below to make common word combinations.**

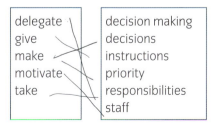

| | |
|---|---|
| delegate<br>give<br>make<br>motivate<br>take | decision making<br>decisions<br>instructions<br>priority<br>responsibilities<br>staff |

## Discussion: Incompatible goals

**The text mentions the often incompatible goals of the finance, marketing and production (or operations) departments. Classify the following strategies according to which department would probably favour them.**

1 a factory working at full capacity
2 a large advertising budget
3 a large sales force earning high commission
4 a standard product without optional features
5 a strong cash balance
6 a strong market share for new products
7 generous credit facilities for customers
8 high profit margins
9 large inventories to make sure that products are available
10 low research and development spending
11 machines that give the possibility of making various different products
12 self-financing (using retained earnings rather than borrowing)

## Listening: Big and small companies ▶1.6

**Listen to three MBA students at the Judge Business School talking about different-sized companies, and answer the questions.**

Krishna Srinivasan (from Malaysia)

Carlo de Stefanis (from Italy)

Olga Babakina (from Russia)

1 Why does Krishna say that company size isn't important? What does he say is important?
2 Why does Carlo recommend university graduates to start in big companies?
3 What does Carlo say are the differences between big and small companies?
4 What does Olga say is more important than company size?
5 What does Olga say about big companies?

## Discussion: Big and small companies

- **How far do you share Krishna and Olga's points of view, and agree with Carlo's advice?**
- **What other benefits of working in a large company can you think of?**
- **What other reasons might make someone prefer to work in a small company?**

- **Do the following statements refer to the advantages of working in a big or a small company?**
  1. You are less likely to be affected by a big reorganization or downsizing or merger or takeover.
  2. You are often responsible for a variety of different tasks.
  3. You can actually see the result of your contribution to the firm.
  4. You can be proud of working for a company with a national or international reputation.
  5. You can become more specialized in your work.
  6. You can probably change departments if you have problems with your colleagues.
  7. You have more independence, and you don't always have to wait for permission from a superior.
  8. You know everyone in the company and the atmosphere is friendlier.
  9. You may be able to go and work in a foreign subsidiary.
  10. Your company will probably be in a better position in an economic downturn or recession.

## Presentation

**Write notes for a short presentation on your company or a company you would like to work for. You should mention:**

- what it does:
  *It designs / makes / provides / distributes / sells / offers / organizes / invests in*, etc.
- where it is located:
  *It has offices / branches / subsidiaries / factories / stores*, etc. in ...
- how it is structured and whether this a reason for its success:
  *It consists of / includes / is divided into / is organized in*, etc.
- why you want to work for this company.

**Then give a short presentation to the class.**

*"I do my part."*

# 4 Managing across cultures

## Aims

- Consider the importance of cultural differences for people working across cultures
- Discuss the conflict between globalization and localization

## Lead-in

- What are the advantages and disadvantages of a multinational company adapting its management methods to the local culture in each country in which it operates?
- To what extent is the culture of your country similar enough to those of neighbouring countries to have the same management techniques? Or do they have very different attitudes to work, hierarchy, organization, and so on? If so, what are these differences?

Krishna Srinivasan (from Malaysia)

Carlo de Stefanis (from Italy)

## Listening 1: Managers and authority ▶1.7

**Listen to two MBA students at the Judge Business School talking about cultural differences, and answer the questions.**

1 What concepts does Krishna say are important in management in Singapore?
2 How does this differ from the European countries Krishna mentions?
3 From what Carlo says, how similar is Italy to Switzerland and Britain?

- **In your country, what gains respect within an organization, long service or achievement?**
- **Can a young, dynamic, aggressive manager with an MBA rise quickly in the hierarchy?**

Richard Lewis

## Reading: Managing across cultures

**Richard Lewis is well known in the field of cross-cultural communication and the author of *When Cultures Collide: Managing Successfully Across Cultures* and *The Cultural Imperative: Global Trends in the 21st Century*. Read about his model of three types of cultures, and answer the questions.**

Managing a global multinational company would obviously be much simpler if it required only one set of corporate objectives, goals, policies, practices, products and services. But local differences – cultural habits, beliefs and principles specific to each country or market – often make this impossible. The conflict between globalization and localization has led to the invention of the word 'glocalization'. Companies that want to be successful in foreign markets have to be aware of the local cultural characteristics that affect the way business is done.

Richard Lewis has classified different cultures according to three 'poles' representing different types of behaviour. Businesspeople in 'linear-active' cultures such as Britain, the USA and Germany are generally organized and rational, try to act logically rather than emotionally, plan in advance, and like to do one thing at a time. They believe in respecting rules, regulations and contracts, and so are what the Dutch theorist Fons Trompenaars calls 'universalists' – they think rules apply to everybody. They are not afraid of confrontation but will compromise when necessary to achieve a deal. They are essentially individualist.

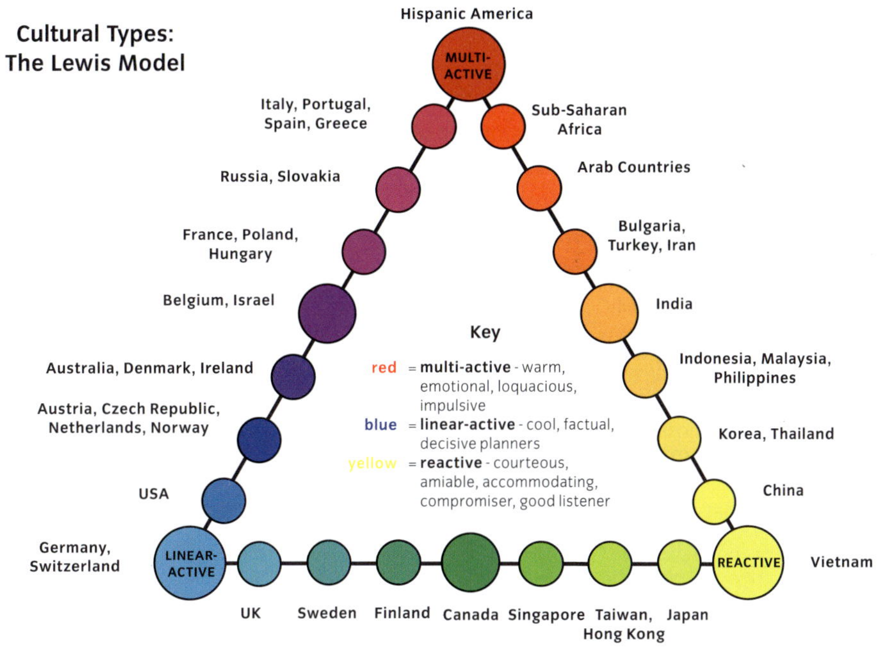


From Richard D. Lewis, *The Cultural Imperative: Global Trends in the 21st Century* (Yarmouth, Maine: Intercultural Press, 2003)

'Multi-active cultures' in Southern Europe, Latin America and Africa attach more importance to feelings, emotions and intuition, and relationships and connections. People like to do many things at the same time; they are flexible, good at changing plans and happy to improvise. They believe in social or company hierarchy, and respect status. They are essentially collectivist, and also what Trompenaars calls 'particularist' – they believe that personal relationships and friendships should take precedence over rules and regulations.

People in 'reactive cultures' in Asia prefer to listen to and establish the other's position, and then react to it. They try to avoid confrontation, and don't want to 'lose face' or cause someone else to. They rarely interrupt speakers and often avoid eye contact. They try to formulate approaches which suit both parties.

Other countries have cultures which show combined characteristics of two of these poles, and can be represented along the sides of a triangle.

## Comprehension

1 Why is it important for companies to be aware of local cultures?
2 What are the differences between individualists and collectivists?
3 Who is more likely to think: 'I'll let them speak first.'
4 Who is more likely to say, about other people: 'They can't be trusted because they will always help their friends or family' – universalists or particularists?
5 Who is more likely to say: 'Oh, you can't trust them; they wouldn't even help a friend'?

## Vocabulary

**Match the words in the box with the definitions below.**

| | | | | | |
|---|---|---|---|---|---|
| collectivist | compromise | confrontation | connections | eye contact | glocalization |
| improvise | interrupt | intuition | logic | lose face | status |

**1** an invented word combining worldwide and regional concerns
**2** thought based on reason and judgement rather than feelings and emotions
**3** a face-to-face disagreement or argument
**4** reducing demands or changing opinions in order to agree
**5** understanding or knowing without consciously using reason
**6** people of influence or importance with whom you are associated
**7** to do something when necessary without having already planned it
**8** respect, prestige or importance given to someone
**9** believing that the group is more important than the individual
**10** to be humiliated or disrespected in public
**11** to cut into someone else's turn to speak
**12** looking directly at the people you are talking or listening to

## Discussion: Managing across cultures

**1** To what extent do you agree that it is possible to sum up national characteristics in a few words? Is there usually some (or a lot of) truth in such stereotypes? Or, on the contrary, do you find such stereotyping dangerous?
**2** If your country is not shown on the diagram, where do you think it should be situated? If your country is shown, do you agree?
**3** Would you say that you, personally, were individualist or collectivist? Particularist or universalist?
**4** What about the majority of people in your country?
**5** Which of the following working practices would be effective or damaging in your country? Why?
 **a** the principle of 'pay-for-performance' for sales representatives – the more they sell, the more they get paid
 **b** having a competition for the 'Employee of the month'
 **c** having a matrix management system
 **d** extensive teamwork

## **Writing:** You and your influences

**Write a short text (100–150 words) explaining which *five* of the factors listed below you think have had the most influence on your behaviour and attitudes. Put them in order of priority.**

- Nature: your genes or DNA, the characteristics you inherited from your parents and were born with, your emotional and physical make-up
- Your family environment in early life
- Your friends and social life, the things you do in your free time
- Primary or secondary school, teachers, and what you learnt
- Higher education: college, university, teachers, colleagues, the subjects you studied (or are studying)
- Your job

- The culture of your particular company
- Your colleagues: the people in your team or department
- Your colleagues: the kind of people who work in your specific area of work
- The characteristics that are considered typical of your country, arising from geography, climate, history, religion, the political, social and economic system, and so on

**Then in groups, report on your choices and explain them.**

## Listening 2: Managers and cultural diversity 1.8

**What would happen if the world became truly globalized, and everyone travelled, or worked with people from different cultures? Listen to three MBA students at the Judge Business School, and answer the questions.**

1. What does Lakshmi describe as an advantage of international management schools?
2. Why does Janine say that American businesspeople now have different attitudes?
3. What skill or ability does Janine say allows people to be more self-aware?
4. What expression does Carlo use to describe corporations becoming truly international?
5. What does Carlo say happens if companies move a lot of executives and managers around?
6. What is the saying or proverb that Janine quotes? What does it mean?
7. What is the Japanese version of this saying that she heard? What does it mean?

**Lakshmi Jaya (from India)**

**Janine George (from South Africa)**

**Carlo de Stefanis (from Italy)**

## Role play: Welcoming American colleagues

**You work in a multinational organization. You have been given the responsibility of mentoring two American colleagues who are coming to work in your office. You have been asked to help them settle in to their new workplace by preparing a short document outlining the general practices they can expect to find when they are living and working in your country.**

**The document could include information about working practices in your office, as well as practical information about your city or country, including advice about transport, and conventions such as tipping in taxis and restaurants.**

**In groups discuss what should go in this document and then present these ideas to the rest of the class.**

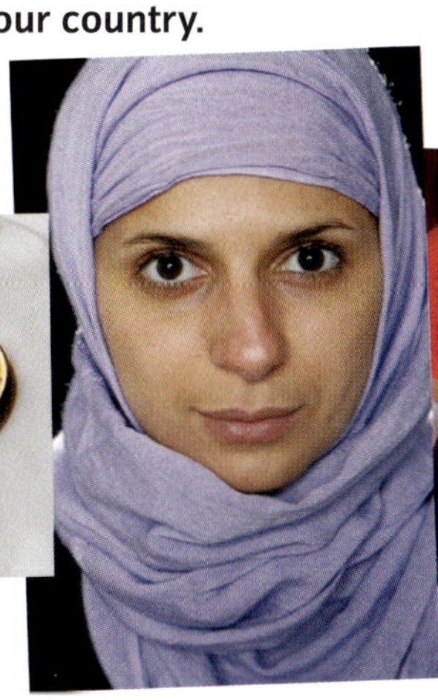

# 5 Recruitment

## Aims

- Consider the different stages of recruitment
- Discuss what makes a good CV/resume and covering letter
- Compare good and bad practice in preparing a CV and covering letter

## Lead-in

- How long do you think recruiters in a Human Resources department spend looking at the average CV or resume for a junior position?
- If 100 young people with very similar experience and qualifications apply for a job, which elements in a CV or resume make a difference, and might lead to a job interview?
- How many times do you expect to apply for a new position during your career? How many times do you expect to change jobs?
- What does this cartoon say about the recruitment process?

*"Résumés over there."*



## Reading: Filling a vacancy

**When employees 'give notice', i.e. inform their employer that they will be leaving the company as soon as their contract allows, in what order should the company carry out the steps listed below? Complete the chart opposite with the letters A–I.**

**A** either hire an employment agency (or for a senior post, a firm of headhunters), or advertise the vacancy

**B** establish whether there is an internal candidate who could be promoted (or moved sideways) to the job

**C** examine the job description for the post, to see whether it needs to be changed (or indeed, whether the post needs to be filled)

**D** follow up the references of candidates or applicants who seem interesting

**E** invite the shortlisted candidates for an interview

**F** make a final selection

**G** receive applications, curricula vitae / resumes and covering letters, and make a preliminary selection (a shortlist)

**H** try to discover why the person has resigned

**I** write to all the other candidates to inform them that they have been unsuccessful

### Vocabulary note

*Curriculum vitae* or *CV* is used in Britain; *resume* is more common in America. *Resume* used to be spelled the French way, with accents on the letter *e* (*résumé*), but it is now often spelled without them. The word has three syllables and the final *e* is pronounced: rez-oo-may /ˈrezʊmeɪ/.

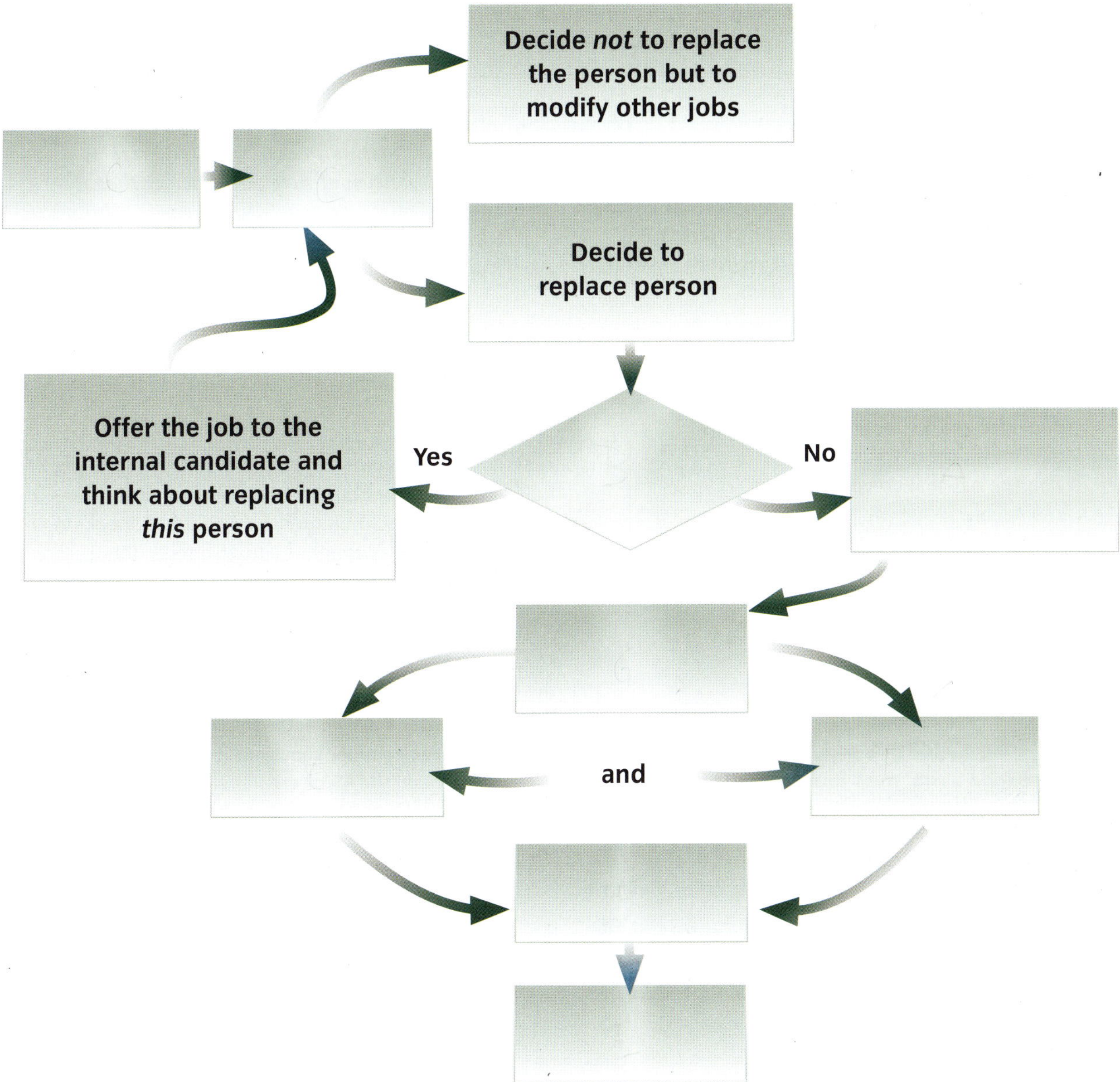


## Reading and discussion: Job applications

When applying for your first job as a business graduate, you are probably only one of many applicants, most of whom will have similar experience and qualifications to your own.

- How can you get your name onto the shortlist for interviews when applying for a job?
- What can you do to impress the organization which is hiring staff?

**Which of the following extracts from a CV/resume and different application letters would help the candidate to get an interview, and why?**

1

Dear Sir or Madam,
I am writing to express my interest in applying for the position of Community Fundraiser advertised in the Morning Herald on 13 May, 20--. I am looking for a challenging entry-level position that allows me to contribute my skills and experience to fundraising for a charity.

2

*I am writing to express my interest in the position of Account Manager that was advertised on your website on 13 February, 20--. I'm extremely interested in this position, and I would like the opportunity for an interview in which I could show you how I can benefit your company.*

3

I play for the university basketball team. We have won the national university championship for the past two years.

4

My parents are French and Russian, and because they work for a multinational company, I grew up in four different countries. I did all my schooling in English, but I speak and write fluent French and Russian. I can also read Italian, Spanish, Romanian and most Slavic languages.

5

Employment

Saturdays, 2006–8, and full-time July 2008, Right Price food store, West End Avenue (shelf-filling).

July 2009, Port Authority Bus Terminal, 8th Avenue (bus cleaner).

August 2009, grape-picking, Napa Valley, California.

November 2009–June 2010, tourist guide at St Patrick's Cathedral, 5th Avenue (Saturdays).

6

**I have travelled extensively during my last three summer vacations. In 20--, I travelled around the Mediterranean (Spain, France, Italy, Greece) for ten weeks. In 20--, I went to Florida for a month, and I spent six weeks in Bali in 20--. I have consequently met a great many people from many different cultures, and I am absolutely convinced that these cross-cultural experiences make me suitable for a position in international marketing, and that your company would have a great deal to gain from employing me.**

7

*Dear Mr/Ms [name],*

*I am applying for the Sales Associate position which we discussed during the Career Fair at the National University in [city] on [date]. I believe my varied sales experience and my Bachelor's degree in Business Administration are an excellent match to the qualifications you are seeking.*

*As you can see from the enclosed resume, I have sold a variety of products in part-time jobs during my studies and have worked in sales departments during two internship positions. This experience, as well as my oral and written communication skills, should prove valuable in increasing [company name]'s sales volume. I am enthusiastic about pursuing a career in sales with [company name] because of your varied product line and international distribution network.*

8 I am seeking a challenging position with a progressive company that will offer opportunities for professional growth and advancement. I am results orientated, a self-starter and a team player. I'm a good communicator, and have excellent project management, interpersonal, people management and negotiation skills. I can also work unsupervised. I am committed, creative, competitive, ambitious, adaptable and flexible. I am good at meeting deadlines, solving problems and making decisions.

9 As you will see from my CV, I scored an average of 91% in my university examinations (94% at the end of the first year, 87% in my second year, and 92% in my final year exams). I stayed on to do a post-graduate degree in finance and banking, and was encouraged to extend my Master's dissertation into a doctorate, which I have done in the past ten months. I expect to be awarded my PhD in six weeks' time.

## Notes on CVs/resumes

- European and Asian CVs generally include photos; US resumes do not.
- British CVs include personal details such as date of birth, marital status, number of children, etc.; US resumes do not.
- British CVs usually include outside work interests (sports, travelling); US ones sometimes don't.
- Your CV should be totally honest; you should emphasize your strengths, but not lie about your experience or skills. It should not say anything that contradicts what you've put on your Facebook page, or similar!
- Leave out information that is irrelevant or that could give some people a chance to discriminate against you (personal details such as your height, weight, health, country of origin, religion, etc.).
- Limit your CV to a maximum of two pages.
- Lay your CV out neatly.
- Check for grammatical and spelling or typographical errors, and do not rely on an automatic spell checker.
- Get someone to check your CV before you send it.

*"Mind if I take this, chief?*
*It's a headhunter who's been after me for weeks."*

**Here is a model skeleton for a CV.**

- **Is this how you would present a CV in your own language?**

# Curriculum Vitae

**Name**
**Address**
**Phone number(s)** [daytime phone number, with the international access code]
**Email address**
**Date of birth** [write the month, e.g. 11 January 1990, because 11/1 = 11 January (GB) and 1 November (US)]
**Nationality** [always begins with a capital letter]
**Marital status** [Single or Married]

**OBJECTIVE**
[what you want to do next is more important than what you have done] e.g. A job in international marketing; A traineeship in trading; Production assistant; Account manager; Financial analyst

**WORK EXPERIENCE**
[in reverse order, starting with the most recent]
e.g. Part-time Technical Assistant, Economics Faculty IT Centre (September 2009–June 2010) (repair and maintenance of department, faculty, staff, and student computers)

**EDUCATION or QUALIFICATIONS**
[in reverse order, starting with the most recent]
20-- Master's Degree in International Management, Bigtown University (expected date of completion July 20--)
20-- Bachelor's Degree in Business Administration, majoring in Finance, Faculty of Business Administration and Economics, Bigtown University
20-- High School Certificate (specializing in maths and science)

**COMPUTER SKILLS**
e.g. Microsoft Word, Excel and PowerPoint, Lotus Notes and Oracle Financials

**LANGUAGES**
e.g. Fluent in Spanish and English, some knowledge of French and Italian.
*or* Arabic (mother tongue), good knowledge of English, elementary knowledge of Spanish.

**HOBBIES AND INTERESTS**
[ideally, these will include hobbies that demonstrate qualities that are relevant to the job you are applying for]

**REFERENCES [or TESTIMONIALS (US)]**
The following people can provide references:
[names and addresses (and phone numbers or email addresses) of two people]

## Notes on covering letters

- The covering letter explains why you want the job.
- It should be specific to the job you are applying for, adapted to the target organization, and show that you know about its activities.
- It should highlight your skills and achievements, and show how your background, training, work experience and abilities relate to the job you are applying for.
- It should use formal language, and demonstrate that you have good written communication skills.

**Here is a model for a covering letter.**

- **How different would a covering letter be in your language?**
- **Would it be more modest, or more assertive in listing your talents?**

Your address
Your email address

Date (23 May 20--)

Company name
Company address

Dear Mr/Ms (Name),

I am writing to apply for the position of ______ advertised on your company's website. Having read the job description, I believe that my academic record and interpersonal skills make me a strong candidate for the position.

I am a final-year student and will shortly be graduating from ______ University with a BA in Business Administration. Last summer I spent three months gaining practical experience in ______ , during a traineeship (BrE) / internship (AmE) at (organization) in (city). My responsibilities there included organizing / implementing / developing / coordinating / analysing ______ .

As you will see from my CV, last year I spent an exchange semester at the University of ______ . My experience of studying in (language) and working in (country) have taught me how to live and work in different environments, and given me some experience of intercultural communication and working with diverse teams.

I am fluent in ______ and English.

I am available for an interview at your convenience and look forward to hearing from you.

Yours sincerely,

Your handwritten signature
Your name, typed

## Discussion: CVs/resumes and covering letters

- **Why is it normal in some countries *not* to include photos or personal details on a CV/resume?**
- **Should a CV really be *totally* honest? Do you think most people are completely honest?**
- **Why might an employer want to know about your hobbies and interests?**
- **Would you *want* to work for someone who might be prejudiced against your country of origin or religion?**
- **Would you target each covering letter if you were applying to 30 companies?**

## Listening 1: Classifying the interviewee ▶1.9

John Antonakis

**John Antonakis is Professor of Organizational Behaviour at the University of Lausanne. Listen to him talking about how to behave at a job interview, and answer the questions.**

1 What does the saying that John Antonakis quotes mean?
2 What does he say an interviewee should do?
3 How does he demonstrate that the saying is true?

## Listening 2: Confirming first impressions ▶1.10

| | |
|---|---|
| *cue* | a sign or signal for someone to do (or in this case, think or believe) something |

**Listen to John Antonakis talking about the psychology of job interviewers, and answer the questions.**

1 Which of the following things does he say?
  - **A** Interviewers make quick decisions about interviewees because they don't have enough information about them.
  - **B** Interviewees can demonstrate their intelligence and personality in a job interview.
  - **C** Interviewers make judgements on the basis of small signals or cues.
  - **D** Interviewers have a fixed idea in their heads as to what a competent person looks like.
  - **E** Interviewers are biased towards people who resemble themselves.
  - **F** Interviewers can either try to make a candidate succeed or fail.
  - **G** Interviewers will alter incorrect first impressions if a candidate answers questions well.

2 What is 'confirmation bias'?

## Listening 3: Preparing for an interview ▶1.11

**Listen to the third part of the interview and make a list of five things that John Antonakis says interviewees should do either before or during an interview.**

## Discussion: First impressions

- **To what extent do you think that *you* judge people as quickly as Antonakis suggests?**
- **How accurate do you think your first impressions about people usually are?**
- **How could interviewers be trained to be less biased?**

## Further tips for job interviews

**Which five of these tips do you think are the most useful?**

- Research the company thoroughly.
- Have complimentary things to say about the company and its products or services.
- Be confident and enthusiastic.
- Be prepared to talk about your strengths and weaknesses.
- Expect questions about difficult situations you have faced, problems you have solved, etc.
- Have examples of successful experiences with groups or teams.
- If you talk about your hobbies, try to say something interesting and memorable (and not just 'music, cinema, travel').
- Have some questions you can ask the interviewer, such as:
  - Can you tell me more about your training programmes?
  - Can you tell me how performance is measured and reviewed?
  - Are there possibilities of promotion for someone whose results are good?
  - Is the company facing any major challenges I don't know about?

## Role play: A job interview

**You will either interview a candidate for a job or be interviewed. Your teacher will give you a role to prepare. But first:**

1. As a class, select a large, international consumer-goods company (food, clothing, electronics, household goods, etc.), and study its website so that you know what the company does, and why you would want to work for it.
2. Choose one of the three positions advertised on page 143.
3. Make appropriate changes to your own CV so that you would be a serious candidate, and prepare yourself for an interview for the job you have chosen.
   - What kind of questions do you think they will ask?
   - What is the best way to answer them?
   - What do they want to hear / not want to hear? etc.

# 6 Women in business

## Aims

- Consider the importance of women in business
- Discuss attitudes towards women in business today

## Lead-in

- What is the ratio of males to females in your business school or place of work?
- If you are in college, what is the ratio of male to female teachers or professors?
- If you are in work, how many female managers are there, especially at higher levels in the organization?
- Why do you think this is?

## Listening 1: Women in business – a strategic issue (1) 1.12

Alison Maitland

**Alison Maitland is the co-author, with Avivah Wittenberg-Cox, of *Why Women Mean Business: Understanding the Emergence of our Next Economic Revolution*. Listen to her talking about women in business, and answer the questions.**

1 What two reasons does Alison Maitland give for saying that the proportion of women in business is a strategic business issue and not a women's issue?

2 What does she mean by 'talent pool'?

## Listening 2: Women in business – a strategic issue (2) 1.13

**Listen to the next part of the interview, where Alison Maitland gives a third very good reason why companies should have a number of women directors or senior managers. What is it?**

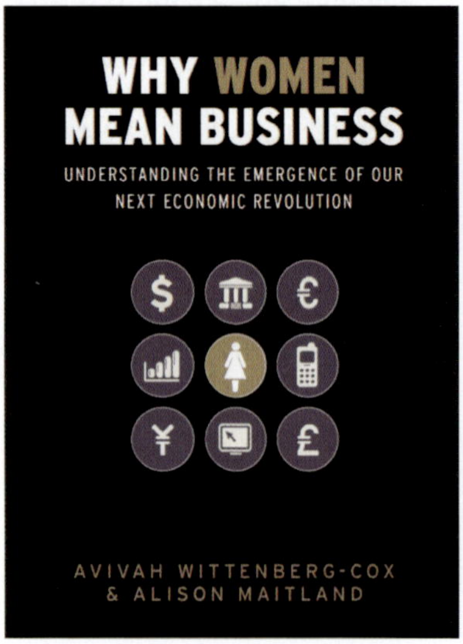


### Vocabulary

**Match the following words and expressions, used by Alison Maitland, with their definitions.**

1 critical mass
2 leadership ranks
3 outperforming
4 profitability
5 return on equity

A doing better than others, financially
B the ability to make a good return on capital invested in the business
C the amount of money a company earns on the investment of its shareholders
D the number of people needed to start and sustain a change
E top levels of management

| 1 | | 2 | | 3 | | 4 | | 5 | |
|---|---|---|---|---|---|---|---|---|---|

## Discussion: The importance of women in business

- **What do the figures about consumer spending decisions made by women (80% in the US, 66% of car purchases in Japan) tell you? What is the situation in your country?**
- **Why do you think that (according to research studies) companies with more than 30% of women on the board of directors or in senior management are so much more profitable than companies without?**

*"I feel like a man trapped in a woman's salary."*

© The New Yorker

## Reading: You're fired!

**Read this extract from an article in the British newspaper *The Guardian*, and answer the questions on the next page.**

# You're fired!

**Imagine you're one of the 13 men on the all-male board of a large company and are told five of you must go to be replaced by women. Unlikely? Not in Norway, where they're enforcing a law that 40% of directors must be female.**

**Yvonne Roberts**

Rolf Dammann, the co-owner of a Norwegian bank, recently had his skiing holiday interrupted by some unwelcome news. The government had published a list of 12 companies accused of breaking the law by failing to appoint women to 40% of their non-executive board directorships. His company, Netfonds Holding ASA, was one of the dirty dozen – attracting international attention.

'I work in a man's world. I don't come across many women and that's the challenge,' Dammann says. 'The law says a non-executive director has to be experienced, and experience is difficult to find in women in my sector. People have had to sack board members they've worked with and trusted for 20 or 30 years, and replace them with someone unknown. That's hard.'

This month, Norway set a new global record. It now has, at 40%, the highest proportion of female non-executive directors in the world, an achievement engineered by the introduction of a compulsory quota. Two years ago, after several years of voluntary compliance had failed to lead to a sufficient number of female board members, 463 'ASAs' – publicly listed companies over a certain size – were told to change the composition of their boards or risk dissolution.

'A woman comes in, a man goes out. That's how the quota works; that's the law,' says Kjell Erik Øie, deputy minister of children and equality, in the centre-left 'Red-Green' coalition government in Oslo. 'Very seldom do men let go of power easily. But when you start using the half of the talent you have previously ignored, then everybody gains.'

In 2002, only 7.1% of non-executive directors of ASAs were female. [...] Business leaders argued that experienced senior women were impossible to find, especially in the oil, technology and gas industries. 'I'm a responsible man,' one CEO told me in Oslo last week. 'I have a duty to do the best I can for our shareholders. I've been forced to appoint two women whom I know are apprentices. Give them ten years and I'd be happy to have them on the board; not now.' [...]

Dammann appointed his two women last June, after what he says was a six-month 'time-consuming' search. He is not a convert to the quota, though.

'I think people will still go to those they have trusted for years, whom they have had to remove from the board,' he says. 'So there will now be a formal and informal system, and that cannot be good for accountability.' [...]

## Comprehension

1 What is the new Norwegian law?
2 What reasons does Rolf Dammann give for not having complied with the new law?
3 What does the CEO say about the two women he has had to appoint as directors?
4 What does Dammann say will happen as a consequence of the new law?

## Vocabulary

**Find words in the article that mean the following:**

1 meet or find unexpectedly or by accident
2 required, obligatory, necessary according to the law
3 an officially imposed number or quantity
4 done by choice, without legal obligation
5 obeying laws or regulations
6 the ending or termination of an organization
7 trainees, people still learning their job
8 someone who changes their beliefs
9 being officially responsible for something

## Discussion: Compulsory quotas

- **What do you think about 'affirmative action' – the imposition of compulsory quotas concerning the number of women board members?**
- **How far do you think affirmative action could also be used for executive board members, and at lower levels in a company?**
- **Should business schools and universities have quotas for female staff and students, or members of ethnic minorities?**

## Questionnaire: Ways of thinking

**Complete the questionnaire opposite about attitudes to job interviews and jobs, and then compare your answers in pairs or groups.**

- **Which of these statements are (more or less) true for you?**
- **Do you think any of these statements reflect mainly masculine or feminine ways of thinking?**

| | Yes | No | Men | Women |
|---|---|---|---|---|
| **1** I'd apply for a job if I thought I covered about 60% of the requirements. | | | | |
| **2** I'd only apply for a job if I thought I covered 100% of the requirements. | | | | |
| **3** I'd always try to negotiate my salary at a job interview. | | | | |
| **4** I'd accept the salary offered at a job interview. | | | | |
| **5** At a job interview, I'd ask: 'What can your company do for my career?' | | | | |
| **6** At an interview, I'd try to show why I deserved the job and what I could do for the company. | | | | |
| **7** I'd lie at a job interview, e.g. about whether I'd be prepared to move abroad in the future. | | | | |
| **8** I wouldn't tell lies at a job interview. | | | | |
| **9** If I do a good job, I will be noticed, promoted and rewarded. | | | | |
| **10** I'd be happy to say that my success is also due to my colleagues, or even to good luck. | | | | |
| **11** Doing a good job is not enough; you have to spend a lot of time telling other people what a good job you're doing. | | | | |
| **12** I prefer relationships between equals to a strict hierarchy. | | | | |
| **13** Hierarchies are necessary, and people obviously want to climb towards the top. | | | | |
| **14** I'd accept a promotion even if I didn't think I was totally ready for it. | | | | |
| **15** If I'm going to succeed and be promoted, someone else will have to lose. | | | | |
| **16** I like to use war metaphors (ready for battle, attack competitors, fight for customers, change tactics, etc.). | | | | |
| **17** I prefer direct, powerful language ('I need you to do this immediately'; 'Come and see me at 11'). | | | | |
| **18** I prefer indirect language ('Sorry, but perhaps you could do it now'; 'Could you come to my office at 11, please?'). | | | | |

## **Role play:** Do we need more women managers?

**The CEO of a large consumer-goods company is worried about the small number of women in senior management positions in the company. He/she has called a meeting of the non-executive directors to discuss what can be done about this. These are people with a long experience in business who oversee the management of the company.**
**Your teacher will give you a role.**

## Writing

**Write a short memo or email (100–150 words) that explains the purpose of the meeting and summarizes the ideas that the CEO thought were the best.**

# 7 The different sectors of the economy

***Aims***

- Consider the different sectors of the economy
- Discuss changes that have taken place in the different sectors of the economy

## **Lead-in:** The economic infrastructure

Identify the most prominent features in these photographs, which illustrate various important elements of the infrastructure of a modern industrialized country.

## **Reading:** Another cup of tea

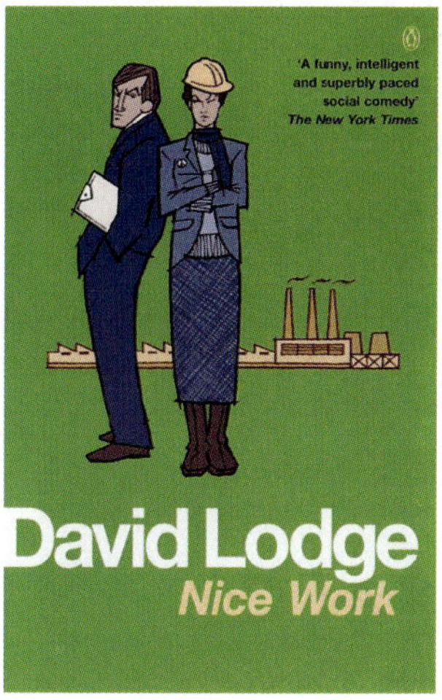


**In this extract from David Lodge's novel *Nice Work*, Robyn Penrose, a university English lecturer, is accompanying Vic Wilcox, the managing director of a manufacturing company, on a business trip to Germany. She looks out of the aeroplane window, and begins to think about the essentially English act of making a cup of tea.**

- **What is the key point that this extract is making about economies?**

Sunlight flooded the cabin as the plane changed course. It was a bright, clear morning. Robyn looked out of the window as England slid slowly by beneath them: cities and towns, their street plans like printed circuits, scattered over a mosaic of tiny fields, connected by the thin wires of railways and motorways. Hard to imagine at this height all the noise and commotion going on down there. Factories, shops, offices, schools, beginning the working day. People crammed into rush hour buses and trains, or sitting at the wheels of their cars in traffic jams, or washing up breakfast things in the kitchens of pebble-dashed semis. All inhabiting their own little worlds, oblivious of how they fitted into the total picture. The housewife, switching on her electric kettle to make another cup of tea, gave no thought to the immense complex of operations that made that simple action possible: the building and maintenance of the power station that produced the electricity, the mining of coal or pumping of oil to fuel the generators, the laying of miles of cable to carry the current to her house, the digging and smelting and milling of ore or bauxite into sheets of steel or aluminium, the cutting and pressing and welding of the metal into the kettle's shell, spout and handle, the assembling of these parts with scores of other components – coils, screws, nuts, bolts, washers, rivets, wires, springs, rubber insulation, plastic trimmings; then the packaging of the kettle, the advertising of the kettle, the marketing of the kettle to wholesale and retail outlets, the transportation of the kettle to warehouses and shops, the calculation of its price, and the distribution of its added value between all the myriad people and agencies concerned in its production. The housewife gave no thought to all this as she switched on her kettle. Neither had Robyn until this moment, and it would never have occurred to her to do so before she met Vic Wilcox.

David Lodge: *Nice Work*

### Comprehension

**In the 20th century, the economy was described as consisting of three sectors:**

- the **primary sector**: agriculture, and the extraction of raw materials from the earth
- the **secondary sector**: manufacturing industry, in which raw materials are turned into finished products
- the **tertiary** or **service sector**: the commercial services that help industry produce and distribute goods to their final consumers, as well as activities such as education, healthcare, leisure, tourism, and so on.

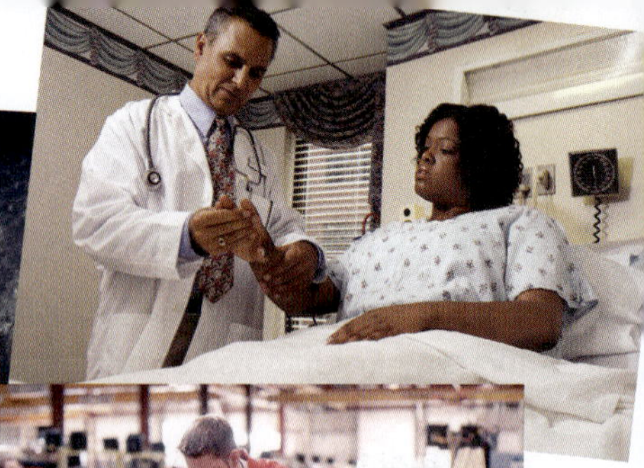

1 In lines 4–7, Robyn sees examples of all three sectors. What are they?
2 The long sentence from lines 11–27 lists a large number of operations belonging to the different sectors of the economy. Classify the 18 following activities from the passage according to which sector they belong to:

| | | |
|---|---|---|
| advertising products | assembling | building |
| calculating prices | cutting metal | digging iron ore |
| distributing added value | laying cables | maintenance |
| marketing products | milling metal | mining coal |
| packaging products | pressing metal | pumping oil |
| smelting iron | transportation | welding metal |

3 Can you think of *three* important activities to add to each list (not necessarily in relation to the kettle)?

## The quaternary sector

**Some people now describe the economy as having a** quaternary sector, **consisting of information services such as computing, ICT (information and communication technologies), consultancy (offering advice to businesses) and R&D (research and development, particularly in scientific fields). Broader definitions add the news media, libraries, universities and colleges, and other intellectual activities including culture generally.**

**In what ways have the activities in the box above been changed by information technology since David Lodge wrote *Nice Work* in the late 1980s?**

## Discussion: Your place in the economy

- **Which sector do you intend to work in or do you already work in? How do you 'fit into the total picture'?**
- **How many people in the tertiary sector have you already spoken to today (travelling to college or work, shopping, eating, and so on)? What about people in the other sectors? When did you last talk to someone who grew or produced food, for example?**
- **What are the (approximate) proportions of the different sectors in your country? How do you expect these proportions to evolve in the future?**

## Reading: Manufacturing and services

**Read the following statements about manufacturing and services in advanced countries.**

- **Which of them are in support of manufacturing in advanced countries, and which are in support of services?**
- **Which of them do you find the most convincing, and why?**

1 A lot of service sector jobs depend on manufacturing industry. Manufacturing companies provide work for accountants, lawyers, designers, marketers, advertisers, salespeople, bankers, engineers, IT specialists, etc.

2 Advanced countries have expertise in higher education, R&D, ICT, business consulting, etc. They should concentrate on these strengths, rather than trying to make things more cheaply than less-developed countries.

3 All the world's major economies – the US, Japan, Germany, France, Britain, Italy, China, etc. – are major manufacturers of exported goods. This obviously needs to continue.

4 Depending on service industries is dangerous; after the financial crisis in 2008, New York and London didn't only lose financial jobs, but also lots of jobs in all the related service industries: law firms, real estate, expensive restaurants, luxury jets, etc. Big cities need factories too.

5 Manufacturing industry will inevitably decline in advanced countries and be replaced by services, because labour costs are too high. Companies will delocalize their manufacturing to low-cost countries.

6 Millions of tourists travel to major cities, and millions of people choose to live in them, because of the arts and entertainment – theatre, music, museums, sport, etc. Manufacturing and heavy industry can and should be done elsewhere.

7 Service functions such as call centres, accounting, writing software, can all be outsourced to companies in cheaper countries. Consequently, advanced countries should concentrate on high-quality manufacturing, which requires skills that cannot be outsourced or delocalized.

### Vocabulary

**Find words in the statements above that mean the following:**

1 products sold to other countries
2 property: buildings such as offices, houses, flats (BrE) or apartments (AmE)
3 work done in return for money
4 to move your factories to another region or country
5 to use other companies to do work your company previously did itself

## **Listening:** The business news ▶ 1.14

**Listen to six business news stories from American radio stations, and complete the chart below.**

| News item | Which industry or industries are mentioned? | Which economic sector or sectors are involved? | Which companies or organizations are named? | Is this good, bad or mixed news for the industry? | What figures are mentioned? |
|---|---|---|---|---|---|
| 1 | | | | | |
| 2 | | | | | |
| 3 | | | | | |
| 4 | | | | | |
| 5 | | | | | |
| 6 | | | | | |

## Writing: The business news

**Write an imaginary business news story (not more than 100 words) involving different industries and economic sectors, and including several figures, and covering everything in the columns.**

# 8 Production

## Aims

- Discuss the process of industrial production
- Consider the global impact of international supply chains

## Lead-in

- What do production and quality managers do?
- What particular skills do you think production and operations managers require? Do you think you have these skills yourself?
- Would you like to work in this field?
- What do you think the objectives of a production department usually are?

*"I'm a local craftsperson – I make money."*
© The New Yorker

## Vocabulary: Industrial production

**Before reading and hearing about industrial production, match up the half-sentences below, which define some basic terms.**

1 **Inventory** (AmE and BrE) or **stock** (BrE) is a company's reserves
2 A **component** is any of the pieces or parts
3 **Capacity** is the (maximum) rate of output
4 **Plant** is a collective word for all the buildings, machines, equipment,
5 **Location** means the geographical situation
6 A **supply chain** is a network of organizations
7 **Outsourcing** means buying products or processed materials
8 **Economies of scale** are the cost savings
9 **Lead time** is the time needed to perform an activity

**A** and other facilities used in the production process.
**B** arising from large-scale production.
**C** from other companies rather than manufacturing them.
**D** involved in producing and delivering goods or a service.
**E** of a factory or other facility.
**F** of raw materials, parts, work in process, and finished products.
**G** such as manufacturing a product or delivering it to a customer.
**H** that can be achieved from a production process.
**I** that make up a product or machine.

| 1 | | 2 | | 3 | | 4 | | 5 | | 6 | | 7 | | 8 | | 9 | |
|---|---|---|---|---|---|---|---|---|---|---|---|---|---|---|---|---|---|
| 1 | F | 2 | ~~F~~ I | 3 | H | 4 | A | 5 | E | 6 | D | 7 | C | 8 | B | 9 | G |

## Reading: Capacity and inventory

**Operations managers have to decide where to manufacture different products, how much productive capacity their factories and plants should have, and how much inventory to maintain. Read the 15 sentences on the next page, and classify them under the six headings (A–F). Some sentences may fall under two headings.**

**A** The consequences of insufficient capacity
**B** The consequences of excess capacity
**C** The advantages of large facilities
**D** The disadvantages of large facilities
**E** The advantages of having a large inventory
**F** The disadvantages of having a large inventory

1 A long lead time may allow competitors to enter the market.
2 As production volume increases, you get economies of scale (the average fixed cost per unit produced decreases).
3 Finding enough workers and coordinating material flows can become difficult.
4 If lead time increases, some customers may go to other suppliers.
5 Lost sales and market share are usually permanent.
6 The working environment might get worse and industrial relations could deteriorate.
7 There are costs of storage, handling, insurance, depreciation, the opportunity cost of capital, and so on.
8 You can be more flexible in product scheduling, and have longer lead times and lower cost operation through larger production runs with fewer set-ups.
9 There is always a risk of obsolescence, theft, breakage, and so on.
10 You can meet variation in product demand.
11 You may be under-utilizing your workforce.
12 You have protection against variation in raw material delivery time (due to shortages, strikes, lost orders, incorrect or defective shipments, etc.).
13 You may be forced to produce additional, less profitable, products.
14 You can take advantage of quantity discounts in purchasing.
15 You may have to reduce prices to stimulate demand.

Alan Goodfellow

## Listening 1: Purchasing ▶ 1.15

**Listen to Alan Goodfellow, Global IT Director of Leica Microsystems, talking about purchasing and manufacturing, and answer the questions. Leica is part of the Danaher group of companies. They make microscopes, imaging systems and medical equipment.**

1 What does he describe as 'one of the main goals of any company'?
2 What is the advantage of being part of a larger group of companies?
3 How does a reverse auction work?
4 Why is it called 'reverse'?
5 What does he mean by 'price isn't everything'?
6 What is the consequence of this?

## Listening 2: Low-cost manufacturing ▶ 1.16

**Listen to Alan Goodfellow talking about manufacturing in Asia, and answer the questions.**

1 What are the advantages of having factories in Singapore and China?
2 Why is this *not* outsourcing?
3 What was the problem with staff in China?

A Leica factory in Singapore

**4** Now listen again, and fill in the gaps in this extract:

Yes, when we first set up the company in China there were a great many problems, mainly to do with [1] ______________ local staff, but particularly [2] ______________ ______________, because the economy was [3] ______________ so much, we found that after training staff, bringing them up to the standards we expected, they were very attractive to other companies and could easily move and take their [4] ______________ elsewhere, so there was a constant process of training and [5] ______________, it was very hard to [6] ______________ staff.

## Reading: 'The Dell Theory of Conflict Prevention'

**In *The World Is Flat: A Brief History of the Twenty-first Century*, the American author Thomas Friedman argues that outsourcing and global supply chains have very positive international consequences.**

**Read the extract. How convinced are you by Friedman's argument?**

THE WORLD IS FLAT

The Dell Theory stipulates: No two countries that are both part of a major global supply chain, like Dell's, will ever fight a war against each other as long as they are both part of the same global supply chain. Because people embedded in major global supply chains don't want to fight old-time wars any more. They want to make just-in-time deliveries of goods and services – and enjoy the rising standards of living that come with that. One of the people with the best feel for the logic behind this theory is Michael Dell, the founder and chairman of Dell.

'These countries understand the risk premium that they have,' said Dell of the countries in his Asian supply chain. 'They are pretty careful to protect the equity they have built up or tell us why we should not worry. […] I believe that as time and progress go on there, the chance for a really disruptive event goes down exponentially. I don't think our industry gets enough credit for the good we are doing in these areas.' […]

There is a lot of truth to this. Countries whose workers and industries are woven into a major global supply chain know that they cannot take an hour, a week, a month off for war without disrupting industries and economies around the world and thereby risking the loss of their place in that supply chain for a long time, which could be extremely costly. For a country with no natural resources, being part of global supply chain is like striking oil – oil that never runs out. And therefore, getting dropped from such a chain because you start a war is like having your oil wells go dry or having someone pour cement down them. They will not come back any time soon.

'You are going to pay for it dearly,' said Glenn E. Neland, senior vice president for procurement at Dell, when I asked him what would happen to a major supply chain member in Asia that decided to start fighting with its neighbour and disrupt the supply chain. […] 'If you follow the evolution of supply chains,' added Neland, 'you see the prosperity and stability they promoted first in Japan, and then in Korea and Taiwan, and now in Malaysia, Singapore, the Philippines, Thailand and Indonesia.' Once countries get embedded in these global supply chains, 'they feel part of something much bigger than their own business,' he said.

## Comprehension

1 Why does Thomas Friedman think countries involved in a major global supply chain are unlikely to start a war?
2 Why does Michael Dell think the computer industry deserves more praise than it gets?
3 What would be the consequences if a country in a major global supply chain did start a war?
4 What consequences has the evolution of supply chains had?

## Vocabulary

A computer like this probably contains components from at least ten countries

**Find the words in the text that mean the following:**

1 firmly fixed in something or part of something
2 the quality of people's lives
3 someone who establishes a company
4 *(in this context)* the potential cost of taking a chance
5 *(in this context)* the value of a business activity
6 causing trouble and stopping something from continuing as usual
7 increasing or decreasing more and more quickly as time passes
8 the obtaining of supplies
9 the state of being successful and having a lot of money
10 the situation when something is not likely to change

## Role play

**In small groups, imagine that you are in a meeting called by the Procurement Manager of a multinational hi-tech manufacturer to discuss potential new suppliers of components.**

**You have chosen to concentrate on three regions: Europe, Asia and South America. What do you think the advantages and disadvantages of these three regions are, in terms of:**

**a** low cost
**b** reliability
**c** a reputation for quality
**d** delivery times to your manufacturing sites
**e** potential future problems that could disrupt supply?

## Writing

**After the meeting, write an email of 100–150 words summarizing what was said about the advantages and disadvantages of the three regions, for each of the five aspects of supply.**

# 9 Logistics

## Aims

- Compare different strategies for stock control and manufacturing
- Discuss potential supply chain risks

## Lead-in

In a manufacturing or retail business, what are the advantages and disadvantages of:

- simply satisfying current demand
- planning to meet (possible) future demand?

## Vocabulary: Pull and push strategies

**You are going to read about *pull* and *push* strategies for stock control and manufacturing. But first, match the words and definitions below.**

| | |
|---|---|
| **1** accurate | **A** a guess of what the size or amount of something might be |
| **2** agile | **B** a statement of what is expected to happen in the future |
| **3** estimate (n.) | **C** able to move quickly and easily |
| **4** forecast (n.) | **D** correct, exact and without any mistakes |
| **5** lean (adj.) | **E** designing and managing the flow of goods, information and other resources |
| **6** logistics | **F** done with the hands |
| **7** manual (adj.) | **G** *(of production)* using small quantities and avoiding any waste |
| **8** replenish | **H** to fill something up again |

## Reading: Pull and push strategies

**These eight paragraphs make up a text about inventories, *pull* and *push* strategies, and Just-In-Time (JIT) production. Put them in the right order to make a logical text. Two have already been done.**

Manufacturing companies can produce according to pull or push strategies. [1]

Historically, Kanban was a manual system in which cards were placed in component bins in warehouses as a signal that items needed replenishing; today, of course, advanced software is used. [ ]

Apart from JIT, other names for pull strategies include lean production, stockless production, continuous flow manufacture and agile manufacturing. In all these systems, nothing is bought or produced until it is needed. [ ]

This replenishment strategy was famously developed as Just-In-Time (JIT) production by Toyota in Japan in the 1950s. The most common JIT system is called Kanban, a Japanese word approximately meaning 'visual card'. [ ]

Supplies are scheduled to meet expected demand, but because demand forecasts are not always accurate, push strategies often incorporate safety stocks and safety lead times. [ ]

In other words, this is a replenishment strategy: both production and suppliers are constantly reacting to the actual consumption of components, rather than planning ahead. [ ]

With a pull strategy, a company manufactures according to current demand, which is satisfied from (a small) inventory. When pieces are removed from stock, replacements are automatically ordered from suppliers. [ ]

With a push strategy such as Manufacturing Resources Planning (MRP), on the contrary, production is based on estimates of future demand, and begins according to the planned production lead time. [7]

## Comprehension: Pull and push strategies

**Now match up the following half-sentences.**

1 *Pull* strategies are based on
2 *Pull* systems only buy or produce
3 *Kanban* systems signal
4 *Push* strategies are based on
5 *Push* strategies often allow for

A current demand.
B estimated future demand.
C safety stocks and lead times.
D that items need to be replaced.
E things when they are needed.

Alan Goodfellow

## Listening 1: Inventory, Kanban and MRP ▶ 1.17

**Listen to Alan Goodfellow of Leica Microsystems talking about inventory levels, and answer the questions.**

1 Why do companies want to keep inventory as low as possible?
2 What do Leica need inventory for?
3 What strategy enables them to keep a low inventory?
4 What changed when Leica was taken over by Danaher?
5 Why does Goodfellow say 'it's not Just-In-Time as such'?

## Listening 2: Leica's supply chain ▶ 1.18

**Listen to Alan Goodfellow talking about Leica's international supply chain, and answer the questions.**

1 What is the difference between Leica's business units and selling units?
2 Does the Singapore factory make all the parts it uses?
3 Why might the Singapore factory send some products to Europe rather than to the end customer?
4 What does he say about languages and currencies?
5 Explain the balance or trade-off between customers' needs and having local stocks or inventories.

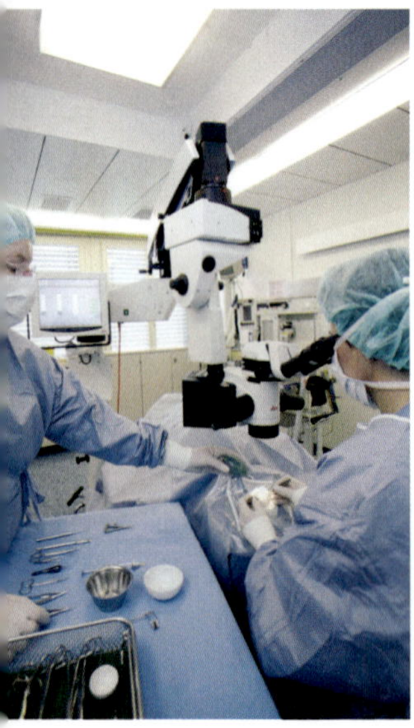

A Leica surgical microscope

## Reading: Supply-chaining

**On the next page there is another extract from Thomas Friedman's book *The World Is Flat: A Brief History of the Twenty-first Century*. Here he is writing about Wal-Mart's supply chain.**

Wal-Marts are large, discount department stores in the US. At the time of writing, Wal-Mart had the largest revenue of any company in the world, and was the world's largest private employer.

**Read the extract. What is Friedman's overall impression of the operation?**

I had never seen what a supply chain looked like in action until I visited Wal-Mart headquarters in Bentonville, Arkansas. My Wal-Mart hosts took me over to the 1.2-million-square-foot distribution center, where we climbed up to a viewing perch and watched the show. On one side of the building, scores of white Wal-Mart trailer trucks were dropping off boxes of merchandise from thousands of different suppliers. Boxes large and small were fed up a conveyor belt at each loading dock. These little conveyor belts fed into a bigger belt, like streams feeding into a powerful river. Twenty-four hours a day, seven days a week, the suppliers' trucks feed the twelve miles of conveyor streams, and the conveyor streams feed into a huge Wal-Mart river of boxed products. But that is just half the show. As the Wal-Mart river flows along, an electric eye reads the bar codes on each box on its way to the other side of the building. There, the river parts again into a hundred streams. Electric arms from each stream reach out and guide the boxes – ordered by particular Wal-Mart stores – off the main river and down its stream, where another conveyor belt sweeps them into a waiting Wal-Mart truck, which will rush these particular products onto the shelves of a particular Wal-Mart store somewhere in the country. There, a consumer will lift one of these products off the shelf, and the cashier will scan it in, and the moment that happens, a signal will be generated. That signal will go out across the Wal-Mart network to the supplier of that product – whether that supplier is in coastal China or coastal Maine. That signal will pop up on the supplier's computer screen and prompt him to make another of that item and ship it via the Wal-Mart supply chain, and the whole cycle will start anew. So no sooner does your arm lift a product off the local Wal-Mart's shelf and onto the checkout counter than another mechanical arm starts making another one somewhere in the world. Call it 'the Wal-Mart Symphony' in multiple movements – with no finale. It just plays over and over 24/7/365: delivery, sorting, packing, distribution, buying, manufacturing, reordering, delivery, sorting, packing …

## Comprehension

**1** Fill in the gaps, and then put the following sentences in the correct order. The first one has been done for you.

| | |
|---|---|
| ___ | A customer buys a product. |
| ___ | A machine reads the [a] ____________ on each box. |
| 1 | A Wal-Mart [b] ____________ picks up [c] ____________ at a supplier's factory or warehouse. |
| ___ | Electric arms guide the boxes off the main [d] ____________ onto another smaller one. |
| ___ | The boxes are placed on a small conveyor belt. |
| ___ | The cashier [e] ____________ the product, which sends a [f] ____________ to the [g] ____________ to produce another one. |
| ___ | The goods are unloaded at Wal-Mart's distribution centre. |
| ___ | The products are [h] ____________ to the [i] ____________ that ordered them. |
| 2 | The small conveyor belt joins a larger one. |
| ___ | This belt leads to another bay where the boxes are [j] ____________ onto Wal-Mart trucks. |

**2** What are the three main metaphors that Friedman uses in this passage? Why does he use them?

## Writing

**Write a brief summary (100–150 words) of the Wal-Mart supply chain.**

## **Reading:** Manufacturing supply chain work flow

**Look at this flowchart for a typical manufacturing supply chain, and number the sentences below in the order that they happen.**

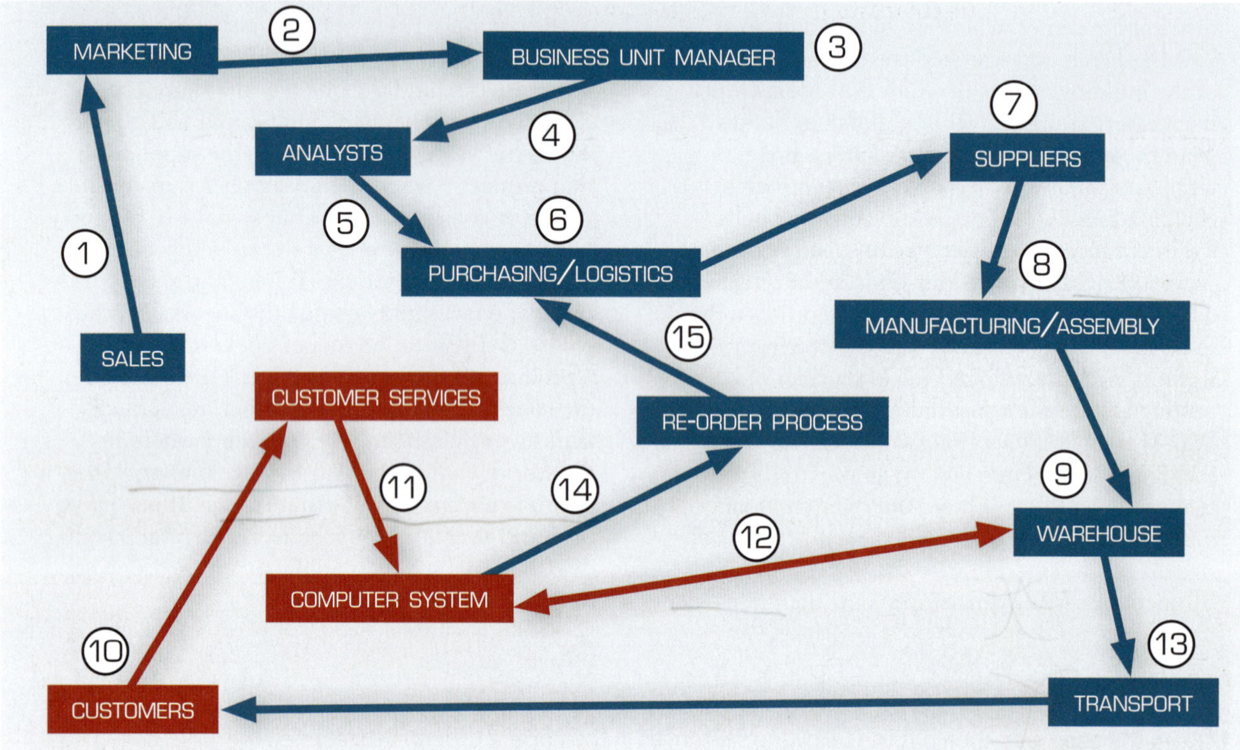


___ The sales department identifies a need for a product, and tells the marketing department about it.

___ As stock has now been used the computer system generates a request for new stock.

___ Customer services take orders and input them to the computer system.

___ Customers place orders through customer services.

___ Finished goods are put into inventory in a warehouse awaiting orders, and the company computer system is updated.

___ Suppliers receive orders and despatch raw materials and components to the manufacturing site on agreed dates.

___ The marketing department researches the project, and forwards a detailed business plan to the Business Unit Manager.

___ The plan is approved and passed to the analysts to prepare and implement the manufacturing process.

___ The analysts pass details of raw materials and components to purchasing.

___ The order is sent to the warehouse.

___ The product is manufactured.

___ The purchasing, logistics and transport departments plan the purchase of materials and their delivery to the manufacturing plant.

___ The re-order process generates a request to the purchasing department to place new orders with the suppliers.

___ The senior business managers make a decision on the project.

___ The transport company collects the consignment and delivers it to the customer.

## Case study: Risk analysis

**Companies might choose not to use suppliers from a country if they are unsure about its future political or financial stability, or about future industrial relations (the possibility of strikes, etc.), or the condition of its infrastructure (roads, railways, power supplies, etc.), or possible changes in the climate, etc.**

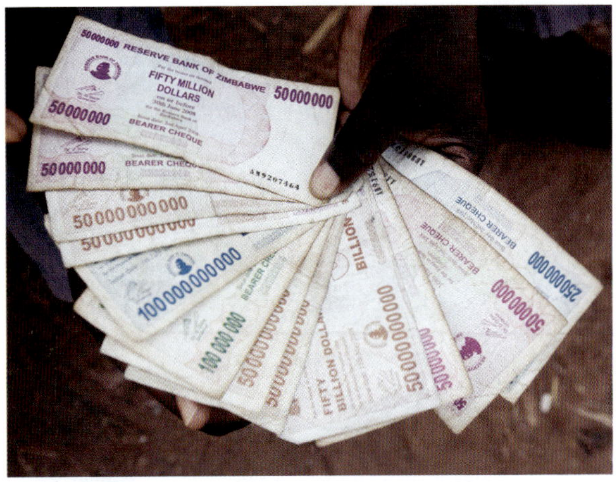

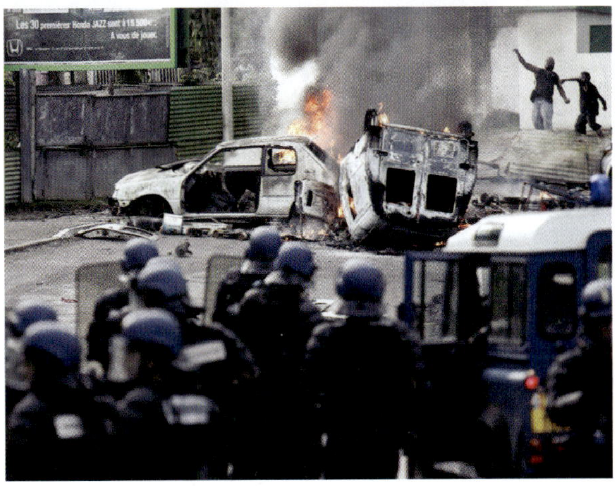

**In small groups, try to identify the potential supply chain risks for the following businesses. How could these risks be minimized?**

- **A car factory in the UK that gets components from British, continental European and Asian suppliers**
- **The fruit and vegetable department of a national supermarket chain**
- **A tourist industry company that hires seasonal workers for different tasks at different times of the year**

### Writing

**Write a short report (100–150 words) summarizing the potential supply chain risks faced by one of the businesses in the Case study, and explaining how they could be minimized.**

# 10 Quality

**Aims**

- Discuss different managerial approaches to quality
- Consider how companies try to ensure quality

## Lead-in

Quality can mean a lot of different things. If you were talking about quality in relation to these products and services, what would you mean?

- a small car (automobile)
- a raincoat
- a laptop computer
- a mobile phone or internet provider
- an insurance company

## Reading and discussion

**A well-known book is *Quality Is Free* by Philip B. Crosby. He writes:**

Doing things right the first time adds nothing to the cost of your product or service. Doing things wrong is what costs money. The typical American corporation spends 15–20 per cent of its sales dollar on reworking, scrapping, repeated service, inspection, testing, warranties and other quality-related costs. Lapses in quality also damage corporate reputations and provoke government regulation. Most, or all, of these headaches could be prevented by a properly managed quality operation. [...]

Quality is not only free but a bountiful source of profits.

**1 Match up the words from the text with the definitions on the right.**

1 bountiful
2 headaches
3 regulation
4 reworking
5 scrapping
6 service
7 warranties

A changing or improving a product or service
B guarantees: written promises to repair or replace products that develop a fault
C providing a large amount of good things
D things that cause difficulties
E official rules or the act of controlling something
F to examine a machine and repair any faulty parts
G getting rid of things which are no longer useful or wanted

| 1 | | 2 | | 3 | | 4 | | 5 | | 6 | | 7 | |
|---|---|---|---|---|---|---|---|---|---|---|---|---|---|

**2 Give some more examples of the expenses companies can avoid by preventing poor quality *before* it happens.**

## Reading: Total Quality Management

**Total Quality Management (TQM) is a management approach designed to improve the production quality of goods and services. Read the text below, and answer the comprehension questions that follow.**

TQM was developed by an American, W. Edwards Deming, in the 1940s, but was first taken up by the Japanese, who adopted it to revive their post-war industry. Following the success of the Japanese in world markets, many American companies began to use it in the 1980s.

TQM (today often just called Quality Management) involves an attitude and a corporate culture that are dedicated to providing customers with products and services that satisfy their needs. Products should have no defects (or 'zero defects') and services should be as close to perfect as possible.

The principle is simply that the company or organization should do the right things, and do them right, the first time and every time, which should eliminate waste from its operations. But because products, services and processes change, everything is capable of being improved all the time.

TQM requires all staff to be involved in the search for continuously improving quality, in all the business's activities – not just production or customer service, but also in marketing, sales, purchasing, design, engineering, R&D, finance, human resources, etc. The organization must make use of the knowledge and experience of its entire staff to identify and correct faulty systems and processes. Production workers should be empowered to stop production to solve problems, as quality is more important than maximizing output or reducing costs.

### Comprehension

**The following five statements are all false. Correct them.**

1 TQM is a Japanese management theory.
2 TQM guarantees 'zero defect' production and no waste.
3 TQM stops when you have the perfect product.
4 TQM concerns production and customer service personnel.
5 TQM involves maximizing output and reducing costs.

**The Toyota Motor Corporation has long been associated with TQM**

## Discussion: Good and bad quality

- **Select an organization whose products could be improved. What improvements could be made that might lead to some of the following outcomes (if applicable)?**
  - improved product reliability
  - improved product durability
  - reduction in the number of complaints
  - reduced waste and product returns
  - improved image
  - increased repurchase rate
  - increased sales and market share
  - improved staff morale and lower staff turnover
- **Could all this be done without increasing costs?**
- **Why do you think the organization has not done these things?**

## Discussion: A four-star hotel

- **What facilities would you expect from a four-star hotel?**

**Denis Frucot**

## Listening 1: Hotel customers and quality ▶ 1.19

**Listen to an interview with Denis Frucot, the manager of a Hotel du Vin, and answer the questions.**

**1** What is the state of affairs that Frucot describes as being 'as simple as that'?
**2** What are his examples of good and bad quality in a bed and breakfast?

## Listening 2: Customer care ▶ 1.20

**Listen to Denis Frucot talking about customer care, and answer the questions.**

**1** What does he say about the Hotel du Vin's level of quality?
**2** What examples does he give of customer care?

## Listening 3: Selecting and training staff ▶ 1.21

**Listen to Denis Frucot talking about his colleagues, and answer the questions.**

**1** How does he select staff when he opens a new hotel?
**2** What two kinds of people does he want in reception, and why?

## **Role play:** A hotel chain in trouble

**A chain of 50 three-star hotels in 15 countries around the world is losing customers and its profits are going down. Something has to be done. The CEO sends the following memo to three senior managers.**

**MEMO** **CITY INN**

Dear colleagues,

As you know, our room occupancy rate has been going down for three years now, and many of our hotels are no longer profitable. This is clearly a long-term trend and not just a temporary problem due to the current economic situation.

There is a lot of competition in the mid-range hotel market, and our brand is continuing to lose customers, which makes it impossible to increase prices. We clearly need to do something quite radical to reverse this trend. One option would be to reduce the quality of the service offered in the hotels, in order to cut costs and save money. Another completely different option would be to reposition the hotels in the market, and target a different type of customer, probably by increasing both services and prices.

I would like to hear your ideas on this subject. I have scheduled a meeting for next Monday at 9.30 in my office. Please prepare some proposals.

occupancy -> Belegung

**Your teacher will give you a role to prepare, working in groups.**

### Writing

**Write an email to the hotel chain's Board of Directors, or a short press release, explaining the decisions that have been taken (100–150 words).**

# 11 Products

## Aims

- Consider the importance of brand recognition
- Discuss the importance of researching a product concept

## Lead-in

- Give three examples of brands to which you are loyal, i.e. which you regularly buy without thinking about it. Why are you loyal to them?
- What products are there for which you are what marketers call a brand-switcher, i.e. you have no preference for or loyalty to a particular brand?
- What products can you think of for which the name of the brand is totally unimportant, so that you don't even notice it?

## Reading: Products and brands

**Read the following text, and write a brief heading for each section.**

1 ______________________________

A product is anything that can be offered to a market that might satisfy a want or need. This means that services, leisure activities, people (politicians, athletes, actors), places (holiday resorts) and organizations (hospitals, colleges, political parties) can also be considered as products.

Most manufacturers divide their products into product lines – groups of closely related products, sold to the same customer groups, and marketed through the same outlets. Because customers' needs and markets are constantly evolving, and because different products are generally at different stages of their life cycles, with growing, stable or declining sales and profitability, companies are always looking to the future, and re-evaluating their product mix.

2 ______________________________

Most products offered for sale by retailers are branded. A brand is a name, or a symbol, or a logo that distinguishes products and services from competing offerings, and makes consumers remember the company, product or service. A brand name can be reinforced by distinctive design and packaging.

The key objective of branding is to create a relationship of trust. Customers have an image of the brand in their minds, combining knowledge about the product and their expectations of it. Some brands are seen as more than just products or services: they successfully represent customers' attitudes or feelings, e.g. Nike, Starbucks, Apple Computer, The Body Shop, etc.

By way of extensive advertising, companies can achieve brand recognition among the general public, including millions of people who are not even interested in the products. Branding is used for B2B (Business-to-Business) marketing of materials and components, as well as for consumer goods in B2C (Business-to-Consumer) marketing.

3 ______________________________

Some companies include their name in all their products (corporate branding), e.g. Philips, Virgin, Yamaha. Other companies do individual branding, and give each product its own brand name, so the company name is less well-known than its brands (compare the name Procter & Gamble with its individual brand names Pampers, Pringles, Duracell and Gillette).

Some companies, such as the major producers of soap powders, have a multi-brand strategy which allows them to fill up space on supermarket shelves, leaving less room for competitors. Even if one brand 'cannibalizes' (or eats into) or takes business away from another one produced by the same company, the sales do not go to a competitor. Having three out of 12 brands in a market generally gives a greater market share than having one out of ten, and gives a company a better chance of getting some of the custom of brand-switchers.

4 ____________________

The brand consultancy Interbrand publishes an annual list of the Best Global Brands, which shows that the worth of a brand can be much greater than a company's physical assets. For example, in the early 2000s, the value of the top ranked brand, Coca-Cola, was calculated at over $70 billion. Consequently, a company's market value (the combined price of all its shares) can be much greater than its book value – the recorded value of its tangible assets such as buildings and machinery. Brand value largely comes from customer loyalty: the existence of customers who will continue to buy the products.

## Comprehension

1. Why do companies' product mixes regularly change?
2. Why do companies brand their products?
3. What is the difference between corporate branding and individual branding?
4. Why do the big soap powder producers have a multi-brand strategy?
5. Why can the market value of companies be much higher than the value of their tangible assets?

## Vocabulary

**Find words or expressions in the text which mean the following:**

1. places of business for selling goods to customers (shops, stores, kiosks, etc.)
2. all the different products, brands and items that a company sells
3. businesses that sell goods or merchandise to individual consumers
4. a graphic image or symbol specially created to identify a company or a product
5. wrappers and containers used to enclose and protect a product
6. the extent to which consumers are aware of a brand, and know its name
7. surfaces in a store on which goods are displayed
8. the sales of a company expressed as a percentage of total sales in a given market
9. consumers who buy various competing products rather than being loyal to a particular brand

## Discussion: Brands and attitudes

**1 What attitude would you associate with the following brands?**

- Apple
- BMW
- Harley-Davidson
- Ikea
- Louis Vuitton
- MTV
- Nike
- Sony

**2 Which brands do you have an emotional attachment to, because they represent your attitudes or feelings?**

Melissa Glass and her partner

## Listening 1: Not just a juice bar ▶ 1.22

**Melissa Glass has opened a chain of juice bars in Switzerland. Listen to her talking about Zeste Juice Bars, and answer the questions.**

**1** What lines of products do Zeste sell?

**2** Why does Melissa Glass say 'we don't consider ourselves just a juice bar'?

## Listening 2: The origin of smoothies ▶ 1.23

**Listen to Melissa Glass talking about where smoothies come from, and why they launched the product in Switzerland, and answer the questions.**

**1** Where did the concept of juice bars originate, and how did it develop?

**2** Where did Melissa and her husband first see the concept?

**3** Why did they decide to open their juice bars in Switzerland?

## Listening 3: Launching the product ▶ 1.24

**Listen to Melissa Glass talking about doing market research and opening the first store, and answer the questions. Then listen again to check your answers.**

**1** Fill in the gaps below in what Melissa says.

We had to do research into [1] ____________, we had to do research into colours, what [2] ____________ where it was going to be the most successful. We knew that obviously we needed [3] ____________-____________ passage. The problem with that in Switzerland is the locations, the places with high passage are extremely expensive, so it's always a balance between getting somewhere that's got enough passage but not too, too expensive, because when you're selling a product that has a cost price of five francs you have to sell a lot of juices and smoothies to cover the base, the [4] ____________ ____________. Apart from that we had to do obviously questionnaire friends, take surveys, we had to do, we also did [5] ____________, [6] ____________, we did a couple of parties at our place to try the different products, and to choose the different smoothies that we were going to start with.

**2** What does 'high-frequency passage' mean?

**3** Why did they give their bars and products English names?

**4** What was their plan after launching in Lausanne?

## **Case study:** Researching a product concept

**In small groups, choose one of the following businesses, and think about how you would go about launching it in your town:**

- a juice bar
- a taxi company
- a home-delivery pizza service
- a gym and fitness centre
- a language school
- another business of your choice.

**Think about:**

1. The product concept: what exactly would the business offer, and how would it differ from similar, competing businesses?
2. The location: what would the ideal location be, bearing in mind that the closer to the town centre and the busier the street, the higher the rent?
3. The name of the business, and the image it wants to project. What kind of design would you use?
4. Pricing: would you try to compete on price, by being cheaper than competitors, or should you try to be better or different, and charge a higher price?

**Once you have some ideas about the product concept, the preferred location, the name and image, and your pricing strategy, decide how you could do some market research to see whether potential customers would be interested. What information would you need? Where could you get it?**

**Could you use the following market research methods?**

- **questionnaire research: asking questions by telephone or personal interviewing**
- **focus group interviews: getting several potential target customers to meet (for a small fee) and discuss the product concept**
- **secondary data: studying government statistics, business newspapers, magazines and trade journals, reports published by private market research agencies, competitors' annual reports, etc.**

**If time permits, carry out the research, and report back.**

## Writing

**Write a short report (150–200 words) *either* outlining your product concept and plans for the business, *or* explaining what research you undertook and what the results were.**

# 12 Marketing

## Aims

- Consider the product life cycle and the role of marketing
- Discuss pricing and distribution strategies

## Lead-in

Here are four definitions of marketing. Which do you prefer, and why?

- Selling means you sell what you make; marketing means you make what you can sell.
- Marketing means the right product, in the right place, at the right price, and at the right time.
- Marketing means identifying customers, defining and developing the products or services they want, and making and distributing them.
- Marketing means anticipating and creating needs: producing useful things customers didn't know they wanted until you produced them.

*"It's all marketing - no one actually wears that stuff."*



## Vocabulary: Basic marketing terms

**Below are some more basic marketing terms. Match up the words in the box to the definitions.**

distribution channel | market opportunities | market penetration | market segmentation | market skimming | price elasticity | product differentiation | product features | sales representative | wholesaler

1 all the companies or individuals ('middlemen') involved in moving goods or services from producers to consumers
2 an intermediary that stocks manufacturers' goods or merchandise, and sells it to retailers and professional buyers
3 dividing a market into distinct groups of buyers who have different requirements or buying habits
4 making a product (appear to be) different from similar products offered by other sellers, by product differences, advertising, packaging, etc.
5 possibilities of filling unsatisfied needs in sectors in which a company can profitably produce goods or services
6 setting a high price for a new product, to make maximum revenue before competing products appear on the market
7 someone who contacts existing and potential customers, and tries to persuade them to buy goods or services
8 the attributes or characteristics of a product, such as size, shape, quality, price, reliability, etc.
9 the extent to which supply or demand (the quantity produced or bought) of a product responds to changes of price
10 the strategy of setting a low price to try to sell a large volume and increase market share

## **Reading:** The product life cycle

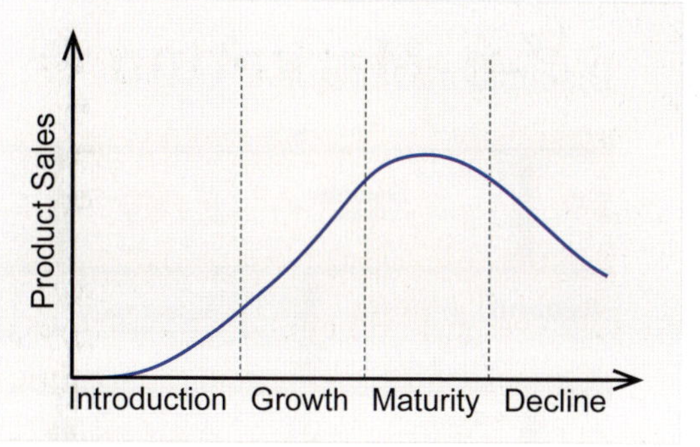


**The graph shows the standard product life cycle. At the introduction stage, sales are low. They rise quickly during the growth stage, level off at the maturity stage, before eventually falling during the decline stage until the product is withdrawn from the market.**

**Which stages do the following sentences about sales, costs, prices and promotion describe?**

**1** Introduction stage **2** Growth stage **3** Maturity stage **4** Decline stage

**Sales:**

___ A Public awareness about the product increases and sales volume rises significantly.

___ B Sales volume peaks.

___ C Sales volume begins to go down.

___ D The sales volume is low and customers have to be persuaded to try the product.

**Costs:**

___ E Costs are high.

___ F The product's features may have to be changed so that it differs from competing brands, which involves new costs.

___ G Costs are reduced due to economies of scale, so profitability increases.

___ H Either costs are too high compared to sales, so the product is discontinued, or the company continues to offer the product to loyal customers, while reducing costs to a minimum.

**Prices:**

___ I The price is either maintained, or greatly reduced to liquidate stock if the product is discontinued.

___ J The company can choose between high skim pricing to recover development costs, or low penetration pricing to build market share rapidly, if there are already competitors.

___ K The price can remain unchanged because demand is increasing but competitors aren't usually yet well established.

___ L Prices may have to be reduced because competitors are established in the market, but companies try to defend their market share while also maximizing profit.

**Promotion:**

___ M Promotion emphasizes product differentiation.

___ N Promotion is aimed at a much broader audience (the majority of the product's users).

___ O At this stage, there is virtually no promotion.

___ P Promotion is aimed at educating potential consumers (innovators and early adopters) about the product, and building product awareness.

## Discussion: Pricing

1 Under what circumstances would manufacturers either set prices that try to maximize profits, or deliberately charge a low price?
2 Give examples of products for which demand is elastic, and which you would only buy (or buy more of) if the price went down.
3 Which products are for you *not* price sensitive, so that you would buy them even if the price increased significantly?
4 If you see a price that is a little less than a round number, e.g. $1.99 or €99.95, does it makes you think of the lower number, e.g. $1 instead of nearly $2, and encourage you to buy the product? If *not*, why do you think most retailers use 'psychological pricing' or 'odd prices' like this?
5 When, as a consumer, have you benefited from a price war when competitors continually lowered prices, trying to get more business? What kind of companies win price wars?

## Discussion: Distribution channels

**Give examples of businesses that would typically use the different channels illustrated in the diagram. (Of course, the same businesses could use different channels for different market segments.) In each case, *why* is this the preferred distribution channel?**

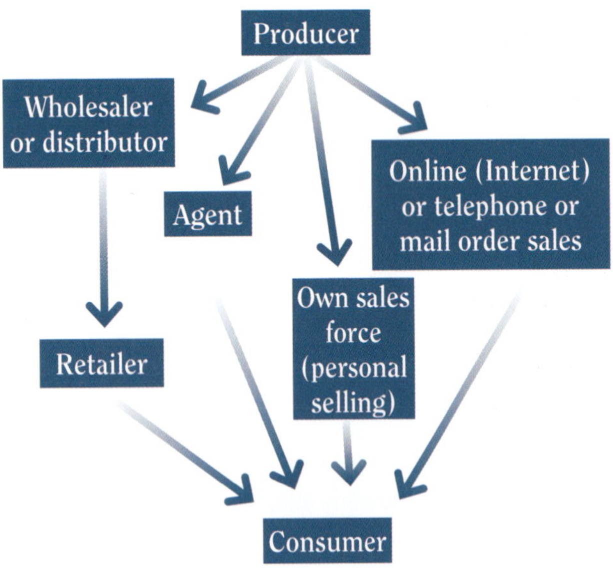

*"On the one hand, eliminating the middleman would result in lower costs, increased sales, and greater consumer satisfaction; on the other hand, we're the middleman.'*

© The New Yorker

## Writing

**Write two or three short paragraphs (60–100 words in total) describing the different distribution channels used for two different products.**

## Reading: Marketing is everything

**Read the following extracts from an article by Regis McKenna in the *Harvard Business Review*, and answer the questions on the next page.**

In 1909, Henry Ford famously said about the Model T:

'Any customer can have a car painted any color that he wants so long as it is black.'

Several decades ago, there were sales-driven companies. These organizations focused their energies on changing customers' minds to fit the product – practicing the 'any color as long as it's black' school of marketing.

As technology developed and competition increased, some companies shifted their approach and became customer driven. These companies expressed a new willingness to change their product to fit customers' requests – practicing the 'tell us what color you want' school of marketing.

Successful companies are becoming market driven, adapting their products to fit their customers' strategies. These companies will practice 'Let's figure out together how and whether color matters to your larger goal' marketing. It is marketing that is oriented toward creating rather than controlling a market.

The old approach – getting an idea, conducting traditional market research, developing a product, testing the market, and finally going to market – is slow and unresponsive.

As the demands on the company have shifted from controlling costs to competing on products to serving customers, the center of gravity in the company has shifted from finance to engineering – and now to marketing.

Marketing today is not a function; it is a way of doing business. Marketing is not a new ad campaign or this month's promotion. Marketing has to be all-pervasive, part of everyone's job description, from the receptionists to the board of directors. Its job is neither to fool the customer nor to falsify the company's image. It is to integrate the customer into the design of the product.

US companies typically make two kinds of mistake. Some get caught up in the excitement and drive of making things, particularly new creations. Others become absorbed in the competition of selling things, particularly to increase their market share in a given product line.

Both approaches could prove fatal to a business. The problem with the first is that it leads to an internal focus. Companies can become so fixated on pursuing their R&D agendas that they forget about the customer, the market, the competition.

The problem with the second approach is that it leads to a market-share mentality. It turns marketing into an expensive fight over crumbs rather than a smart effort to own the whole pie.

The real goal of marketing is to own the market – not just to make or sell products. Smart marketing means defining the whole pie as yours. In marketing, what you lead you own. Leadership is ownership.

That is why marketing is everyone's job, why marketing is everything and everything is marketing.

1 According to McKenna, what did sales-driven companies try to do?
2 Why did some companies become customer driven?
3 What does he say market-driven companies do?
4 What does McKenna mean when he describes the old approach as 'unresponsive'?
5 Why has the main focus of companies moved first from finance to engineering, and then from engineering to marketing?
6 What two negative descriptions of marketing does he reject?
7 What does he say about customers and market-driven companies?
8 What is wrong with focusing on R&D (research and development) and creating new products?
9 What is wrong with focusing on increasing market share?
10 Explain in your own words what he describes as the real job or goal of marketing.

- **Do you think Regis McKenna's account of the role of marketing is realistic?**
- **Would it work for all industries and markets, or only particular ones?**

**Advertising pamphlets on a Swiss bus**

## Listening 1: Promoting a juice bar ▶ 1.25

**Listen to Melissa Glass, who you heard in Unit 11, explaining how Zeste tried to promote their juice bar, and answer the questions.**

1 What was the first form of marketing (or promotion) they tried?
2 Why were they sure it would work?
3 What concept was used for the advertising campaign, and what was the problem with it?

## Listening 2: The most effective form of promotion ▶ 1.26

**Listen to Melissa Glass talking about a successful form of promotion, and answer the questions.**

1 According to Melissa, what is the most effective form of promotion?
2 Does it have a temporary or a permanent effect?
3 Why do you think this form of promotion works better than advertising?

**A Zeste Juice bar**

## Case study: Promoting a new product

**Plan a marketing campaign for a new product or service. This could be the product or service you researched in Unit 11. Would you use advertising? Publicity? Sales promotions? If so, why and where and how?**

# 13 Advertising

## Aims

- Analyse the different kinds of sales promotions
- Discuss what makes a successful advertising campaign

## Lead-in

- To what extent do you think your purchases are influenced by advertising?
- How many advertising messages do you think you see or hear on an average day?
- How many times do you think you have to see an ad or a brand name before you remember it?
- When has advertising ever persuaded you to buy things you don't need, or even things you don't want?

## **Reading:** Advertising and viral marketing

**Read the text below and on the next page and decide which paragraphs should be given the following headings:**

**A** Advertising spending and sales
**B** How companies advertise
**C** Word-of-mouth advertising and viral marketing
**D** Potential drawbacks of advertising

__B__ Advertising informs consumers about the existence and benefits of products and services, and attempts to persuade them to buy them. Most companies use advertising agencies to produce their advertising for them. They give the agency a statement of the objectives of the advertising campaign, known as a brief, an overall advertising strategy concerning the message to be communicated to the target customers, and a budget. The agency creates advertisements (often abbreviated to adverts or ads), and develops a media plan specifying which media – newspapers, magazines, the Internet, radio, television, cinema, posters, mail, etc. – will be used and in which proportions.

__A__ It is always difficult to know how much to spend on advertising. Increased ad spending *can* increase sales, but many companies just spend a fixed percentage of current sales revenue, or simply spend as much as their competitors (the comparative–parity method). On the other hand, lots of creative and expensive advertising campaigns, including television commercials that lots of people see and remember, and which win prizes awarded by the advertising industry for the best ads, *don't* lead to increased sales.

__D__ Advertising is widely considered to be essential for launching new consumer products. Combined with sales promotions such as free samples, price reductions and competitions, advertising may generate the initial trial of a new product. But traditional advertising is expensive, it doesn't always reach the target customers, and it isn't always welcome if it does reach them. People might choose to look at posters in the street or on public transport (and virtual ones in computer and video games), or look at the ads in newspapers and magazines, but many other ads interrupt them when they're trying to do something else, like read a web page, listen to the radio, or watch a TV programme or a film.

_C_ This is why the best form of advertising has always been word-of-mouth advertising: people telling their friends about good products and services. For example, at the end of the last century, more and more people were saying to their friends 'Have you used Google? It's great.' Today, word-of-mouth has developed into viral marketing: companies succeed in getting people to spread commercial messages, like a virus, via peer-to-peer (P2P) networks on the Internet. The classic example is Hotmail, which added a little advertisement for itself at the bottom of every email sent using a Hotmail address. In the mid-1990s, the number of users increased from 500,000 to 12 million within a year. More and more companies are trying new strategies like setting up blogs or online forums, commenting on other people's blogs and social networking websites, making podcasts, and putting videos on YouTube, and hoping that people will use the 'Share' function to send a link to all their contacts. Viral marketing allows companies to inform and persuade, and create a 'buzz', so that an idea spreads very quickly, at very little cost.

## Comprehension

**Read the text again and answer these questions.**

1 What are the two functions of advertising? Advertising
2 What is the role of advertising agencies?
3 What three different methods of determining advertising spending are mentioned?
4 What does the text describe as disadvantages of traditional advertising?
5 What ways of using the Internet to advertise are mentioned? Peer to peer

## Vocabulary

**Find the words in the text that mean the following:**

1 companies that design advertising for clients ad agency
2 the advertising of a particular product or service during a particular period of time campaign
3 the statement of objectives that a client works out with an advertising agency
4 a defined set of customers whose needs a company plans to satisfy target customers/audience
5 the amount of money a company plans to spend in developing its advertising and buying media time or space budget
6 the choice of where to advertise in order to reach the right people media plan
7 choosing to spend the same amount on advertising as one's competitors competitive-parity method
8 a small amount of a product given to customers to encourage them to try it free samples
9 free advertising, when satisfied customers recommend products to their friends
10 trying to get consumers to forward an online marketing message to other people viral marketing

## Writing

**Write short summaries (30–50 words) of**

- **the disadvantages of traditional advertising,**
  **and**
- **the advantages of viral marketing.**

*"How else are we going to pay for the war?"*

## Discussion: Advertising and promotions

**How responsive are you to advertising and sales promotions? Classify the following techniques.**

| I find these advertising and sales promotions techniques: | interesting and effective | interesting but not very effective | both irritating and ineffective |
|---|---|---|---|
| Advertisements in the cinema product placement ✓ | | | X |
| Radio commercials | | | X |
| Television commercials | | | X |
| Advertisements in newspapers and magazines | X | | |
| Posters on advertising hoardings (BrE) or billboards (AmE) | | X | |
| Advertisements inside or outside buses | | X | |
| Backlit posters in display boxes | | X | |
| Neon signs on walls in city centres | | | X |
| Direct mail (or junk mail) you find in your letter box | | X | |
| Flyers (or fliers, or handbills) handed out on the street | | | X |
| Discount coupons in newspapers to cut out and present at a supermarket checkout | X | | |
| Point-of-sale displays next to checkout counters in stores | | | X |
| Free samples of products given away in public places | X | | |
| Free promotional items like T-shirts, caps, pens, mouse pads or mugs, with a company's name or logo or slogan on them, given away at sporting events, etc. | X | | |
| Telephone marketing: people phoning you at home trying to sell you things | | | X |
| Text or picture messages (SMS/MMS) received on your mobile or cell phone | | | X |
| Banner advertisements at the top or bottom of a web page | | | X |
| Pop-up pages on the Internet | | | X |
| Spam emails | | | X |

**If your answers are predominantly 'irritating and ineffective', do you think advertising and promotions work? Is it possible that the hundreds of billions of dollars spent on advertising around the world are being wasted?**

## Listening: Radio commercials ▶ 1.27, 28, 29

**Listen to three American radio commercials or advertisements.**

- **What are they advertising?**

**Listen again to each of the commercials in turn and answer the following question for each one:**

- **How does this ad work? What message or idea or image or atmosphere is the advertiser trying to create?**
- **Which of these three ads do you prefer, and why?**

## Scripting a radio commercial

**In small groups, write a script for a 20-second commercial to be played on a popular English-language radio station, advertising either a well-known product exported by your country, or some form of travel to your country. Remember that you have to persuade and inform, and are not supposed to say anything misleading or untruthful – although of course in this case you are free to invent the name of a company, the details of its service, and so on. You may use music and sound effects if you have access to them. If not, merely indicate what you would use in addition to a voice or voices. Ideally, you should actually record your commercial.**

## Discussion: Successful advertising

- **What do you think makes an advertisement memorable:**
  humour? originality? the use of famous actors or personalities? endless repetition? nudity? other elements?
- **Do you find the advertisements on television generally:**
  informative? persuasive? amusing? well made? artistic? worth watching? an annoying interruption to the programmes? sometimes better than the programmes?
- **Give examples of ads that you have enjoyed.**
- **Give examples of ads that have persuaded you to buy the product.**
- **Do these examples coincide?**
- **Have you ever passed on advertising material by email, or discussed products in blogs or online forums, thereby helping advertise an organization's products or services?**

# 14 Banking

**Aims**

- Consider banking products and services and different types of banks
- Discuss the subprime crisis and microfinance

## Lead-in

- Which of the following banking products or services do you find the most useful or necessary?

| | |
|---|---|
| a current account (BrE) or checking account (AmE) | buying or selling foreign currency for travelling (BrE) or traveling (AmE) |
| a savings or deposit account (BrE) or time or notice account (AmE) | a mortgage (a loan to buy property (BrE) or real estate (AmE)) |
| cashpoints (BrE) or ATMs (Automated Teller Machines, AmE) | an overdraft (the possibility to borrow money by spending more than you have in your bank account) |
| a chequebook (BrE) or checkbook (AmE) | |
| a credit card | investment advice |
| a debit card | internet banking (payments, transfers) |
| a loan | telephone banking (payments, transfers) |

- What other banking services do businesses use?

## Reading: Banks and financial institutions

**Insert the names of the following types of financial institutions in the spaces in the text.**

commercial banks    hedge funds    investment banks    Islamic banks
non-bank financial intermediaries    private banks    stockbrokers

Retail banks or [1] ______________ (often called High Street banks in Britain) receive deposits from, and make loans to, individuals and small companies. [2] ______________ work with big companies, giving financial advice, raising capital by issuing stocks or shares and bonds, arranging mergers and takeover bids, and so on. They also generally offer stockbroking and portfolio management services to rich corporate and individual clients. Wealthy individuals can also use [3] ______________, which provide them with banking and investment services, and [4] ______________, which are private investment funds for wealthy investors (both individuals and institutions) that use a wider variety of (risky) investing strategies than traditional investment funds, in order to achieve higher returns.

In the USA, where many banks went bankrupt following the Wall Street Crash in 1929, a law was passed in 1934 (the Glass-Steagall Act) that separated commercial banks and investment banks or stockbroking firms. For the rest of the 20th century, there were regulations in the US, Britain and Japan that prevented commercial banks from doing investment banking business. In other countries, including Germany and Switzerland, large banks did all kinds of financial business. But starting in the 1980s, many rules were ended by financial deregulation, and Glass-Steagall was repealed in 1999. Large banks became international conglomerates offering a complete range of financial services that were previously provided by banks, [5] ____________________ and insurance companies.

[6] ____________________, in Islamic countries and major financial centres, offer interest-free banking. They do not pay interest to depositors or charge interest to borrowers, but invest in companies and share the profits (or losses) with their depositors.

Some car manufacturers, food retailers and department stores now offer products like personal loans, credit cards and insurance. Technically these are not banks but [7] ____________________.

## Vocabulary

**1 Find the words or expressions in the text which mean the following:**

1. money placed in a bank
2. a sum of money borrowed from a bank
3. the money invested in a business
4. certificates representing part-ownership of a company
5. certificates of debt issued by governments or companies to raise money
6. when one company combines with another one
7. when one company offers to buy or acquire another one
8. buying and selling stocks or shares for clients
9. all the investments owned by an individual or organization
10. the profits made on investments
11. unable to pay debts or continue to do business
12. the ending or relaxing of legal restrictions
13. a group of companies, operating in different fields, which have joined together
14. the price paid for borrowing money, paid to the lenders

**2 Match up the verbs in the left-hand box with the nouns in the right-hand box to make common verb–noun combinations found in the text above.**

| | |
|---|---|
| charge | pass |
| do | pay |
| give | provide |
| issue | raise |
| make | receive |
| offer | share |

| | |
|---|---|
| advice | loans |
| bonds | profits |
| business | interest |
| capital | services |
| deposits | stocks or |
| laws | shares |

**What other verb–noun combinations can you make with these words?**

## Listening 1: Commercial banking ▶ 1.30

Tony Ramos

**Listen to Tony Ramos, a recruitment manager at HSBC in London, talking about investment and commercial banking, and answer the questions.**

1 How does Tony Ramos describe commercial banking? 'A kind of ________ ________ ________.'

2 What was Tony Ramos's job before he moved into recruitment?

3 What does he say commercial banking actually consists of? Fill in the gaps.

> '... you're kind of working in a [1] ________ ________, you're working you know with, like, [2] ________ ________, kind of what the day-to-day job consists of, actually [3] ________ ________ ________ people with their businesses, [4] ________ ________ ________ those businesses, seeing those [5] ________ ________ ...'

4 What does he say students wrongly think it consists of?

HSBC headquarters in London

## Reading: The subprime crisis and the credit crunch

**Deregulation in the 1980s was one of the factors that led to the subprime crisis. Read about the crisis and then put the sentences below in the right order.**

When American house prices began to fall in 2007, many 'subprime' borrowers, defined as those with poor credit ratings and consequently a high risk of default, stopped paying their mortgages, as their debt was greater than the value of their house. Unfortunately, the institutions which had issued the mortgages had created financial products called mortgage-backed securities (MBS) and collateralized debt obligations (CDO), which had been bought by many financial institutions including investment banks, hedge funds, insurance companies, pension funds, mutual funds, and so on. This process is called securitization: financial assets like mortgages which produce a cash flow are pooled (grouped together) and converted into securities that are then sold to investors.

MBSs and CDOs give their buyers the right to receive the payments on the underlying mortgages, and banks bought them because they believed that house prices would continue to rise, and households would continue to make their mortgage payments. But when many subprime borrowers stopped paying, the value of subprime related securities fell dramatically. Many banks in the USA, Britain and elsewhere lost billions of dollars on their MBSs; some went bankrupt, and others had to be rescued by governments. It is estimated that banks around the world will eventually have to write off $1.5 trillion of worthless subprime MBSs (now often referred to as 'toxic debt'). These losses destroyed much of the capital of the world banking system, leading to a credit crisis or a 'credit crunch': a massive reduction in the amount of credit available for banks to lend to other banks, businesses and households.

___ American house prices fell and many borrowers stopped repaying.

___ Lenders granted mortgages to 'subprime' borrowers.

___ Some went bankrupt, and others had to be rescued by governments.

___ The mortgage lenders sold mortgage-backed securities to financial institutions.

___ The value of MBSs fell to almost zero and many banks lost billions of dollars.

___ There was a credit crisis as there was little capital left for lending and borrowing.

## Vocabulary

**Match up the words and definitions.**

**1** credit rating
**2** default
**3** collateralized
**4** cash flow
**5** write off

**A** cancel a bad debt or a worthless asset from an account
**B** estimates of people's ability to fulfil their financial commitments
**C** failure to repay a loan
**D** the money generated by an investment
**E** with property or another asset used as a guarantee of payment

## Discussion

- **Who do you think was responsible for the subprime crisis? What did the financial industry do wrong?**

## Listening 2: Microfinance ▶ 1.31

- **Do you know (and can you explain) what 'microfinance' is?**

Anna-Kim Hyun-Seung

**Anna-Kim Hyun-Seung from South Korea is a former MBA student from the Judge Business School in Cambridge who works in the not-for-profit sector. Listen to her talking about microfinance, and answer the questions.**

**1** In microfinance, what replaces normal financial collateral?
**2** What is the 'risk-management tool' that Anna-Kim mentions?
**3** Why is lending money to poor people not necessarily as risky as it sounds?
**4** Why are conventional banks now developing microcredit products?
**5** In which three continents are there successful microfinance schemes?

## Discussion

- **What do you think of this kind of banking initiative? What other initiatives like this have you read about or heard of?**

## Role play: Microfinance

**A major bank has been rescued by the government after losing billions of euros on speculative investments. But it has lost a lot of customers and now has a very bad reputation. One of the directors thinks that the way the bank can regain public trust and restore its reputation is to enter the microfinance market in developing countries. He/she calls a meeting to explain the idea to colleagues. Your teacher will give you a role to prepare. Take part in the meeting to decide what to do.**

## Writing

**Write minutes of the meeting explaining what decision was taken, and why.**

# 15 Venture capital

## Aims

- Consider how venture capitalists invest
- Discuss the contents of business plans
- Compare different possible investments

## Lead-in

- If you were starting a *new* company, how could you try to raise money?
- What are the main ways that *established* companies raise capital?

### Listening 1: Background experience 1.32

Chris Smart

**Listen to Chris Smart of Acacia Capital Partners, a venture capital firm, talking about the investments his company makes. Answer the questions.**

**1** What fields do Acacia Capital Partners invest in?
**2** Which industries does he mention that the partnership doesn't invest in?
**3** What happened when Chris Smart previously ran a non-specialized multi-disciplinary fund, and why?

## Listening 2: Investing for ten years 1.33

**1** Where does Chris Smart say venture capitalists get most of their money from? Fill in the gaps.

… so they equally have to raise that money from a [1] ______ ______ , and that in the most general terms is the insurance, it's the insurance industry, so [2] ______ ______ and [3] ______ ______ provide [4] ______ funding to venture capitalists. It is actually a very small percentage, so they will put one to three per cent of their [5] ______ ______ , and no more, into venture capital.

**2** Chris Smart says 'they've got five years to reap' – what does he mean by this?
**3** What is (in theory) the ten-year investment cycle?
**4** What does Chris Smart say 'actually happens'?
**5** What should happen at the end of the cycle?

## Listening 3: Managing new companies 1.34

**1** How does Chris Smart describe the sector he works in?
**2** What does he say about the managers in this sector?
**3** What can the venture capital industry provide apart from capital?
**4** What should a start-up do if they do not have the right managerial skills in the company?

## Listening 4: Successes and failures ▶ 1.35

1 What term does Chris Smart use that means knowing that some investments will fail?
2 How does he describe the average technology venture capital portfolio?
3 Which very successful businesses does he mention?
4 What are the names of the venture capital companies that helped them, and made 'phenomenal returns'?

### Discussion

- **From what Chris Smart says in the four extracts, what kind of skills do you think you would need to be successful in venture capitalism?**
- **Would you be good at it?**

## Reading: A business plan

**If you are starting a business, you have to get capital from investors. In order to persuade them to invest, you need, among other things, to write a business plan. Here are ten standard elements of a business plan, in alphabetical order. In what order do you think they should come in the actual plan?**

___ **Appendix or Appendices** – curricula vitae or resumes of the managers, and any other necessary documents (e.g. promotional materials for your products)

___ **Competition** – specifies the existing competitors to your product or service, reviews their strengths and weaknesses, predicts how they will react when you enter the market, analyses the possibilities of future competitors entering the market, and describes how the company plans to overcome them

___ **Competitive advantage** – describes the sustainable competitive advantage the new business has over its competitors and the strategy for maintaining it over the long term (e.g. management strengths, innovative technology, product features, pricing, etc.)

___ **Customer profile** – gives details about the customers you plan to cater to (market segments, age, sex, lifestyle, interests, geographic location, etc.)

___ **Executive summary** – a one-page summary or overview of what the business plan is about and what it will contain (e.g. what sort of company it is, what the product or service is and what is special about it, who the managers are, how much money you need, and what you will use it for)

___ **Financial analysis** – gives details of the business's performance (if it is already operating), and existing finance and assets, sales forecasts, and projected financial statements. It will specify the minimum level of sales required to achieve the break-even point, and make projections for future revenue. It will specify current and long-term financing requirements and give details of previous investment. It will outline an exit strategy for investors.

___ **Implementation plan** – describes sales and marketing and operational strategies, including what pricing strategy you will use and why, sales and distribution strategy, promotional strategy (public relations, advertising, sales promotions, etc.)

___ **Management team** – gives information about the founders, directors, advisors, etc., and their previous business record and experience, and about the key personnel, or the human resources plan if key staff still need to be appointed

___ **Market opportunity** – briefly describes what the company or business plans to do, the target market, its needs, current products and services and why they are inadequate, and how the new product or service fills the gap

___ **Product or service** – describes its features and the benefits for the customers, emphasizing differences, improvements and innovations compared with other products or services on the market

## Vocabulary

**1 Find words in the business plan text that mean the following:**

1 what an organization can do better than its competitors
2 able to continue over a period of time
3 the sales businesses expect to achieve in a particular period of time
4 where total costs equal total income from sales and the company makes neither a profit nor a loss
5 the total income received by a business before any expenses are paid
6 an investor's plan for getting their investment back and potentially realizing a profit
7 the people who establish a company or other organization
8 the people who are employed in an organization

**2 Use the words from the previous exercise to fill in the gaps below.**

1 Company __________ are often much too optimistic, and make unrealistically high __________ __________.
2 If a start-up's __________ __________ doesn't appear to be __________, e.g. because of the threat of new entrants, investors won't be interested.
3 It took three years for our __________ to reach our __________ __________, but in the fourth year we finally made a profit.
4 Big companies sometimes lose some of their best __________ to start-ups, and this can happen to start-ups too once they have become established.
5 An investor's __________ __________ can be sabotaged by events such as a suddenly falling stock market.

## Role play: Investing in start-ups

**Imagine that you are investment managers for a large financial institution such as a pension fund or an insurance company that has decided to invest up to 2% of its assets in start-up companies.**

**It will not be difficult to find companies in which to invest, because you regularly receive propositions from venture capital firms. But first, you want to establish a strategy. Which industries or industry sectors do you think you should invest in? Which industries have the most potential? Which industries or technologies probably present the fewest risks? If you are going to invest in companies in your own country, in which industries does it have expertise or a competitive advantage?**

**Choose three of the sectors listed on the next page. Prepare a short presentation of your strategy in small groups. Then change groups and explain your strategy to your colleagues, and then present your decisions to the class.**

A laboratory

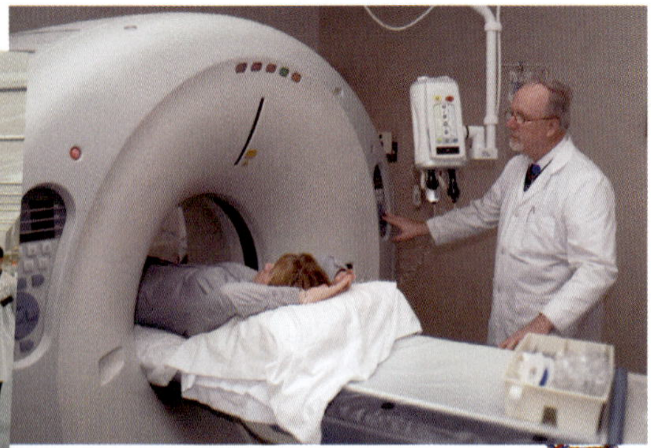

A CT scanner

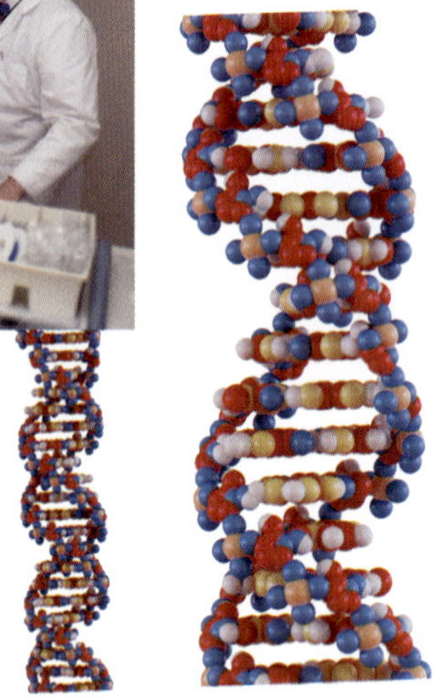

A model of DNA

Solar panels

A microprocessor

- computer and video game technology
- DNA sequencing and genetic medicine
- fuel-efficient aeroplane (BrE) or airplane (AmE) technology
- genetically modified food
- high-speed rail transport
- hybrid (petrol and electric battery) automobile technology
- microprocessors using nanotechnology
- mobile telephone technology
- nuclear energy
- nuclear medical imaging
- solar energy technology
- wind energy technology
- other?

## Writing

**Write a 100–150 word summary of your group's investment decisions.**

# 16 Bonds

United States Department of Treasury Building, Washington, DC

## Aims

- Consider the different types of bonds
- Discuss mortgage-backed securities and bond funds

## Lead-in

- What are the two main ways governments can raise money?
- What are the two main ways established companies can raise money?
- What are the advantages and disadvantages of bonds for companies and investors?

## Reading: Bonds

**Read the text and underline the answers to the questions above.**

Companies finance most of their activities by way of internally generated cash flows. If they need to raise more money to expand their operations they can either issue new shares – selling them to their existing owners or on the stock market (equity finance) – or borrow money (debt finance), usually by issuing bonds. Companies generally use an investment bank to issue their bonds, and to find buyers, which are often institutional investors like insurance companies, mutual funds and pension funds.

Bondholders get back their original investment (or 'principal') on a fixed maturity date, and receive interest payments (the 'coupon') at regular intervals (six-monthly or annually) until then. Most bonds have fixed interest rates.

For investors, bonds are generally safer than stocks or shares, because if an insolvent or bankrupt company sells its assets, bondholders are among the creditors who might get some of their money back. On the other hand, in the medium or long term, shares generally pay a higher return than bonds. For companies, the advantage of debt financing over equity financing is that bond interest is tax deductible: companies deduct their interest payments from their profits before paying tax, while dividends paid to shareholders come from already-taxed profits. But debt increases a company's financial risk: bond interest has to be paid, even in a year without any profits to deduct it from, and the principal has to be repaid when the debt matures, whereas companies are not obliged to pay dividends or repay share capital.

If tax revenue is insufficient, governments also issue bonds to raise money, and these are considered to be a risk-free investment. In the US there are Treasury notes (with a maturity of two to ten years) and Treasury bonds (with a maturity of ten to 30 years), while in Britain government bonds are known as gilt-edged stock or just gilts.

Bonds are saleable instruments that can be traded on the secondary bond market. Banks and brokerage companies act as market makers, quoting bid and offer prices for bonds with a very small spread or difference between them. The price of bonds varies inversely with interest rates. If interest rates rise, so that new borrowers have to pay a higher rate, existing bonds lose value. If interest rates fall, existing bonds paying a higher interest rate than the market rate increase in value. Consequently the yield of a bond – how much income it gives – depends on its purchase price as well as its coupon.

## Comprehension

**Are the following statements true or false?**

1 Companies regularly finance their activities by issuing bonds.
2 Bond-issuing companies use investment banks to find investors.
3 Bonds are repaid at 100% when they mature, unless the borrower is insolvent.
4 Bondholders get their money back if a company goes bankrupt.
5 Bond coupons are generally lower than share dividends.
6 For profitable companies, there are tax advantages to issuing stocks or shares rather than bonds.
7 Governments systematically finance public spending by issuing bonds.
8 A bond paying 5% interest would lose in value if interest rates fell to 4%.

## Vocabulary

**1 Find words in the text that mean the following:**

1 the money a company receives minus the money it spends during a certain period
2 part ownership of a company in the form of stocks or shares
3 funds operated by investment companies that invest people's money in various assets
4 funds that invest money that will be paid to people after they retire from work
5 the amount of capital making up a bond or other loan
6 the length of time for which a bond is issued (until it is repaid)
7 the amount of interest that a bond pays
8 unable to pay debts
9 people or institutions to whom money is owed
10 payments by companies to their shareholders
11 businesses that buy and sell securities
12 the price at which a buyer is prepared to buy a security at a particular time
13 the price at which a seller is prepared to sell a security at a particular time
14 the rate of income an investor receives from a security

**2 Match up the verbs on the left with the nouns on the right to make common verb–noun combinations found in the text. Some of the verbs and nouns are used more than once.**

| | |
|---|---|
| borrow | raise |
| deduct | receive |
| finance | repay |
| issue | sell |
| pay | |

| | |
|---|---|
| (a rate of) interest | interest payments |
| a return | money |
| activities | principal |
| assets | shares |
| bonds | tax |
| dividends | |

**What other verb–noun combinations can you make with these words?**

## Listening: Bonds and subprime mortgages 2.2

Teresa La Thangue

**Listen to Teresa La Thangue of the Financial Services Authority in London talking about how subprime mortgages, which were discussed in Unit 14, affected bonds in the US. Answer the questions.**

1 What terms does Teresa La Thangue use to describe totally safe government bonds?
2 Why were mortgage-backed securities traditionally considered to be very safe?
3 How does she explain the term 'subprime'?
4 What happened to mortgage-backed bonds in the US?
5 What did the credit rating agencies do wrong?
6 What has been the consequence of this?

### Discussion

- **How easy is it to get a mortgage in your country?**
- **Do banks tend to lend to people who might not be able to repay?**
- **Did the banks in your country buy American subprime bonds? If so, why?**

## Reading: How to profit from bonds

**Read the three extracts from newspaper articles on the next page, and answer these questions.**

1 What are the three classes of bonds mentioned?
2 What, according to the journalists and the experts quoted, is happening that makes each type of bond a good investment opportunity?
3 Why is the government buying back billions of pounds worth of bonds?
4 What kind of companies issue high-yield bonds?
5 What is the risk involved with buying high-yield bonds, and how can it be reduced?

### Vocabulary

**Find words in the articles that mean the following:**

1 rose quickly
2 to revive or stimulate something
3 a standard used when comparing other things
4 a period when the economy is contracting (*three different words*)
5 an improvement or increase in prices
6 failing to repay a loan
7 another word for going bankrupt

"LET'S RENAME IT 'THE LOSERS' FUND' AND MARKET IT TO PEOPLE WITH LOW SELF-ESTEEM."

www.cartoonstock.com

## Discussion

- **What has happened to bond prices since the predictions on page 84 were made during the recession in 2008/9? Were the journalists and experts correct?**

# Rush to buy government bonds

UK government bonds soared for a second day yesterday after the Bank of England unveiled plans to buy billions of pounds of assets to kickstart the economy. Fund managers and speculators rushed to buy government bonds, known as gilts, driving up prices. Benchmark 10-year gilt prices saw their biggest one-day jump in 17 years yesterday.

The central bank will create new money to buy £75bn of assets, mainly gilts, at a series of auctions over the next three months. Another £75bn could follow. Many economists believe the unprecedented measures should be enough eventually to lift the economy out of its worst slump since the 1930s.

John Wraith of RBC Capital Markets expects the rally in the gilt market to continue for some time. 'A lot of people will now want to own gilts on the assumption that prices will keep on rising,' he said.

*The Guardian*

## Corporate bonds: the only 'hot' story in town

Good news is thin on the ground for investors. Only brave hearts would look at getting back into the stock market at the moment, as it is still unclear whether we are headed for a worldwide recession or depression.

So any area of investment that promises growth is going to spark more than a little interest. And it's the unglamorous world of corporate bonds that is catching the attention of those in the know. These bonds, it seems, are the one potentially 'hot' investment of 2009.

'They represent the opportunity of a generation, offering both capital growth and relatively high income,' says Meera Patel, senior analyst at independent financial adviser Hargreaves Lansdown. With the world economy speeding downwards, companies that were once thought ultra-safe are now being forced to offer higher returns to investors.

*The Independent*

## Why high-yield bonds are only for the brave

For UK investors, opportunities are currently on offer within high-yield bonds. Having been generally overlooked by most investors over the past decade, this asset class has started to grow in popularity, partly due to the staggeringly high yields they have offered since the world plunged into recession last year.

Patrick McCullagh, head of European and UK credit research at Schroders, expects high-yield bonds to be offering more attractive opportunities than the investment-grade corporate bonds that are currently in favour.

High-yield bonds are investments in the debt of companies that are deemed – by a ratings agency such as Standard & Poor's – to have a greater chance of defaulting on their loans. The lower a company's rating, the more likely they are to go bust, but the more investors will be paid for accepting that increased risk. It means that fund managers who choose wisely can make decent money from this area.

*The Independent*

## **Case study:** Investing in funds

**In pairs or small groups, look at the advertisements opposite for different bond funds offered for sale by banks.**

**Imagine that you have $30,000 or €30,000 or £20,000 (etc.) to invest in bonds.**

- **Which fund or funds would you choose? Why?**
- **What might be the risks associated with each fund?**

## Writing

**Write a short report (100–150 words) explaining and justifying your choices.**

**This could begin:** We decided to invest in ... because ...

1

## Renewable energy fund

This fund invests in small firms that lead the global market in manufacturing equipment for generating wind power, building wind farms and producing solar energy systems. Energy is now being produced at competitive prices from wind and solar sources at suitable locations, offering customers an attractively priced, reliable and environment-friendly supply. Investors have an opportunity to benefit from the industry's high rate of growth by investing in its leading players.

2

## Emerging markets fund

This fund aims to achieve a high and steady income and an above average yield, whilst taking into account the security of capital. The fund invests in debt securities in various currencies issued by governments, institutions and companies in emerging markets in four continents. Emerging markets today account for one third of economic activity worldwide and three-quarters of global growth. They are additionally profiting from their strong competitive position as production locations.

3

## High-yield US fund

This fund aims to achieve a high level of income, although considerable fluctuations in price cannot be ruled out. The fund invests at least two-thirds of its assets in US-denominated non-investment grade bonds issued by US companies.

4

## Luxury goods fund

This fund invests in companies that produce high-priced prestigious branded luxury goods that enjoy stable demand even during tough times for the overall economy. Economic growth in emerging markets is leading to greater purchasing power and opening up significant new sales markets for luxury goods firms.

5

## Ethical growth fund

This fund aims to achieve the highest possible capital growth while investing only in ethically or socially responsible companies. The fund invests in companies whose products and services generate long-term economic, ecological and social benefits. It avoids companies with interests in armaments, tobacco, alcoholic beverages, gambling, pornography, non-medical animal testing, intensive farming, and nuclear energy.

6

## Global microfinance fund

This fund invests in all segments of the global microfinance markets. Loans are administered by established microfinance institutions on three continents. The fund aims at long-term growth in value that is higher than the fund currency's money market value. Microfinance clients operate in an environment that is largely separate from developments in the global markets. They consequently offer excellent possibilities for diversification.

7

## Protection fund

This fund aims to achieve a steady inflation-protected return in euros. The fund invests its net assets worldwide, in accordance with the principle of risk-spreading, in medium to high quality inflation-linked debt securities.

8

## Dynamic international fund

This fund aims to achieve high and steady long-term earnings by investing in Eurobonds across the entire range of borrower ratings and maturities. Investments are made globally with no restrictions as to country, currency or sector. Sizeable short-term price fluctuations are possible.

# 17 Stocks and shares

## Aims

- Consider the uses of stocks and shares and ways of talking about price changes
- Discuss different possible investments

## Lead-in

If you have money to invest, what are the advantages and disadvantages of:

- putting it under the mattress
- buying a lottery ticket
- taking it all to Las Vegas or Monte Carlo
- depositing it in a bank
- buying gold
- buying a painting (Matisse, Van Gogh, etc.)
- investing in property or real estate
- buying bonds
- buying stocks or shares
- investing in a hedge fund
- giving it away?

## Reading: Stocks and shares

**Match up the half-sentences below, which make up a text about stocks and shares.**

1 Successful companies can issue stocks or shares (certificates representing part ownership of the company)
2 Offering these stocks for sale to financial institutions and the general public changes the business
3 Selling stocks for the first time is called an IPO or initial public offering in the US
4 Companies use an investment bank to find buyers, and to underwrite the stock issue,
5 Stocks and shares are also known as equity or equities; the most common form
6 After shares have been issued they can be traded on the secondary market at
7 Some stock exchanges have automatic computerized trading systems that match up buyers and sellers; others have market makers –
8 Stock prices rise and fall depending on supply and demand,
9 Consequently the nominal value of a share – the price written on it – is rarely the same as its market price –
10 Companies either distribute part of their profits to shareholders as an annual dividend,
11 Stock markets are measured by stock indexes (or indices),
12 A period during which most stocks (and the stock index) are rising is called a bull market,

**A** and a flotation or an IPO in Britain.
**B** and one in which most of them fall in value is a bear market.
**C** the stock exchange on which the company is listed or quoted.
**D** from a private to a public company, and is called going public.
**E** i.e. how many sellers and buyers there are.
**F** i.e. to guarantee to buy the stocks if there are not enough other buyers.
**G** is called common stock in the US, and ordinary shares in Britain.
**H** or keep the profits in the company, which also causes the value of the stocks to rise.
**I** the price it is currently being traded at on the stock exchange.
**J** to raise capital to expand their operations.
**K** traders in stocks who quote bid (buying) and offer (selling) prices.
**L** which show changes in the average prices of a selected group of important stocks.

| 1 | J | 2 | | 3 | | 4 | | 5 | | 6 | | 7 | | 8 | | 9 | | 10 | | 11 | | 12 | |
|---|---|---|---|---|---|---|---|---|---|---|---|---|---|---|---|---|---|---|---|---|---|---|---|

## Discussion

1 Many economists argue that it is (theoretically) impossible to regularly outperform the stock market, as all available information is already factored into a company's share price. So analysing a company's finances, or trying to discover or predict patterns in price movements, is a waste of time. What implications does this have for investors?
2 Imagine that you have just come from a secret meeting of a company's board of directors, which has made a decision that you know will financially ruin some close friends of yours unless they can sell some shares before the board's decision becomes known. You are having dinner at their home that same evening. Should they expect you to warn them? Should you do so?
3 How can you make money from a falling stock market (when prices are going down)?

## **Listening:** A financial news report ▶2.3

**Listen to an extract from a financial market report on an American radio station. The newsreader mentions the prices of the following securities, currencies and commodities. In each case, does she say that the price has risen, fallen, or stayed almost the same?**

| | Risen | Fallen | Unchanged |
|---|---|---|---|
| The Dow-Jones | | | |
| The S&P 500 | | | |
| The NASDAQ | | | |
| Shares in Germany | | | |
| Shares in France | | | |
| Shares in Britain | | | |
| Shares in Japan | | | |
| Shares in Australia | | | |
| The dollar against the euro | | | |
| The dollar against the pound | | | |
| The dollar against the yen | | | |
| Gold | | | |
| Oil | | | |

### British and American usage

The terms *stocks* and *stockholders* are used in the USA, and *shares* and *shareholders* in Britain. In Britain, *stock* can also mean securities such as government bonds. The terms *stock exchange, stock market* and *stockbroker* are used in all English-speaking countries. The most common type of equity is called *common stock* in the US, and *ordinary shares* in Britain. Some companies also have *preferred stock* (AmE) or *preference shares* (BrE) that receive a fixed dividend.

"Today share prices fell sharply on the fear that share prices might fall sharply."

www.cartoonstock.com

*"Will you please try to get your mind off of the S.&P. Index?"*

## Vocabulary

**Rather than endlessly repeating the words 'rose' and 'fell', financial journalists use a large number of verbs and phrases to describe the movements of security prices. Classify the following sentences, according to whether you think the verb or expression means:**

**A** to rise after previously falling **B** to rise a little **C** to rise a lot
**D** to fall a little **E** to fall a lot

**1** ___ Volkswagen shares rocketed after the revelation that Porsche has upped its stake in the company to 74%.

**2** ___ The Sensex index of the Bombay Stock Exchange crashed on Monday on fears of a recession in the US.

**3** ___ Visa shot up yesterday on the NYSE on its first trading day, rising as high as $69 a share.

**4** ___ The Footsie revived a little in London in the afternoon, gaining 30 points in late trading.

**5** ___ After the strong gains of last week, Asian shares slipped on fears of a looming recession.

**6** ___ In Milan, the S&P/MIB index plummeted, after the unions called for a three-day general strike next week.

**7** ___ Leading shares were slightly weaker in Switzerland, the Swiss Market Index losing 20 points.

**8** ___ Share prices recovered in Hong Kong today, the Hang Seng finishing up ten points.

**9** ___ On the São Paulo exchange, the Bovespa Index advanced a little, up 12 points.

**10** ___ Chinese shares jumped after a two-thirds cut in a securities trading tax.

**11** ___ Even after the government bailout, Citigroup is continuing to plunge, now down to $1.95.

**12** ___ Most shares were a little stronger in Madrid this morning, when the exchange reopened after yesterday's public holiday.

## **Reading:** Hedge funds

**Hedge funds are private investment funds for wealthy investors that trade in securities and derivatives, and try to get high returns whether markets move up or down. Read the following extract from Geraint Anderson's book *Cityboy*, which explains one of the major strategies of hedge funds, and answer the questions.**

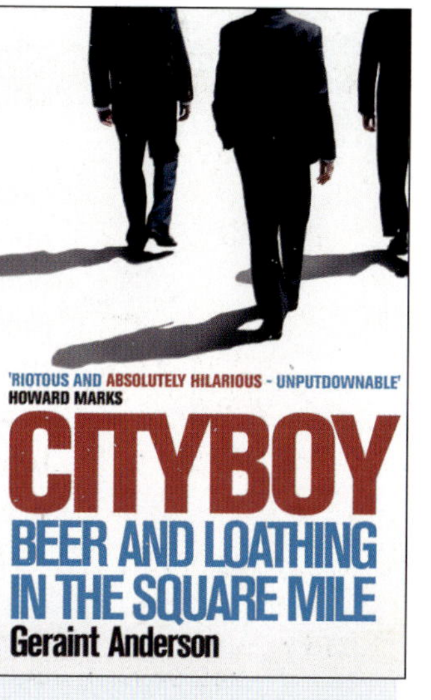


The rise of hedge funds began in earnest around 2001. By then stock markets had been in decline for around a year after the bursting of the tech bubble. With no end to the bear market in sight investors wanted to make returns that were not geared to the performance of the stock market. They wished to make an absolute return even if stock markets fell. They demanded what Cityboys, in their never-ending mission to confuse the general public, like to call 'Alpha' not 'Beta'. Hence, hedge funds became increasingly popular since, unlike conventional 'long-only' funds, they can 'short' shares. That is to say, they can sell shares they don't own by borrowing them off a conventional fund so that when the share price falls they make a profit by buying them back at a cheaper price. As the bear market continued cash began pouring into these funds. [...] As these hedge funds multiplied and grew, investment banks had no choice but to prioritize them relative to their old, traditional long-only clients because some of these crazy guys *really* like trading shares. Whilst your typical pension fund might, on average, hold on to a share for a year or more I've seen certain hedge funds buy in the morning and sell in the afternoon. Hell, I've even seen buy and sell orders in the same stock within an hour! On certain days, one of the biggest hedge funds, GLG, has been said to be behind five per cent of all the trades in the FTSE 100.

1 What does 'the bursting of the tech bubble' mean?
2 Anderson calls the people working in the financial industry 'Cityboys'. What implied meanings does this word convey?
3 What is Anderson implying by 'their never-ending mission to confuse the general public'?
4 Explain in your own words how hedge funds make money by shorting shares.
5 Why did 'investment banks [have] no choice but to prioritize' hedge funds?

**Vocabulary note**

*Alpha:* A risk-adjusted measure of the active return on an investment, i.e. the return that exceeds normal compensation for the risk involved. A high value for alpha implies that a stock or fund has performed better than would have been expected given its beta.

*Beta:* A measure of the elasticity or relative volatility of a security: the rate at which its price moves up and down compared to the market as a whole.

## Role play: Investing a client's money

**Imagine that you are an asset manager, investing money for a client. In pairs or small groups, select ten different securities, and invest an imaginary €100,000 in them (or the equivalent in your local currency), dividing up the sum as you wish. Your client does not particularly want to take risks.**

**Choose several** blue chips **– shares in large, well-established companies with a good reputation for quality and profitability – as well as two companies that have only been listed or quoted on a stock exchange for less than a year (this information can be found in the financial pages of newspapers and on financial websites). You can choose companies on any major stock exchange, but remember that if you buy stocks in foreign currencies there is a risk of exchange rate movements.**

**A safe investment for part of the sum would be an** index fund **or** tracker fund **or** exchange-traded fund (ETF) **that seeks to replicate the performance of an entire market (e.g. the S&P 500), so it won't lose (or gain) more than the market as a whole. Major banks sell shares in funds like these (similar to the bond funds mentioned in Unit 16). Another possibility, if you expected interest rates to fall in the near future, would be to include some** bonds **in the portfolio.**

**Follow the progress of your portfolio in the financial press or on the Internet. Depending on the length of your course, select a date to make a short presentation reporting on the how well or badly the portfolio has done, and attempting to provide reasons or explanations for any price changes.**

# 18 Derivatives

**Aims**

- Consider the uses of derivatives
- Discuss the dangers of derivatives

## Lead-in

- What are the main types of derivatives?
- What are they used for?

**Trader's $29 Billion Bet Brings Down Barings Bank**

**Daiwa Bank Says Trader Lost $1.1 Billion on Deals in US**

**Long-Term Capital Management: Fallen Hedge Fund To Receive $3.5 Billion Bailout**

**Allied Irish Bank: Trader's Losses Total $750 Million**

**Financial Weapons Of Mass Destruction Designed By Madmen: Was Warren Buffett Right?**

**Rogue Trader Loses Société Générale 4.9 Billion Euros**

- The headlines above suggest that derivatives are potentially much more risky than other financial products. Why?
- Can you remember any other examples of financial institutions that have lost huge sums of money on derivative deals that went wrong?
- The American investor Warren Buffett is said to be the second richest man in the world (after Bill Gates). What do you think about his assessment of derivatives in the headline above?

## **Vocabulary:** Derivatives

**Before reading and hearing about derivatives, match up the half-sentences below which define some basic terms.**

1. **Derivatives** are financial instruments whose prices are dependent upon, or derived from,
2. A **future** is a contract agreement to buy or sell a security, commodity or financial instrument
3. An **option** offers the buyer the right, but not the obligation,
4. **Commodities** are raw materials or primary products such as
5. **Hedging** means making contracts to buy or sell commodities or financial assets
6. **Speculation**, on the contrary, means buying assets in the hope of making a capital gain
7. An **interest rate swap** is an agreement to exchange future interest payments
8. A **currency swap** is an agreement between two parties who exchange principal and fixed rate interest payments

**A** at a predetermined price, at a predetermined point the future.

**B** by selling them later at a higher price (or selling ther in the hope of buying them back at a lower price).

**C** in the future, at a pre-arranged price, as a protection against price changes.

**D** metals, cereals, coffee, etc., that are traded on spec markets.

**E** to buy (call option) or sell (put option) an asset at an agreed-upon price (the strike price), either during a certain period of time, or on a specific date.

**F** underlying assets such as stocks, bonds, commodities, currencies, interest rates and market indices.

**G** on a loan in one currency for principal and fixed rate interest payments on an equal loan in another currency.

**H** with another company or financial institution, e.g. a floating rate loan for a fixed interest rate loan.

| 1 | | 2 | | 3 | | 4 | | 5 | | 6 | | 7 | | 8 | |
|---|---|---|---|---|---|---|---|---|---|---|---|---|---|---|---|

### Discussion

**What could the following people or companies do, using futures and derivatives?**

1. A cocoa grower who thinks the price might drop and a chocolate manufacturer who thinks the price might rise.
2. A company with a lot of fixed interest debt that expects interest rates to fall.
3. An investor who expects the price of a stock to fall in the next few weeks or months.
4. An investor who expects the price of a stock to rise in the next few weeks or months.
5. Are the financial instruments in your answers to 1– what people call 'win–win situations' or 'zero-sum games'? Can you explain these terms?

## **Listening:** Hedge funds and structured products 2.4

**Listen to Teresa La Thangue of the Financial Services Authority, which regulates the financial industry in Britain, talking about hedge funds and structured products, and answer the questions.**

1. Why can't individuals (retail investors) invest in hedge funds in Britain?
2. In what way have hedge funds changed since they began?
3. What are the five forms of investment that Teresa La Thangue mentions in relation to hedge funds?
4. Retail investors can buy structured products from banks. What constraint must banks obey when developing these products?

**Teresa La Thangue**

## **Reading:** Spread-betting

**Read the text below, from *Times Online*, and answer these questions.**

1 Find an expression that means 'having a bet'.
2 In which expressions does the journalist indicate that you are likely to lose?
3 Is it true that 'your potential losses are unlimited'?
4 Are all the examples given in the article about gambling?

**TIMESONLINE**

NEWS COMMENT BUSINESS MONEY SPORT

### Things to know about spread-betting

Once the preserve of City dealers, spread-betting – which enables you to gamble on the direction of shares, commodities or stock market indices – is becoming more popular among ordinary investors, with as many as 150,000 now taking part.

### Health warning

Spread-betting is gambling, not investing. You are taking a punt on the future movement (either up or down) of a share price, index or a commodity. Remember that the odds are in the spread-betting company's favour and that your potential losses are unlimited.

### Tax break

As spread-betting is gambling, all profits are free of capital gains tax – that's if you make any profits, of course.

### How it works

The spread-betting company will quote a bid (selling) and offer (buying) price for the FTSE 100 index, say 5,016 and 5,018. The difference between these prices is the spread. If you think that the index will rise, you might 'buy' at £10 a point at 5,018. If you allow your bet to run until the market's close and the FTSE rises to 5,053, your profit will be the difference between the closing price of 5,053 and the opening price you were quoted (5,018) times £10, giving a total of £350. If you wanted to bet that the market will fall, you would 'sell' at 5,016, hoping that it would drop below this level.

### Pain barrier

Set up a 'stop-loss' limit, which will close your trade at a set level if the price moves against you.

### Correct timing

Some spread-betting participants close their trades daily, but you can leave positions for longer. A woman who took out two bets on shares in Google at £1 a point and £2 a point held her positions open for more than two months. She made £27,000 profit.

### Risk reduction

Some investors use spread-bets to hedge, or protect, their positions. But the usual risk warnings apply. For example, someone with £10,000 invested in a FTSE 100 tracker fund and who is worried about a fall in the stock market could 'hedge' the position by selling the FTSE 100 index on a spread-bet. If the index closes at 5,386, an investor can sell at £1.86 a point (£10,000/5,386). For every point the FTSE 100 falls, the investor will make £1.86 on the bet to cover losses in the tracker fund.

## Discussion: Investing, speculating and gambling

**invest** *verb*
**investment** *noun*

to put money, effort, time etc. into something to make a profit or get an advantage

**speculate** *verb*
**speculation** *noun*

to buy and sell in the hope that the value of what you buy will increase and that it can then be sold at a higher price in order to make a profit

**gamble** *verb*
**gambling** *noun*

1 to do something risky that might result in loss of money or failure, hoping to get money or achieve success

2 to risk money, for example in a game or on a horse race

*Cambridge Advanced Learner's Dictionary*

- **From what you know about stocks, bonds, currencies, futures, options, swaps, and structured products involving combinations of these assets, would you say buying and selling each of them is a matter of:**

  **a** investment
  **b** speculation, or
  **c** gambling?

## Role play: Financial instruments

**Trainees in an investment bank are being tested on their knowledge of financial instruments (bonds, stocks, derivatives, etc.). The training manager gives them questions to answer. Your teacher will give you a role and some questions.**

## Writing

**Write the answers to one of the sets of questions, either as a short training memo for junior bank staff, or as an information leaflet for bank customers.**

# 19 Accounting and financial statements

## Aims

- Consider the different types of accounting and financial statements
- Discuss a company's financial results

*"Perhaps we could find a way to redefine 'profit'."*



## Lead-in

- What is accounting?
- What skills do you think accountants need?
- Do you think you have these skills? (What are *your* assets and liabilities?)
- If you have not yet chosen a career, could it be accountancy?

## Vocabulary

**1 Which basic accounting words are defined below?**

**1** all the money received from business activities during a given period
**A** assets **B** income **C** transactions

**2** all the money that a business spends on goods or services during a given period
**A** debts **B** expenditure **C** liabilities

**3** a financial operating plan showing expected income and expenditure
**A** account **B** budget **C** financial statement

**4** anything owned by a business – cash, buildings, machines, equipment, etc.
**A** asset **B** income **C** revenue

**5** all the money that a company will have to pay to someone else in the future, including debts, taxes and interest payments
**A** debits **B** expenditure **C** liabilities

**6** an entry in an account, recording a payment made
**A** credit **B** debt **C** debit

**7** an entry in an account, recording a payment received
**A** credit **B** debit **C** income

**8** adjective describing something without a material existence, which you can't touch
**A** current **B** intangible **C** tangible

**9** adjective describing a liability which has been incurred but not yet invoiced to the company
**A** accrued **B** deferred **C** receivable

**10** delayed or postponed until a later time
**A** deferred **B** payable **C** retained

**2 How well do you know the different types of accounting and the different branches of the accounting (or accountancy) profession? Match the terms with the definitions in the box below.**

accounting   auditing   bookkeeping   cost accounting
'creative accounting'   managerial or management accounting   tax accounting

**1** calculating all the expenses involved in producing something, including materials, labour, and all other expenses

2 calculating how much an individual or a company will have to pay to the local and national governments (and trying to reduce this to a minimum)
3 inspecting and reporting on accounts and financial records
4 preparing financial statements showing income and expenditure, assets and liabilities
5 providing information that will allow a business to make decisions, plan future operations and develop business strategies
6 using all available accounting procedures and tricks to disguise the true financial position of a company
7 writing down the details of transactions (debits and credits)

- **Which of these areas of accounting do you find the most interesting?**

**3 Match up the names of the financial statements with the definitions below.**

| | | |
|---|---|---|
| **1** Balance sheet (or Statement of financial position) | **2** Cash flow statement | **3** Income statement (or Statement of income, Profit and loss statement, or Profit and loss account) |

**A** a statement giving details of money coming into and leaving the business, divided into day-to-day operations, investing and financing
**B** a statement showing the difference between the revenues and expenses of a period
**C** a statement showing the value of a business's assets, its liabilities, and its capital or shareholders' equity (money the business has that belongs to its owners)

**4 Make common word combinations with the verbs and nouns below.**

| | |
|---|---|
| calculate<br>keep<br>pay<br>receive<br>record<br>value | assets<br>expenditure<br>income<br>liabilities<br>records<br>taxes<br>transactions |

## Reading 1: Google Inc. Balance sheet

**Look at the balance sheet opposite, and answer these questions.**

1 Which lines on the balance sheet do the definitions below it refer to? (Two have been done as examples.)
2 Which two figures have to be the same (to balance), by definition?
3 How much money had the company already paid in advance for goods and services, on the date of the 2008 balance sheet?
4 At the 2008 balance sheet date, which is greater, the amount of capital the shareholders have paid into the company, or the amount of profit that has not been spent?
5 At the 2008 balance sheet date, which total is higher – the money Google currently owes, or the money that it is owed?

## Google Inc.
### Balance Sheet

| In Millions of $ | As of 2008-12-31 | As of 2007-12-31 |
|---|---|---|
| Cash & Equivalents | 8,656.67 | 6,081.59 |
| Short Term Investments | 7,189.10 | 8,137.02 |
| Total Receivables, Net | 2,642.19 | 2,162.53 |
| Prepaid Expenses | 1,404.11 | 694.21 |
| Other Current Assets, Total | 286.11 | 213.79 |
| **Total Current Assets** | **20,178.18** | **17,289.14** |
| Property/Plant/Equipment, Total – Gross | 5,233.84 | 4,039.26 |
| Goodwill, Net **(10)** | 4,839.85 | 2,299.37 |
| Intangibles, Net | 996.69 | 446.60 |
| Long Term Investments | 85.16 | 1,059.69 |
| Other Long Term Assets, Total | 433.85 | 201.75 |
| **Total Assets** | **31,767.57** | **25,335.81** |
| Accounts Payable | 178.00 | 282.11 |
| Accrued Expenses | 1,824.46 | 1,575.42 |
| Other Current Liabilities, Total | 299.63 | 178.07 |
| **Total Current Liabilities** | **2,302.09** | **2,035.60** |
| Deferred Income Tax | 12.51 | 0.00 |
| Other Long Term Liabilities, Total | 1,214.11 | 610.53 |
| **Total Liabilities** | **3,528.71** | **2,646.13** |
| Common Stock, Total | 0.31 | 0.31 |
| Additional Paid-In Capital | 14,450.34 | 13,241.22 |
| Retained Earnings **(8)** | 13,561.63 | 9,334.78 |
| Other Equity, Total | 226.58 | 113.37 |
| **Total Equity** | **28,238.86** | **22,689.68** |
| **Total Liabilities & Shareholders' Equity** | **31,767.57** | **25,335.81** |

1. all the money belonging to the company's owners
2. assets whose value can only be turned into cash with difficulty (e.g. reputation, patents, trade marks, etc.)
3. capital that shareholders have contributed to the company above the nominal or par value of the stock
4. expenses such as wages, taxes and interest that have not yet been paid at the date of the balance sheet
5. money owed by customers for goods or services purchased on credit
6. money owed to suppliers for purchases made on credit
7. money paid in advance for goods and services
8. profits that have not been distributed to shareholders
9. tangible assets such as offices, machines, etc.
10. the difference between the purchase price of acquired companies and their net tangible assets
11. the total amount of money owed that the company will have to pay out

## Listening: Valuing assets ▶2.5

Richard Barker

**Richard Barker is the director of the MBA programme at the Judge Business School of Cambridge University, and an expert on international accounting. Listen to him talking about valuing assets, and answer the questions.**

1. What examples does Richard Barker give of assets that are difficult to value?
2. How does he define a company's annual profit or loss?
3. Why is the estimated value of an airport runway probably not very objective?
4. How does he define or explain depreciation?

### Discussion

- **How would you put a value on your college or university? What are its major assets – buildings and equipment, or people and their skills, knowledge and reputations?**
- **In most countries, companies record the historical cost of their assets – their original purchase price, and not their (estimated) current selling price or replacement cost. Why?**
- **Should companies record raw materials, work-in-progress, and their inventory of products ready for sale at their cost price, or their current market price (the price at which they could be sold)?**
- **Give some examples of companies whose value largely derives from intangible assets such as their well-known brands, or their good reputation.**

## Reading 2: Google Inc. Income statement

**Look the income statement opposite. Which lines refer to the following?**

1. money received from investments
2. money spent in order to produce income in the future
3. the expenses specific to providing the company's services
4. additional expenses involved in running the company

### Vocabulary: Cash flow statement

**Cash flow statements contain three categories: Cash from Operating Activities (Ops.), Cash from Investing Activities (Inv.) and Cash from Financing Activities (Fin.). Which categories do the following items belong to (as positive or negative amounts)?**

| | Ops. | Inv. | Fin. |
|---|---|---|---|
| Amortization (loss of value of intangible assets) | | | |
| Changes in the size of the inventory | | | |
| Depreciation (loss of value of tangible assets) | | | |
| Dividends paid | | | |
| Income taxes paid | | | |
| Payments to suppliers for goods and services | | | |
| Payments to employees | | | |
| Proceeds from issuing shares or debt | | | |
| Purchases or sales of property, plant and equipment | | | |
| Receipts from the sale of goods or services | | | |
| Repurchase of company shares or repayment of debt | | | |

## Google Inc. Income Statement

| In Millions of $ | 12 months ending 2008-12-31 | 12 months ending 2007-12-31 |
|---|---|---|
| **Total Revenue** | **21,795.55** | **16,593.99** |
| Cost of Revenue, Total | 8,621.51 | 6,649.09 |
| **Gross Profit** | **13,174.04** | **9,944.90** |
| Selling/General/Administrative Expenses | 3,748.88 | 2,740.52 |
| Research & Development | 2,793.19 | 2,119.98 |
| Unusual Expense (Income) | 1,094.76 | 0.00 |
| **Total Operating Expense** | **16,258.34** | **11,509.59** |
| **Operating Income** | **5,537.21** | **5,084.40** |
| (Non-operating) Interest Income Net | 311.89 | 594.28 |
| Other, Net | 4.50 | (4.70) |
| **Net Income Before Tax** | **5,853.60** | **5,673.98** |
| **Net Income After Tax** | **4,226.86** | **4,203.72** |

### Vocabulary note

Google's financial statements use American terms, which sometimes differ from British ones.

| American English | British English |
|---|---|
| Accounts Payable | Creditors |
| Receivables or Accounts Receivable | Debtors |
| Additional Paid-in Capital | Share Premium |
| Annual Stockholders Meeting | Annual General Meeting |
| Common Stock | Ordinary Shares |
| Net income | Profit |

## Role play: Presenting a company's results

**The Chief Financial Officer of Google Inc. is going to present the company's results at the Annual Stockholders Meeting. He/she will refer to the Balance Sheet and Income Statement, and explain which figures have increased and which have decreased. In groups, prepare the presentation.**

**If this is a homework task to prepare for the next lesson, you could look up more recent figures on the Internet on sites such as http://investor.google.com, http://finance.yahoo.com and http://moneycentral.msn.com, rather than use the figures given here. You could also use the company's website or the Internet to find details about acquisitions, product developments, and so on, which might explain any changes.**

**Alternatively, you could present the accounts of a company you work for or have worked for or know well.**

# 20 Market structure and competition

## Aims

- Consider the standard structure of markets for products and services
- Discuss existing and potential industrial clusters

## Lead-in

Think of durable consumer goods that your family possesses – perhaps a car, a computer, a television, a music player, a camera, a cooker, a fridge, furniture, and so on. Think also of your favourite clothes. Think of the brands of food and drink you habitually consume, and personal hygiene products you use.

In each case, do you know whether the company that makes them is:

- the *market leader* (with the biggest market share)
- the *market challenger* (the second-biggest company in the industry)
- or one of many smaller *market followers*?

*"I'm looking for something slightly more perfect."*



If you have bought products that are *not* produced by the market leader or a well-known market challenger, is the reason:

- chance
- price
- because they have a *unique selling proposition*: something that makes them different from any other product, and which appeals to you
- because you need something special, and are part of a particular small *niche* or *market segment*?

Have you bought products sold by *new entrants* to a market which later became big and successful companies? Give examples.

## Reading: Market structure

**Read the text and insert these words in the gaps:**

differentiated market challenger market followers market leader market segmentation market share niche unique selling proposition (or USP)

In most markets there is a definite [1] ____________ : the firm with the largest [2] ____________ . This is often the first company to have entered the field, or at least the first to have succeeded in it. In many markets, there is often also a distinct [3] ____________ , with the second-largest market share. In the car hire business, the challenger actually advertised this fact for many years: Avis used the slogan 'We're number two.

We try harder,' and got closer to the leader Hertz. The second-largest company in an industry can either attempt to attack the leader, or to increase its market share by attacking various 4 ________________ .

Most of the smaller companies in any industry present no threat to the leader. Many of them concentrate on 5 market segmentation: selling profitable 6 niche products that are in some way 7 differentiated from the products of larger companies, and which have growth potential. A smaller competitor which does not differentiate its product is in a dangerous position: if its product does not have a 8 unique selling proposition there is no reason for anyone to buy it. This is especially true in recessions when, for psychological reasons, distributors, retailers and customers all prefer to buy from big, well-known suppliers.

**In many industries, there is a leader, a challenger, and many followers**

## Vocabulary

**Before listening to a company director talking about industrial evolution, match up the words and definitions below.**

| | | | | |
|---|---|---|---|---|
| address or tackle | attorney | cluster | disrupt | dominate |
| entrepreneur | headhunter | landlord | patent | vulnerable |

**1** a group of similar things (e.g. companies) situated close together
**2** a person or organization that owns a building or an area of land and rents it to other people
**3** a person who starts their own business, especially when this involves taking risks
**4** a recruiter of important personnel for companies
**5** an alternative American term for a lawyer
**6** likely to be attacked
**7** the official legal right to make or sell an invention for a particular number of years
**8** to have control over something, or to be the most important person or thing
**9** to prevent something from continuing as expected
**10** to try to deal with a problem

Charles Cotton

## Listening 1: Early stage companies ▶2.6

**Charles Cotton is the former CEO of a high-tech company in California, and is currently a director of several high-tech companies. You will hear him talking about how early stage companies can either change existing industries or create and dominate whole new ones.**

- **Charles Cotton mentions some of the most successful internet-based companies of the previous 20 years. What do you think these are?**

**Listen to Charles Cotton and answer the questions.**

1 How does he describe 'the perspective of an early stage company'?
2 Which companies does he mention?
3 What does he mean when he says some industries are 'defined by the new entrants'?

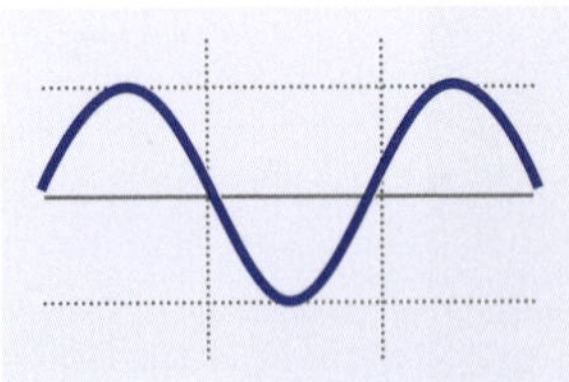

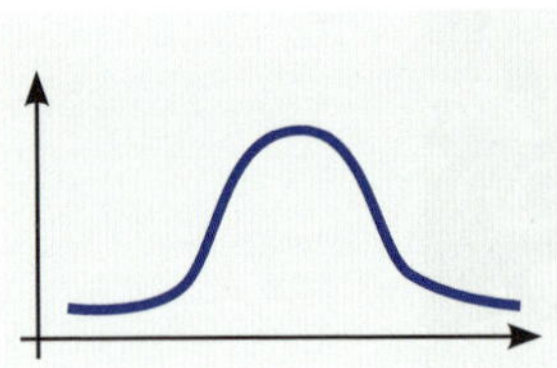

## Listening 2: Sine waves and bell curves ▶2.7

- **Charles Cotton says that industries go through 'sine waves or bell curves'. Can you explain these terms?**

**Listen to Charles Cotton talking about how industries evolve, and answer the questions.**

1 What was Google's problem at the time the recording was made?
2 Fill in the gaps below.

> ... you know, a [1] ______ moves in to being a [2] ______ player, potentially with other strong players, but over time their position is, becomes more [3] ______, and they are, they find themselves being [4] ______ ______ by younger, newer, fresher, more exciting new ideas.
>
> So, [5] ______, new ideas, [6] ______, address, tackle, [7] ______ ______ existing, [8] ______-______ industries and structures, but it's an [9] ______.

## Discussion: Clusters

**You will hear Charles Cotton talking about industrial clusters: groups of companies in the same industry that establish themselves in the same area.**

- **Which industries do you associate with the following places:**
  Bangalore Detroit Hollywood Las Vegas Paris Silicon Valley
  the area around Bordeaux?
- **Can you think of any other industrial clusters?**
- **Why do start-ups often situate themselves near other companies in the same industry?**
- **Why do similar shops and restaurants often do business right next to each other?**

## Listening 3: Clustering ▶2.8

1 What are the two 'well-established examples' of clusters that Charles Cotton cites?
2 What are the four others?
3 What is the reason for clusters having evolved in these particular places?
4 What do people moving into a business environment need?
5 Fill in the gaps below.

So some of the other factors that make clusters successful are all of the supporting services like the lawyers, the accountants, the [1] ______ ______, the [2] ______, the recruiters, the people who provide catering services for the companies that come along, the [3] ______ and so on, so you get this vast circle of activity around, around a cluster, which then builds into something more than what starts as a [4] ______ cluster into a, into an [5] ______ cluster itself.

## Listening 4: Software-based clusters ▶2.9

- **You will hear Charles Cotton talk about countries with excellent and inexpensive software programmers and developers. Which countries do you think these are?**

**Now listen, and answer these questions.**

1 Who does Charles Cotton describe as 'the most creative people on the planet'?
2 Why did they need to become so good at what they did?
3 What is their advantage over competitors from the other country he mentions?

## Listening 5: Clusters of the future ▶2.10

1 Which three large countries does Charles Cotton talk about?
2 What factors do they have in common that will make them successful?

- **Do you agree with Charles Cotton? Can you see any other countries successfully developing economic clusters? In what fields?**

## **Case study:** Encouraging clusters

**Imagine that you (in pairs or small groups) have been invited by the government (in your country, or the country in which you are studying) to advise them about economic development.**

**The government wants to encourage clusters – groups of interconnected companies that will be able to exchange information, ideas and innovations, and associated suppliers and service providers. They hope that clusters of businesses will develop a competitive advantage over other countries or regions.**

- **The following factors are generally important in the development of clusters:**

  - a skilled workforce that meets the needs of the industry
  - a good infrastructure (roads, utilities, communications)
  - a good education system providing specialized training
  - already-existing companies in a growing industry
  - a good business environment (simple procedures for starting new businesses, no 'barriers to entry' for new companies, reasonable tax rates, etc.)
  - a network of small companies that could supply inputs (components, machinery) and business services to the core industry
  - a government department that can provide information, research and technical support
  - a spirit of collaboration as well as competition
  - venture capital firms and other sources of finance
  - mobility: people can easily move to a thriving economic region (e.g. there are possibilities to buy, sell and rent accommodation, and enrol children in schools)

- **Can you think of any other factors that could be important?**
- **Which of these factors does your country possess?**

**Prepare a short presentation for the government, explaining:**

- **what actions they could take to increase the chances of a successful cluster developing**
- **which industries should be encouraged**
- **in which sector of the economy.**

**Then present your ideas to another group, or to the whole class.**

### Writing

**Write a short briefing document (150–200 words) to present to the government, summarizing your group's conclusions and recommendations.**

# 21 Takeovers

**Aims**

- Consider the reasons for takeovers and mergers, and competition laws
- Discuss whether dominant companies are bad for competition

## Lead-in

- Why do companies take over other companies?
- How do companies take over other companies?
- What is a merger?
- Have there been any big takeovers or mergers in the news recently?
- Why do you think they happened?

## Reading: Takeovers, mergers and buyouts

**Read the text below, and underline the answers to the first three questions above.**

Successful companies have to find ways of using their profits. Sometimes they develop new products or services, perhaps to diversify and enter new markets, but sometimes it is easier to take over other companies with existing products and customers. Acquiring a competitor in the same field of activity (horizontal integration) gives a company a larger market share and reduces competition. If a company is too big to buy, it may be possible to merge with it: to combine the two companies to form a single new one. Companies can also acquire businesses involved in other parts of their supply chain (vertical integration), generally to achieve cost savings. Backward integration involves acquiring suppliers of raw materials or components; forward integration is buying distributors or retail outlets.

One way to acquire part-ownership of a company is a raid, which simply involves buying as many of a company's stocks as possible on the stock market. Because this increases demand, the stock price will immediately rise. A raid is unlikely to result in the acquisition of a controlling interest. More often, a company will launch a takeover bid: a public offer to a company's stockholders to buy their stocks at a certain price (above the current market price) during a limited period of time. If all the stockholders accept the bid, the buyer has to purchase 100% of the company's stocks, even though they only need 50% plus one (or in practice, perhaps much less) to gain control of a company. If the board of directors of a company that is subject to a bid agrees to a takeover, it is a friendly bid (and if the stockholders sell, it becomes a friendly takeover); if the company does not want to be taken over, it is a hostile bid (or hostile takeover).

Companies are frequently encouraged to take over other companies by investment banks, which generally have large mergers and acquisitions departments with lots of researchers analysing the value of listed companies. Banks also advise companies involved in mergers and takeovers, earning high fees in the process.

Takeovers can lead to the formation of large conglomerates, which in turn can lead to a contrary phenomenon: leveraged buyouts or LBOs. Buyouts occur when financiers (corporate raiders or private equity funds) consider that a conglomerate resulting from a series of takeovers has not achieved synergy but instead has become inefficient, and so is undervalued on the stock market. In other words, the conglomerate's market capitalization is lower than the value of its total assets, including land, buildings, pension funds, etc. Raiders can borrow money, usually by issuing bonds (leveraged means largely financed by borrowed capital), and buy the companies. They then either sell off the subsidiaries, or close them and sell the assets, which is known as asset-stripping. The raiders then pay back the bonds while making a large profit. Until the law was changed, raiders were also able to buy companies and take possession of their pension funds.

Although raiders had a very bad reputation in the 1980s – a famous book about a huge LBO was called *Barbarians at the Gate* – private equity funds are more respected today for buying companies and making them more efficient prior to reselling them.

*"The employees have to assume a share of the blame for allowing the pension fund to become so big and tempting."*



## Vocabulary

**Find the words in the text that mean the following:**

1. to become more varied or different (e.g. by selling different products)
2. places where goods are sold (shops, stores, kiosks, markets, etc.)
3. a sufficient number of stocks in a company to be able to decide what to do (at an Annual General Meeting)
4. public companies whose stocks are traded on a stock exchange
5. amounts of money paid for services
6. companies that own or control several smaller businesses selling very different products or services
7. the combined power or value of a group of things working together which is greater than the total power or value achieved when each is working separately
8. the total value of a company on the stock exchange (the price of all its stocks)
9. companies that are owned by a larger parent company
10. a sum of money reserved to pay a company's retired employees

## Comprehension

**Explain the following in your own words:**

1. the difference between horizontal and vertical integration
2. the difference between backward and forward integration
3. the difference between a raid and a takeover bid
4. the difference between a friendly and a hostile bid
5. asset-stripping

## Discussion

- **All public companies face the permanent risk of takeover bids. Is this a good thing for business? What are arguments in favour of and against takeovers and buyouts?**

Rory Taylor

## Listening 1: The role of the Competition Commission ▶ 2.11

**You will hear Rory Taylor of the Competition Commission in London talking about its work.**

- **What do you think a Competition Commission does?**

**Listen to Rory Taylor, and answer the questions.**

1 What is the alternative American term for a competition investigation organization?
2 When is the Competition Commission asked to investigate companies?
3 What is the hypothetical situation that Rory Taylor mentions?
4 What have lots of companies told the Commission about their attitude to competition in their business?
5 What do you think Rory Taylor means by these phrases?
   a a free market attitude
   b a competition regime
   c a necessary check and balance
   d over-interventionist

**Are supermarkets abusing their dominant position?**

## Listening 2: Market investigations ▶ 2.12

**Listen to Rory Taylor talking about market investigations.**

1 Fill in the gaps.

> You won't generally come across too many markets where there's one dominant [1] ________ outside the, sort of, [2] ________ ________ and the [3] ________ . We used to do, under the previous legislation, what were called monopoly investigations, but now they're known as [4] ________ ________ , as to some extent that reflects that you're not usually looking at one player dominating one particular market but maybe a small [5] ________ . That's not necessarily a bad thing, it all depends on the structure of that market and to what degree they're competing with each other. We've just been looking at the [6] ________ market, that's ... I would say using, using the term advisedly, dominated by big four supermarkets, certainly got the [7] ________ ________ of the ... people's shopping, but at the same time they're competing very vigorously with each other, so that's not necessarily anything we'd, we'd look to intervene in.

2 Give synonyms for 1, 5 and 7.

3 Give explanations or definitions for:

2 ____________________________________________

3 ____________________________________________

6 ____________________________________________

## **Listening 3:** Breaking the law and abusing a dominant position 2.13

**Listen to Rory Taylor talking about ways in which companies can break competition law, and answer the questions.**

**1** Which of the following things does Rory Taylor say?

Sometimes there isn't much competition in a market because:

**a** there are large companies which have done nothing wrong, but just acted in the ways successful companies do.

**b** companies abuse their dominant position.

**c** companies are collaborating and working on projects together.

**d** rival companies agree to charge the same prices.

**2** Which two official bodies does he mention?

**3** What can companies be fined 10% of their turnover for?

### Discussion

- **Rory Taylor mentions 'abuse of a dominant position', but he doesn't explain this. What do you think it means? Can you give an example?**
- **Do you know why the European Competition Commission started a case against Microsoft?**

## **Role play:** Is this company restricting competition?

**Imagine that a very successful company is being investigated by your country's Competition Commission or Antitrust Authority. The company argues that it is successful because it is efficient and innovative, and provides products or services that customers want, and which are better than those offered by competitors. The competition authority is worried that the company is so large that it is restricting competition.**

**Two representatives of the company meet a representative of the competition authority. Your teacher will give you a role.**

**But first, as a class, choose an industry (e.g. computer software, mobile/cell phone networks, pharmaceuticals, retail banking, insurance, satellite television, groceries, furniture, etc.) in which there is an imaginary, highly successful company to investigate and defend.**

### Writing

**Write a short summary (150–200 words) of the company's arguments in defence of its high market share, or the competition authority's reasons for recommending an investigation into the company.**

# 22 Government and taxation

## Aims

- Consider the role of government intervention in the economy
- Discuss government spending and taxation

## Lead-in

Some people argue that too much regulation is bad for business, and that governments interfere with 'market forces'.

*"No, I didn't. I never said there should be no government regulation."*



Could any of the following activities not be undertaken or regulated by the government, but left to the private sector and the market system in your country?

- education
- healthcare
- low-income housing
- defence (the armed services – army, navy, air force)
- the police, the justice system, prisons, and so on
- public transport (trains, buses, and so on)
- social security (unemployment and sickness benefits, old age pensions)
- working conditions (working hours, child labour, minimum wages, and so on)
- traffic regulations (driving tests, speed limits, seat belts, the alcohol limit, parking restrictions, the safety of cars, the size and weight of lorries and trucks, and so on)
- health, safety and cleanliness regulations (concerning factories, shops, restaurants, food, medicines, the disposal of chemical and nuclear waste, and so on)
- the sale of alcohol, drugs, guns, and so on

## Reading: The role of government

**The American economist Milton Friedman was well-known for his views on government. Read the extracts from *Free to Choose* by Milton and Rose Friedman on the next page.**

- **What is the Friedmans' opinion of the activities of the US government?**

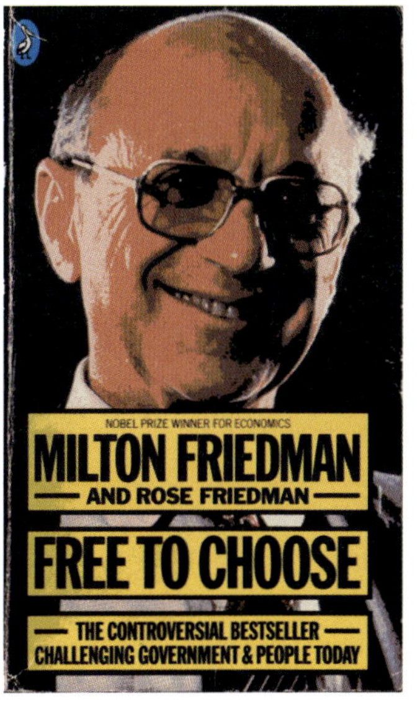

Though the United States has not adopted central economic planning, we have gone very far in the past 50 years in expanding the role of government in the economy. That intervention has been costly in economic terms. The limitations imposed on our economic freedom threaten to bring two centuries of economic progress to an end. Intervention has also been costly in political terms. It has greatly limited our human freedom.

An essential part of economic freedom is freedom to choose how to use our income: how much to spend on ourselves and on what items; how much to save and in what form; how much to give away and to whom. Currently, more than 40% of our income is disposed of on our behalf by government at federal, state and local levels combined.

As consumers, we are not even free to choose how to spend that part of our income that is left after taxes. Our physician is not free to prescribe many drugs for us that he may regard as the most effective for our ailments, even though the drugs may be widely available abroad. We are not free to buy an automobile without seat belts.

Another essential part of economic freedom is freedom to use the resources we possess in accordance with our own values – freedom to enter any occupation, engage in any business enterprise, buy from or sell to anyone else, so long as we do so on a strictly voluntary basis and do not resort to force in order to coerce others.

Today you are not free to offer your services as a lawyer, a physician, a dentist, a plumber, a barber, a mortician, or engage in a host of other occupations, without first getting a permit or licence from a government official. You are not free to work overtime at terms mutually agreeable to you and your employer, unless the terms conform to rules and regulations laid down by a government official.

You are not free to set up a bank, go into the taxicab business, or the business of selling electricity or telephone service, or running a railroad, busline, or airline, without first receiving permission from a government official.

Although these examples only scratch the surface, they illustrate the fundamental proposition that freedom is one whole, that anything that reduces freedom in one part of our lives is likely to affect freedom in the other parts.

Freedom cannot be absolute. We do live in an interdependent society. Some restrictions on our freedom are necessary to avoid other, still worse, restrictions. However, we have gone far beyond that point. The urgent need today is to eliminate restrictions, not add to them.

**Vocabulary notes**

on our behalf = for us
physician (AmE) = doctor (BrE)
drugs (AmE) = medicines (BrE)
to resort to force = to use violence
to coerce = to make people do something against their will
mortician (AmE) = undertaker (BrE): someone who arranges funerals
a host of = a large number of

## Comprehension

1 What do the Friedmans think will be the consequence of increased government intervention in the economy?
2 In which sentence do they criticize taxation?
3 What do they say about medical and road safety legislation?
4 What is the only restriction they believe to be necessary regarding professional occupations, business and trade?
5 What is their objection to the law regarding labour contracts?

Discussion

- **How would you characterize the Friedmans' politics?**
- **How far do you agree with them, concerning any of the specific examples they give of government legislation?**

## Vocabulary

**Before listening to an economist talking about government intervention in the economy, match up the words and definitions below.**

1 allocation (of resources)
2 commercialize
3 externalities
4 infrastructure
5 optimal
6 outcome
7 unfettered

A basic systems and services such as transport and power supplies
B distribution according to a plan
C not limited by any rules or controls
D positive or negative consequences (benefits or costs) of economic activities experienced by other people
E the best or most likely to bring success
F the result or effect of an action or situation
G to organize something to make a profit

Michael Kitson

## Listening: Government intervention 2.14

**Michael Kitson is Senior Lecturer in international macroeconomics, and Director of the Management Studies Tripos, at Cambridge University. Listen to him talking about the role of government.**

- **Is he is in favour of government intervention?**

**Listen again and answer the questions below.**

1 Fill in the gaps.

> The second effect is whether we think unfettered [1] ________ ________ alone can ensure the long-term [2] ________ allocation of resources and long-term [3] ________ ________. Markets are very important, I'm not denying that, but so is the role of government to actually help markets work better. Often economists talk about notions of [4] ________ ________ or the fact that markets are not working properly.

2 What reasons does Michael Kitson give for government spending on education and health?
3 Why don't firms invest in very early-stage technologies?
4 What other areas or activities does Kitson mention?

- **How far do you agree with Kitson about these various forms of spending?**

## **Discussion:** Taxation 1

**All government spending has to be paid for by taxation.**

- **Which different taxes can you name?**
- **The same amount of money can be taxed more than once. Can you give any examples of this?**

*'In this world nothing can be said to be certain, except: death and taxes!'* (Benjamin Franklin, 1789)

*"Can't we put in something about rich white guys don't have to pay taxes?"*



## Vocabulary

**Which terms are defined below?**

**1** The tax people pay on their wages and salaries is called
**A** capital transfer tax **B** income tax **C** wealth tax

**2** A tax on wages and salaries or on company profits is a
**A** direct tax **B** indirect tax **C** value-added tax

**3** A tax levied at a higher rate on higher incomes is a called a
**A** flat tax **B** progressive tax **C** regressive tax

**4** A tax paid on property, sales transactions, imports, and so on is a/an
**A** direct tax **B** indirect tax **C** value-added tax

**5** A tax collected at each stage of production, excluding the already-taxed costs from previous stages, is called a/an
**A** added-value tax **B** sales tax **C** value-added tax

**6** Profits made by selling assets are generally liable to a
**A** capital gains tax **B** capital transfer tax **C** wealth tax

**7** Gifts to family members over a certain value are often liable to a/an
**A** capital gains tax **B** inheritance tax **C** value-added tax

**8** The annual tax imposed on people's fortunes (in some countries) is a
**A** added-value tax **B** capital gains tax **C** wealth tax

**9** Making false declarations to the tax authorities is called
**A** fiscal policy **B** tax avoidance **C** tax evasion

**10** Reducing the amount of tax you pay to a legal minimum is called
**A** creative accounting **B** tax avoidance **C** tax evasion

**11** Countries where taxes are low, where multinational companies often set up their head offices, are known as
**A** money launderers **B** tax harbours **C** tax havens

**12** A small mistake or exception in a tax law, which allows you to avoid paying something, is called
**A** an escape **B** an excuse **C** a loophole

## **Discussion:** Taxation 2

**1** Which of the taxes mentioned above do you have in your country?
**2** Is there a flat rate of income tax (the same for everybody) or is it progressive? Which system do you prefer?
**3** Do you prefer direct or indirect taxes?

**4** Read the following statements. Which of them are in favour of taxation and government spending, and which against?

| | | | | | | |
|---|---|---|---|---|---|---|
| **In favour** | | | | | | |
| **Against** | | | | | | |

**5** Which of the statements do you find the most convincing, and why?

1 All businesses require public roads to allow staff, supplies and customers to get to them.

2 A wealth tax taxes money that has already been taxed before, perhaps many times, and is therefore unethical.

3 As Adam Smith wrote: 'The subjects of every state ought to contribute toward the support of the government in proportion to their respective abilities; that is, in proportion to the revenue which they respectively enjoy under the protection of the state.'

4 The money people earn is their money, the result of hard work.

5 Income tax penalizes all income-generating activity, which makes everyone poorer.

6 If the general population is unhealthy, and unable to work, firms won't find either enough staff or customers.

7 People will stay away from retail outlets in areas of environmental damage or urban decay.

8 Taxing savings and capital gains encourages consumption and reduces capital accumulation and therefore reduces everyone's future prosperity.

9 Some people are born intelligent and others stupid. Some people are born beautiful and others ugly. So why shouldn't some people be born rich?

10 Unequal income distribution and poverty always lead to crime.

11 Redistributive taxation is, quite simply, theft.

12 How would companies get qualified staff without the public education system?

13 Society creates the conditions under which financial success is possible, and it therefore has a rightful claim to a share of that success, in the form of taxes.

## Presentation: Taxation and government spending

**Prepare a brief talk (or a written report) giving arguments both in defence of and against taxation and government spending, but preferably with a conclusion coming down on one side or the other. You can use your own opinions as well as those expressed in this unit.**

# 23 The business cycle

## Aims

- Consider the causes of the business cycle
- Discuss whether governments can or should influence the business cycle

## Lead-in

- How well is the global economy doing at the moment?
- How well is the economy doing in your country?
- When was the last significant change to the economy, and what was the most probable cause?
- When do you expect the economic situation to change, and why?
- What are the main causes of the alternate periods of growth and contraction of the business cycle?

## Vocabulary 1: The business cycle

**Before reading about the business cycle, match up the words and definitions below.**

balance of payments   consumption   demand   downturn   expectations
gross domestic product (GDP)   save   supply   upturn

1 a decline in economic activity downturn
2 an increase in economic activity upturn
3 beliefs about what will happen in the future expectations
4 purchasing and using goods and services consumption
5 the difference between the funds a country receives and those it pays for all international transactions balance of payments
6 the total market value of all the goods and services produced in a country during a given period GDP
7 the willingness and ability of consumers to purchase goods and services demand
8 the willingness and ability of businesses to offer goods or services for sale supply
9 to put money aside to spend in the future save

## Reading 1: What causes the business cycle?

**Read the text and fill in the gaps with words from the exercise above.**

The business cycle or trade cycle is a permanent feature of market economies: [1] GDP alternately grows and contracts. During an [2] upturn, parts of the economy expand to the point where they are working at full capacity, so that production, employment, business investments, profits, prices, and interest rates all tend to rise. A long period of expansion is called a boom. But at some point there will inevitably be a [3] downturn. The economy will hit a peak and start to contract again, the demand for goods and services will decline and the economy will begin to work at below its potential. Investment, output, employment, profits, commodity and share prices, and interest rates will generally fall. A downturn that lasts more than six months

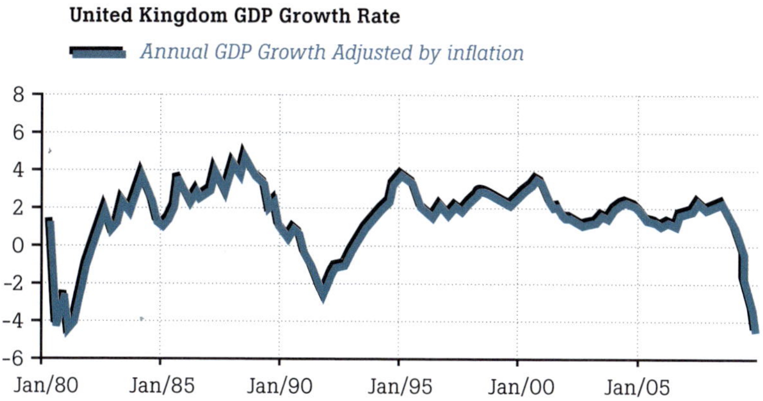


is called a recession; one that lasts for a year or two is generally called a depression or a slump. Eventually the economy will bottom out, and there will be a recovery or an upturn.

The most probable cause of the business cycle is people's spending or [4] ______________ decisions, which in turn are based on [5] ______________ . A country's output, investment, unemployment, [6] ______________ , and so on, all depend on millions of decisions by consumers and businesses on whether to spend, borrow or [7] ______________ . When economic times are good or when people feel confident about the future, they spend, and run up debts. At a certain point, spending has to slow down and debts have to be paid. If interest rates unexpectedly rise, a lot of people find themselves paying more than they anticipated on their mortgage or rent, and so have to consume less. Similarly, if people are worried about the possibility of losing their jobs in the near future they tend to start saving money and consuming less, which leads to a fall in [8] ______________ , and consequently a fall in production and employment. Investment is closely linked to consumption, and only takes place when demand is growing. As soon as demand stops growing, investment in new factories, machines, etc. falls, which contributes to the downturn. But if [9] ______________ exceeds demand, prices should fall, and encourage people to start buying again. Eventually the economy will reach a trough or bottom out, and there will be a recovery or an upturn.

This is the internal (or endogenous) theory of the business cycle; there are also external (or exogenous) theories, which look for causes outside economic activity, such as scientific advances, natural disasters, elections or political shocks, demographic changes, and so on. The economist Joseph Schumpeter believed that the business cycle is caused by major technological inventions (e.g. the steam engine, railways, automobiles, electricity, microchips), which lead to periods of 'creative destruction' during which radical innovations destroy established companies or industries.

*"We're still the same, great company we've always been, only we've ceased to exist."*



## Comprehension

**Complete the following sentences.**

1 A downturn begins when ...
2 People spend, and borrow money, when ...
3 People tend to spend less when ...
4 When interest rates rise ...
5 Companies only invest while ...
6 Creative destruction means that ...

Discussion

- **What examples can you give of 'creative destruction' occurring at the moment?**
- **During a downturn, to what extent should the government intervene in the economy, by creating demand or jobs? How could it do these things?**
- **What are the economic arguments against such governmental spending?**

## Vocabulary 2: Fiscal and monetary policy

**1 Before reading about the government and the economy, match up the following words and definitions.**

| | |
|---|---|
| **1** equilibrium | **A** an amount of money that is smaller than is needed (e.g. when spending exceeds revenues) |
| **2** deficit | **B** an excess: a quantity that is larger than is needed |
| **3** surplus | **C** a state of balance, for example when supply is the same as demand |
| **4** fiscal policy | **D** government or central bank actions concerning the rate of growth of the money in circulation |
| **5** monetary policy | **E** government actions concerning taxation and public expenditure |
| **6** money supply | **F** the economic theory that government monetary and fiscal policy should stimulate business activity and increase employment in a recession |
| **7** Keynesianism | **G** the total amount of money available in an economy at a particular time |

| 1 | | 2 | | 3 | | 4 | | 5 | | 6 | | 7 | |
|---|---|---|---|---|---|---|---|---|---|---|---|---|---|

**2 Match up the words below into pairs with similar meanings.**

| | | | |
|---|---|---|---|
| boost | decrease | depression | excess |
| expand | expenditure | grow | output |
| production | recovery | reduce | slump |
| spending | stimulate | surplus | upturn |

**3 Match up the words below into pairs with opposite meanings.**

| | | | | |
|---|---|---|---|---|
| boom | contract | demand | depression | |
| endogenous | expand | exogenous | | |
| peak | save | spend | supply | trough |

## Listening 1: Consumption and the business cycle 2.15

**Listen to Michael Kitson, who you heard in Unit 22, talking about the causes of the business cycle, and answer the questions.**

1 What does Kitson say many economists believed a year or so previously?*
2 According to Kitson, were they right?
3 What does Kitson say causes economic booms?
4 What about depressions?

Michael Kitson

* Kitson was talking in early 2008.

## Listening 2: Keynesianism ▶ 2.16

**Listen to Michael Kitson talking about Keynesianism, the economic theory named after John Maynard Keynes, and answer the questions.**

**1** Fill in the gaps below.

> ... we still have the business cycle, OK, we can still have the possible problems of a [1] ___________, which makes the argument for what I think is standard Keynesianism, the way you [2] ___________ budget [3] ___________ or budget [4] ___________ depending on whether the economy's [5] ___________ or is in [6] ___________. OK, and the government's golden rule in the UK is consistent with that, in general. If the economy's turning down it may make sense for governments to have budget deficits, and to keep [7] ___________ in the economy. That's the Keynesianism argument about ironing out the business cycle, which I think is important because recessions can have very long-term [8] ___________ effects.

**2** Which of the following do you think is the British government's 'golden rule' of fiscal policy? The government should:

**A** cut taxes and increase spending in the months before an election.
**B** ensure that there is never a budget deficit.
**C** only borrow to invest for the future and not to fund current spending, which should be paid for with today's taxes.
**D** spend any budget surplus on boosting or stimulating the economy.

**3** What does 'ironing out' mean?

**John Maynard Keynes**

## Reading 2: Keynesianism and monetarism

**Read the following text and decide which paragraphs could be given these headings:**

**A** Countercyclical policies don't work until too late
**B** Keynesianism returns
**C** The Keynesian argument
**D** The lesson of the 1930s
**E** The monetarist argument

______ The great depression of the 1930s demonstrated that, at least in the short term, the market system does not automatically lead to full employment. John Maynard Keynes argued that market forces could produce a durable equilibrium with high unemployment, fewer goods being produced, fewer people employed, and reduced rates of income and investment. Classical economic theory stated that in the long run, excess savings would cause interest rates to fall and investment to increase again; Keynes famously riposted that 'In the long run, we are all dead.'

______ He therefore recommended governmental intervention in the economy, to counteract the business cycle. During an inflationary boom, governments could decrease their spending or increase taxation. During a recession, on the contrary, they could increase their expenditure, or decrease taxation, or increase the money supply and reduce interest rates, so as to boost the economy and increase output, investment, consumption and employment.

______ In the 1950s and 1960s, monetarist economists, most notably Milton Friedman, began to argue that Keynesian fiscal policy had negative effects in the long term. They insisted that money is neutral, meaning that in the long run, increasing (or inflating) the money supply will only change the price level (lead to inflation) and have no effect on output and employment. They argued that governments should abandon the attempt to manage the level of demand in the economy. On the contrary, they should try to make sure that there is constant and non-inflationary growth in the money supply.

______ Monetarists and believers in free markets argue that since governments aren't able to foresee a coming recession any more quickly than the companies that make up the economy, their fiscal measures usually only begin to take effect when the economy is already recovering, and simply make the next swing in the business cycle even greater.

______ By the beginning of the 21st century, the argument that free markets and competition are efficient, and should be allowed to operate with a minimum of governmental intervention, seemed to be dominant. But when the subprime crisis occurred in 2008, and financial institutions and large automobile companies began to go bankrupt, Keynesianism suddenly came back into fashion. Governments around the world poured huge amounts of money into the economy. Monetarists were outnumbered, but continued to argue that this would inevitably lead to massive inflation in the future.

## Comprehension

**Match up the following half-sentences.**

**1** Keynes argued that left to itself, the free market system
**2** In classical theory, if consumption and investment fall, excess savings should
**3** Keynesians argue that during an inflationary boom governments should
**4** Keynesians argue that during an economic downturn governments should
**5** Monetarists argue that in the long run,
**6** Monetarists also believe that Keynesian fiscal measures
**7** There was a revival in Keynesian policies and government intervention

**A** cause interest rates to fall and investment to increase again.
**B** decrease their spending or increase taxation
**C** does not guarantee full employment.
**D** in 2008, when major financial institutions began to go bankrupt.
**E** increase their spending or the money supply.
**F** increasing the money supply merely leads to inflation.
**G** only begin to take effect too late, when an upturn is already beginning.

| 1 | | 2 | | 3 | | 4 | | 5 | | 6 | | 7 | |
|---|---|---|---|---|---|---|---|---|---|---|---|---|---|
| 1 | C | 2 | A | 3 | B | 4 | ~~BA~~ F | 5 | E | 6 | G | 7 | D |

## Discussion: Government intervention

- **Which of the arguments in the text above do you find the most convincing?**
- **Which is more important, fighting inflation or unemployment?**
- **In an economic crisis, should governments rescue banks that have taken too big risks, and large companies in old industries, or rather invest in new, efficient start-up companies in innovative new industries such as information technology, biotechnology, nanotechnology, wind and solar power, etc.?**
- **Which companies in your country are 'too big to go bankrupt'?**
- **Which industries should the government invest in?**

# 24 Corporate social responsibility

## Aims

- Consider the responsibilities of business
- Discuss the ethics of various business practices

## Lead-in

*Latin expression meaning 'let the buyer beware'

- Which of the views expressed in the illustration do you agree with?

## **Reading:** Profits and social responsibility

**Four of the views expressed in the illustration on the previous page are referred to in the following text. Which are they?**

Pure free market theorists argue that the function of a business is to make profits. Milton Friedman, for example, argued that any corporate action inspired by 'social responsibility', rather than the attempt to maximize profits, is 'unbusinesslike'. In an article called 'The social responsibility of business is to increase its profits,' he argued that people who say that business has 'responsibilities for providing employment, eliminating discrimination, avoiding pollution', and so on, are 'undermining the basis of a free society'. For Friedman, 'only people can have responsibilities', and not corporations:

> In a free enterprise, private-property system, a corporate executive is an employee of the owners of the business. He has direct responsibility to his employers. That responsibility is to conduct the business in accordance with their desires, which generally will be to make as much money as possible, while of course conforming to the basic rules of the society, both those embodied in law and those embodied in ethical custom.

Therefore, 'to say that the corporate executive has a "social responsibility" in his capacity as businessman' is to say that 'he is to act in some way that is not in the interest of his employers'. Because if an executive makes 'social' expenditures he is:

> spending someone else's money ... Insofar as his actions in accord with his 'social responsibility' reduce returns to stockholders, he is spending their money. Insofar as his actions raise the price to customers, he is spending the customers' money. Insofar as his actions lower the wages of some employees, he is spending their money.

Furthermore, such actions are 'undemocratic' as they involve corporations taking on responsibilities that should be the government's: taxation and expenditure, and solving social problems. If the elected government is not taking certain actions, it is because the voters did not want it to do so. Any such action 'harms the foundations of a free society' and reveals an unfortunate 'suicidal impulse' in businessmen.

Friedman does not seem to consider the possibility that stockholders might prefer to receive lower dividends but live in a society with less pollution or less unemployment and fewer social problems.

An alternative view to the 'stockholder model' exemplified by Friedman's article is the *stakeholder* model. According to this approach, business managers have responsibilities to all the groups of people with a stake in or an interest in or a claim on the firm. These will include employees, suppliers, customers and the local community, as well as the stockholders. Proponents of the stakeholder approach argue that all these groups should be represented on a company's board of directors.

## Comprehension

1 According to Friedman, why should business executives only seek to maximize profits?
2 Who are the employers of corporate executives?
3 In what negative way do 'socially responsible' actions affect stockholders, customers, and employees?
4 According to Friedman, in what way are 'socially responsible' actions by businesses 'undemocratic'?
5 According to the text, what other desires might stockholders have, apart from making as much money as possible?
6 What is a 'stakeholder'?

## Vocabulary

**1 Find words in the text that mean the following:**

1 treating some people in a worse way than you treat other people
2 making something weaker
3 an economic system in which anyone can raise capital, form a business, and offer goods or services
4 complying with or following (rules, etc.)
5 expressed, given a material form
6 according to generally accepted beliefs based on morals
7 a usual way of behaving
8 to the degree or extent that
9 causes damage to
10 supporters, people who argue in favour of something

**2 Match up the verbs and nouns below to make word combinations from the text.**

| | |
|---|---|
| avoid | business |
| conduct | discrimination |
| conform to | employment |
| eliminate | expenditures |
| increase | money |
| make | pollution |
| maximize | profits |
| provide | rules |
| undermine | the basis (of a free society) |

## Discussion

**How far do you agree:**

- **that doing anything other than maximizing profits is unbusinesslike?**
- **that stockholders or shareholders generally wish to make as much money as possible? (Notice the 'generally'.)**
- **that corporate social expenditure simply means spending someone else's money?**
- **that solving social problems is uniquely the job of the democratically elected government?**
- **that a company's other stakeholders are much less important than the stockholders?**

**If you don't agree, why not? How can you oppose these arguments?**

## Listening 1: Socially responsible investment ▶ 2.17

Anna-Kim Hyun-Seung

**Listen to Anna-Kim Hyun-Seung, who you heard in Unit 14, talking about socially responsible investment, and answer the questions.**

1. Which expression about business does Anna-Kim attribute to Milton Friedman? What does it mean?
2. What assumption is Friedman's argument based on?
3. According to what Anna-Kim says, what do you think 'socially responsible investment' means?
4. How significant does Anna-Kim say socially responsible investment is?

## Listening 2: Different stakeholder groups ▶ 2.18

**Listen to Anna-Kim.**

1. Fill in the gaps.

> I think it is very important to respond to different stakeholder groups, because obviously companies tend to be more [1] ________ to the [2] ________ rather than other stakeholders, but I think when a company really considers different stakeholder groups seriously, including their [3] ________, including their own [4] ________, then they are likely to have more genuine corporate social responsibility [5] ________ and [6] ________. For example, there are companies which are probably doing very good things for the community, for the external society, so that they can really improve their [7] ________ with their external stakeholders, but for example, if they are not very nice to their own employees, if there is something going wrong within their [8] ________ ________ management, with regard to [9] ________ ________, low-cost [10] ________ ________, working hours, then probably they don't really have a good response from their own employees, who are their own internal stakeholders, so I think it is very important to listen to all different stakeholders, internal and external, to develop a holistic approach to corporate social responsibility.

2. What does Anna-Kim say genuine corporate social responsibility involves?
3. Why is it not sufficient for a company to do things for the community?

## Discussion

**Although he dismissed the notion of social responsibility, Milton Friedman still argued that a business must conform to the basic rules of society. Do you think the following activities, several of which are not illegal, conform to the basic rules of society?**

1 Bribing corrupt foreign officials in order to win foreign orders, on the grounds that where bribery is a way of life, you have no alternative if you want to win a contract
2 Industrial espionage: spying on competitors' research and development departments with concealed cameras and microphones, bribing their employees, etc., rather than doing your own expensive R&D
3 Selling supposedly durable goods with 'built-in obsolescence', i.e. which you know will not last more than a few years
4 Spending money on lobbying, i.e. trying to persuade politicians to pass laws favourable to your particular industry
5 Telling only half the truth in advertisements, or exaggerating a great deal, or keeping quiet about the bad aspects of a product
6 'Whistle blowing', i.e. revealing confidential information to the police or to a newspaper, e.g. that a company is breaking health and safety regulations and therefore putting people's lives in danger

## Role play: Problems at a clothes manufacturer

**The CEO of an outdoor and sports clothing manufacturer in an advanced industrial country calls an emergency meeting to discuss two problems. Firstly, sales have started to fall in an economic downturn, the company's inventory is growing, and the production level is clearly too high. A decision has to be made about whether to lay off some staff. Secondly, a researcher has reported that one of the chemicals the company uses in its products is harmful to the environment. Your teacher will give you a role to prepare.**

### Writing

**Write a short report (100–150 words) summarizing the decisions taken at the meeting.**

# 25 Efficiency and employment

## Aims

- Discuss the potential conflict between business efficiency and employment
- Consider cases of rationalization and downsizing

## Lead-in

- How important to you is job security?
- How many different employers do you expect to have in your career?
- Would you prefer to have a single full-time job, or various part-time activities?
- Which economic sectors are expected to create jobs in your country?
- In which sectors are jobs expected to disappear?
- Is technological progress creating or destroying jobs, on balance?

## Vocabulary

**1 Match up the words in the box with the definitions below.**

| | | | | |
|---|---|---|---|---|
| casual work | contract work | delayering | downsizing | flexible labour market |
| job sharing | outsourcing or contracting-out | rationalization or restructuring | | |
| relocation or delocalization | rightsizing | | | |

1 a situation in which it is easy for companies to hire non-permanent staff
2 decreasing the number of permanent employees working for an organization
3 using other businesses as subcontractors to supply components or services
4 employing two or more people on a part-time basis to perform a job normally available to one person working full time
5 moving some of a business's activities (e.g. accounting, production) to another place or country
6 removing unproductive parts of the management hierarchy to make organizations more flexible and efficient
7 reorganizing a company, business or system in a new way to reduce costs and improve efficiency and effectiveness
8 temporary employment by an organization to do a specific project or piece of work
9 temporary employment that is not regular or fixed
10 another way of saying downsizing, though it could also describe increasing the size of an organization, perhaps as an attempt to correct a previous downsizing

*"Burns, you've done a good job downsizing, but we've decidied to outsource your function."*

2 **Which of the following words have a similar meaning to employ someone, and which mean the same as to dismiss someone?**

appoint engage fire hire lay off let go
make redundant recruit sack take on

**Are there any differences among the words in the different groups?**

3 **Fill the gaps in the sentences with words from the exercises above.**

1 As an IT specialist, I mainly do ________ ________ for local companies, two or three months at a time.

2 ________ is expensive for employers, as having two members of staff instead of one involves extra costs.

3 Big companies abolished a lot of middle management positions by ________ in the 1980s.

4 We ________ our accounting and IT services to Indian companies last year, but we would never ________ our manufacturing.

5 When they ________ the company, 1,000 people were made ________ .

## Discussion

- **What notable cases of restructuring or downsizing or delocalizing have there been in the news recently? What was the reaction?**
- **In a situation where there is growing unemployment, what are the advantages and disadvantages of the following partial solutions?**
  - job sharing
  - decreasing working hours
  - lowering the age of retirement
  - staff training programmes
  - increasing the number of public sector jobs (i.e. those paid for by national or local government)

## Listening 1: Efficiency and the number of employees ▶2.19

Anna-Kim Hyun-Seung

**Listen to Anna-Kim Hyun-Seung, who you heard in Units 14 and 24, talking about alternatives to laying off employees, and answer the questions.**

1 What do companies normally do when they increase their efficiency?
2 What is the alternative that Anna-Kim Hyun-Seung mentions?
3 What were the consequences for the employees in the case mentioned?

## Listening 2: Efficiency, training and productivity ▶ 2.20

**Listen to Anna-Kim talking about a Korean company, and answer the questions.**

1 What do Yuhan-Kimberly do?
2 Why do they have a good reputation?
3 What was the company's solution to the problem they faced?
4 What were the consequences?

- **Do you think the situation described here is exceptional, or could more companies do the same thing?**

## Discussion: The postal service

- **In your country, is the postal service public or private? (i.e. is it a nationalized industry, or a private company with shareholders?)**
- **Is it profitable?**
- **Is it a monopoly?**
- **What do you know about post offices in other countries?**
- **Should everybody have the right to the same postal services, whether they live in a large city, or in a very remote part of the countryside?**
- **If a business is considered to offer a public service, should it be allowed to rationalize or restructure or downsize or outsource or delocalize?**

## Role play: Reorganizing the postal service

**This role play is about a plan to restructure and modernize a postal distribution system, which will also result in serious downsizing.**

## Reading

The post office in a country of about 10 million people has recently been privatized. Now it wants to become more efficient, so as to be more competitive when the market is opened to international competition.

There is already a lot of competition for express mail – companies such as DHL, FedEx and UPS – but the law will soon allow post offices to compete for local business in other countries, e.g. delivering mail to businesses and homes in large cities. Furthermore, the volume of mail has decreased by 10% in the past ten years, and is expected to decrease by another 10%. Since the spread of email and electronic signatures, the amount of inter-company mail has declined by over 60%, but commercial mail still represents 85% of the post office's turnover.

There is already a plan to close 25% of post offices – the smaller, unprofitable ones in small towns and villages. Now the post office wants to reduce the number of sorting offices from the existing 25, spread all over the country, to three.

The plan is to build three large new sorting offices on cheap land outside big cities, with good access to railways and motorways. They would be of equal size, in the west, centre and east of the country. They would use new automated machines.

The restructuring would save €200 million a year in salaries and increased efficiency.

The number of sorting staff would be reduced from 10,000 to about 5,500, although many of them would now have to work at night and would have to travel further to work. The post office would try to find jobs for the other 4,500 people elsewhere in the organization (in post offices and in technical and maintenance jobs). It is also promising a €100 million redundancy package and training programmes.

The trade unions are obviously against this proposal, and so are the local governments in areas where many jobs would be lost. Between them, they have put forward various alternative plans, whereby the post office builds five, or six or eight new centres instead of only three, or three main ones but also several secondary ones, in order to preserve jobs all over the country. On the contrary, the local governments in the areas where the three new centres are planned are wholly in favour of the project.

## Comprehension

1 What does the post office want to do?
2 Why do they say this is necessary?
3 What are the advantages and disadvantages?
4 Who is for and who is against the plan?

## Role play

**The CEO of the post office invites the Financial Director, the Human Resources Director, and a Trade Union Representative to a meeting to discuss the proposed restructuring of the sorting offices. Your teacher will give you a role.**

## Writing

**Write a short report (100–150 words) outlining what was decided at the meeting.**

# 26 Exchange rates

## Aims

- Consider the causes of exchange rate fluctuations
- Discuss the desirability of a tax on currency transactions

## Lead-in

- Why do companies, institutions and people buy and sell currencies?
- How is the value (the exchange rate) of the money in your pocket determined?
- Has the value of your currency increased or decreased in the past few weeks or months? Why?

## Reading: Exchange rates

**Read the text below and decide which paragraphs could be given the following headings:**

**A** Counteracting speculation
**B** Gold convertibility
**C** Market forces
**D** Market interventions
**E** Parity and speculation

__B__ An exchange rate is the price at which one currency can be exchanged for another (e.g. how many euros are needed to buy a pound). For a quarter of a century after World War II, the levels of most major currencies were fixed (or 'pegged') against the US dollar, and the dollar was pegged against gold. One dollar was worth 1/35 of an ounce of gold, and the Federal Reserve guaranteed that it could exchange this amount of gold for every dollar in existence. These fixed exchange rates could only be adjusted (revalued or devalued) with the agreement of the International Monetary Fund. This system of gold convertibility ended in 1971 because after inflation in the USA, the Federal Reserve did not have enough gold to guarantee its currency.

__C__ Since that time there has been a system of floating exchange rates in most western countries. This means that exchange rates are determined by supply and demand – the quantities of currencies bought and sold in the foreign exchange markets. If there are more buyers of a currency than sellers, its price will rise; if there are more sellers, it will fall. Proponents of floating exchange rates, such as Milton Friedman, argued that currencies would automatically settle at stable rates which would reflect economic realities more precisely than calculations by central bank officials. Yet they underestimated the extent of speculation, which can push currencies away from levels that reflect underlying economic conditions.

E In theory, exchange rates should give purchasing power parity (PPP). In other words, the cost of a given selection of goods and services would be the same in different countries. So if the price level in a country increases because of inflation, its currency should depreciate – its exchange rate should go down so as to return to PPP. In fact, this does not happen because rates are influenced by currency speculation. Financial institutions, companies and rich individuals all buy currencies, looking for either higher interest rates or short-term capital gains if a currency appreciates. Only about 5% of the world's currency transactions are related to trade – individuals or organizations buying foreign currencies because they want to buy goods and services from abroad – and foreign travel. The remaining 95% are purely speculative.

A Exchange rate changes brought about by speculation clearly cause problems for industry. Although it is possible to some extent to hedge against currency fluctuations by way of futures contracts, forward planning is difficult when the price of raw materials bought from abroad, or the price of your products in export markets, can rise or fall rapidly. This was a major reason for the establishment of the euro, the common currency in much of Europe.

D Governments and central banks sometimes try to change the value of their currency. They intervene in exchange markets, using their foreign currency reserves to buy their own currency to raise its value, or selling their currency to lower its value. But speculators have much more money than a government has in its reserves, so attempts to 'manage' a floating exchange rate have limited success. For example, in 1992 the Bank of England lost over £3 billion in one day trying to protect the value of the pound sterling. Speculators were trading so much currency that it was impossible for intervention by a central bank to influence the floating rate.

## Comprehension

**Write *questions* to which these could be the answers, according to the text.**

1 A system in which the Federal Reserve could exchange gold for all the paper money, if necessary
2 Because of inflation
3 By the number of buyers and sellers
4 The cost of a given selection of goods and services would be the same
5 To get a higher interest rate or make a capital gain
6 About 95%
7 By buying futures contracts
8 By buying or selling their currency on the exchange markets
9 Because speculators have much more money than governments

## Vocabulary

**Find words in the text that mean the following:**

1 to increase the value of a currency in an otherwise fixed system
2 to decrease the value of a currency in an otherwise fixed system
3 adjective describing a rate that changes or varies
4 people who argue in favour of something
5 to fall in value in a market system
6 to rise in value in a market system
7 to attempt to protect oneself against future price changes
8 continuous changes in a price or value
9 agreements to buy something at a fixed price several months ahead

## Discussion

- **What is the price of gold today? (It is certainly a lot higher than $35!)**
- **What percentage of your currency is backed by gold?**
- **Should governments or central banks try to intervene in currency markets?**
- **Should speculators be prevented or discouraged from trading in currencies – over $1.8 trillion dollars are traded every day – or should they have the right to do whatever they like with their assets?**
- **How could currency speculation be discouraged?**

## Listening 1: Currency flows and the Tobin Tax ▶ 2.21

Michael Kitson

**Listen to Michael Kitson, who you heard in Units 22 and 23, talking about a possible way of limiting currency speculation, and answer the questions.**

1 What is 'hot money'?
2 What are the 'real effects' of financial crises that Kitson mentions?
3 What is a Tobin Tax?
4 What is 'highly leveraged' currency trading?
5 What would be the probable effect of the Tobin Tax?
6 What has happened that makes some people think a Tobin Tax could now be introduced?

## Listening 2: Developing Africa ▶ 2.22

James Tobin (1918–2002), Nobel Prize for Economics winner in 1981

**Listen to Michael Kitson talking about how the Tobin Tax could be spent, and answer the questions.**

1 Why don't individual firms invest a lot of money in Africa?
2 What would be the benefits of spending the money generated by the Tobin Tax in Africa?

## Case study: A currency transaction tax

**A proposal has been made to impose a currency transaction tax (CTT) that would be collected from dealers in international currency markets, by financial clearing or settlement systems.**

**The idea behind the Tobin Tax was to slow down capital flows across borders, to make governmental monetary policy more effective, and to prevent or manage exchange rate crises. The CCT, on the contrary, is not designed to change foreign exchange market behaviour, but only to raise money without disrupting the market. But of course taxing foreign exchange transactions would increase the spread, or the difference between bid (buying) and ask (selling) prices at which trades would be profitable, and so would reduce the number of transactions. It is estimated that this would be by 14%.**

**The proposed tax rate is 0.5 basis points. A basis point is 1/100th of 1%, so the tax would be 0.005% of the amount of currency traded. Buying and then selling a currency would involve a tax of 1 basis point.**

**It is calculated that a CTT of 0.5 basis points on all major currencies would yield an annual revenue of over $33 billion. Taxing only transactions involving the US$ against all other currencies would raise over $28 billion, as most foreign exchange transactions involve the dollar.**

- **In small groups, imagine that you have been invited to advise the government on how the proceeds of a currency transaction tax should be spent, and where.**

  **Select five of the following suggestions, and number them in order of priority:**

_____ Cleaning up pollution

_____ Developing alternative energy installations

_____ Disaster aid (future earthquakes, hurricanes, floods, etc.)

_____ Disease prevention (AIDS and other diseases)

_____ Education and literacy (for children and adults)

_____ Funding microfinance schemes (see Unit 14)

_____ Health clinics and hospitals

_____ Humanitarian aid for refugees from wars, famine, or political persecution

_____ Land preservation and environmental restoration (planting trees, etc.)

_____ Monitoring and protecting endangered species

_____ Removing landmines

_____ Other: ______________________________________

## Writing

**Write a brief summary (150–200 words) of your group's decisions.**

# 27 International trade

## Aims

- Consider the theory of free trade
- Discuss the advantages and disadvantages of international trade

## Lead-in

- Look around you. How many things can you see that were imported from another country?
- How much of the food you've eaten in the last 24 hours came from abroad?
- What are your country's major trading partners?
- What are your country's most important exports?
- Does your country try to restrict imports?

## Vocabulary

**Before listening to Michael Kitson talking about international trade, match up the half-sentences below defining key terms.**

1 **Free trade** means imports and exports of goods and services
2 **Protectionism** means restricting imports
3 **Trade barriers** are
4 A **tariff** is
5 A **quota** is
6 **Absolute advantage** means a country's ability to
7 **Comparative advantage** means a country's ability to
8 An **infant industry** is one that is
9 A **strategic industry** is one that is

**A** a maximum quantity of goods of a specific kind that can be imported into a country.
**B** a tax charged on imports.
**C** by way of trade barriers such as tariffs and quotas.
**D** government policies or regulations that restrict international trade.
**E** in an early stage of development and which cannot survive competition from foreign companies.
**F** particularly important to a country's economy.
**G** produce goods at a lower cost than any other country.
**H** produce particular goods more efficiently (using fewer resources and at a lower cost) than some other countries.
**I** without any government restrictions.

| 1 | | 2 | | 3 | | 4 | | 5 | | 6 | | 7 | | 8 | | 9 | |
|---|---|---|---|---|---|---|---|---|---|---|---|---|---|---|---|---|---|

## Listening 1: Free trade ▶ 2.23

**Listen to Michael Kitson talking about the consequences of free trade, and answer the questions.**

1 What are the problems with economic models?
2 What is the standard argument for free trade?
3 What is the example Kitson gives?
4 Who loses in this example, and why?
5 What is Kitson's suggested alternative to 'unfettered free trade'?

Michael Kitson

## Listening 2: Exceptions to free trade ▶ 1.24

**Listen to Michael Kitson talking about exceptions to free trade, and answer the questions.**

1 Why would the developing country not want to specialize only in cloth?
2 What would help or enable the country to move into new sectors?
3 What reasons does Kitson give for considering an industry or sector as strategic in an advanced country?
4 What example does he give of a strategic industry, and what are its advantages?

Ha-Joon Chang

## Reading: Education and protection

**The Korean economist Ha-Joon Chang is the author of several books including *Bad Samaritans – Guilty Secrets of Rich Nations and the Threat to Global Prosperity*. Here is part of an interview about this book. Read it and answer the questions below.**

To explain this idea in the book I use the example of my young son. This little guy is perfectly capable of making a living. He's already eight now, but when I wrote the book he was six. Millions of children work in developing countries from the age of four or five, as did millions of children in rich countries in the 19th and early 20th century. Maybe I should send my son to the labour market and make him get a job. If he can earn his own living, that's a lot of money saved for me. But more importantly, this will expose him to competition and make him a very productive person.

Well, of course I don't do this. He is quite a clever kid and maybe if I support him for another 12 or 15 years, he could become a software engineer or brain surgeon or nuclear physicist. Of course, there's a danger that he might turn out to be a total waste of time, but that's a risk I'm willing to take. I know for sure that if I kick him into the labour market now, he will become a shoe-shine boy, and will maybe grow up to be a street hawker, but he will never be a brain surgeon or a nuclear physicist.

The analogy is: When you are trying to get into a more difficult and thereby higher-return activity, developing countries have to invest in it. The investment comes in the form of protection, which makes, for the moment, your local consumer use expensive and inferior domestic products. But unless you do that, these industries are not going to grow. You accept that you will use inferior products from inefficient producers for the time being. In the meantime, you do certain things to make sure that these firms grow up, i.e. they increase their productivity and eventually give you cheaper domestic goods, create jobs and stimulate other activities. In the end, you are better off that way.

So, inefficiency is part of the deal. Only you are deliberately creating these inefficiencies with the view of becoming even more efficient than otherwise possible.

1 Explain in detail the analogy Chang makes between child labour and free trade (or between education and protectionism).
2 What is the short-term disadvantage of protecting growing industries?

Discussion

- **Which industries or sectors could be usefully protected in your country, until they had a comparative advantage?**
- **To what extent would you be prepared to use inferior, expensive products from inefficient producers? What if you thought this 'might turn out to be a total waste of time'?**

## Vocabulary

**Before discussing arguments for and against free trade, match up these words and definitions.**

copyright dumping generic subsidize trademark

1 a cheaper copy of a product that is not marked with the producer's name
2 a name or a symbol showing that a product is made by a particular producer and which cannot be legally used by anyone else
3 selling unwanted goods very cheaply, usually in other countries
4 the legal right to control the production and selling of a book, play, film, photograph, piece of music, etc.
5 to pay part of the cost of something

## Reading and discussion: For and against free trade

**Although many economists favour free trade, there is also a lot of opposition. There have been huge and violent protests at meetings of the World Trade Organization (WTO).**

- **Classify the statements on the next page: which are in favour of, and which against, free trade and the policies of the WTO?**
- **Which set of arguments do you find the most convincing?**

A Free trade and international supply chains lead to peace and stability (see Unit 8).

B WTO policies prohibit developing countries from protecting infant industries until they are internationally competitive, although the rich countries that dominate international trade all did this.

C Free trade guarantees the largest possible foreign markets for producers and exporters.

D The WTO defends 'Trade Related Intellectual Property' rights (TRIPs), granting pharmaceutical companies patents, copyrights and trademarks which deny poor countries access to lifesaving medicines and generic drugs.

E Free trade guarantees consumers the lowest possible prices.

F Lowering trade barriers also breaks down other barriers between peoples and nations.

G The price of exported goods does not reflect the environmental cost of transporting them.

H Instead of promoting internationally recognized labour and environmental standards, free trade makes it easier for production to go where the labour is cheapest and environmental costs are low.

I Free trade, comparative advantage and specialization always lead to economic growth and development.

J Total world trade in 2000 was 22 times higher than in 1950, and as a result people were much more prosperous.

K The WTO classifies most environmental, labour, health and safety protection laws as illegal 'barriers to trade'; it has ruled against the US Clean Air Act and parts of the US Endangered Species Act.

L Free trade ensures secure supplies and a greater choice of components and raw materials for producers, and of products and services for consumers.

M The WTO has ruled that governments cannot take into account 'non-commercial values' such as human rights, opposing child labour, etc.

N WTO policies allow rich countries to dump heavily subsidized industrially produced food in poor countries, which damages local production.

| | | | | | | | |
|---|---|---|---|---|---|---|---|
| **In favour** | | | | | | | |
| **Against** | | | | | | | |

## Presentation

**Prepare a brief talk (or a written report) summarizing either the arguments in favour of free trade, or those against. You can use your own opinions and examples as well as those expressed in this unit.**

# 28 Economics and ecology

### Aims

- Discuss global warming
- Consider possible solutions to global warming, and their economic consequences

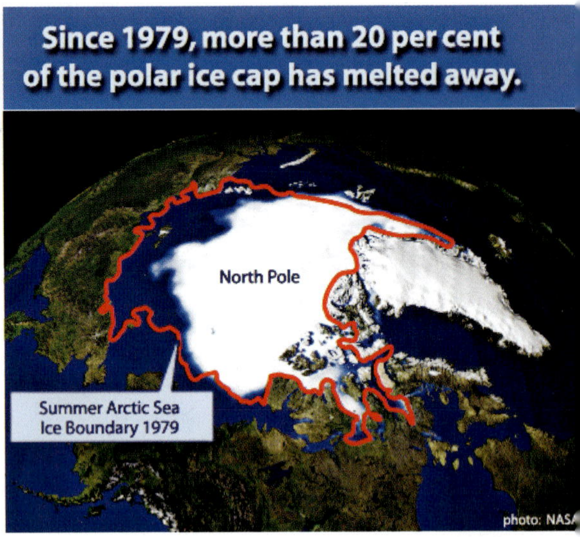
Since 1979, more than 20 per cent of the polar ice cap has melted away.
North Pole
Summer Arctic Sea Ice Boundary 1979
photo: NASA

## Lead-in

- What is causing global warming?
- What are the possible solutions?
- Are these solutions being implemented, and if not, why not?
- Does there have to be an international response to global warming, or can individual governments take measures? If so, what?
- Are you concerned about your carbon footprint: the sum of all the $CO_2$ emissions that are directly and indirectly associated with your activities? (You can calculate this at http://www.carbonfootprint.com/calculator.aspx) For example, do you avoid flying, or pay for carbon offsetting when you fly: funding an equivalent carbon dioxide saving somewhere else?

## Reading: The economics of climate change

**Read the following extract from an article by a French economist, Christian Gollier, about climate change.**

- **What does he say is more important than cutting carbon dioxide emissions?**

Christian Gollier

The Stern Review asserts that most of the consequences of global warming will not appear before the year 2100. For example, it is assumed in the report that the mean losses in global per-capita GDP resulting from climate change will be 2.9% in 2100 and 13.8% in 2200. Thus, future generations will bear most of the costs stemming from global warming. A crucial question, then, is to determine how much current generations should be ready to pay to reduce these future costs. We all agree that one euro obtained immediately is better than one euro obtained next year, mostly because of the positive return we can get by investing this euro. This argument implies that costs and benefits occurring in the future should be discounted at a rate equal to the rate of return of capital over the corresponding period.

Because it is hard to predict the rate of return of capital for the next two centuries, the Stern Review follows another approach, which consists of evaluating explicitly the welfare effect of global warming for each future generation.

The welfare approach to discounting is based on the assumption that future generations will be richer than current generations. In a nutshell, one should not be ready to pay one euro to reduce the loss borne by future generations by one euro, given that these future generations will be so much wealthier than us. Using the argument retrospectively, we enjoy a real GDP per capita that is approximately 50 times larger than Europeans who lived during the Napoleonic wars, and it would not have been a good idea for them to make much effort for our welfare.

By investing in technologies to reduce the impact of climate change in the distant future, we redistribute wealth from the poor current generations to the wealthy future ones. Nevertheless, it is a fact that we do not presently implement policies (fighting malaria, improving access to clean drinking water …) today that would be highly cost-effective and would benefit people in the poorest nations. The priority should be put on helping people currently living below the poverty line rather than on fighting global warming. Worse, by actually focusing on climate change, we are going to force developing countries to divert some of the benefits of their growth, which is so useful to fight poverty, towards cutting carbon dioxide emissions, which is primarily a concern of the wealthy.

## Comprehension

1 Why does Christian Gollier think it is not necessary to invest today in technologies that will reduce the future impact of climate change?
2 Why would the benefits, in the distant future, of spending money today be small?
3 What policies does Gollier say would help people in poor countries today?
4 What effect does Gollier say cutting carbon dioxide emissions will have on poor countries?

## Vocabulary

**1 Find words or expressions in the text that mean the following:**

1 average mean
2 to accept or tolerate or endure something unpleasant bear
3 originating or developing as the result of something stemming from
4 an extremely important or necessary thing to ask crucial question
5 reduced discounted
6 the amount of income received each year from an investment, expressed as a percentage of the total amount invested rate of return
7 in summary, briefly or simply in a nutshell
8 producing very good results for the amount of money concerned highly cost-effective
9 least wealthy countries poorest nations
10 the minimum level of income necessary to meet basic needs poverty line

**2 Match up the verbs and nouns below to make word combinations.**

| | |
|---|---|
| bear | benefits |
| benefit | $CO_2$ emissions |
| cut | costs |
| discount | global warming |
| fight | impact |
| help | people |
| implement | policies |
| redistribute | poverty |
| reduce | wealth |

## Discussion

- **How far do you agree with Christian Gollier that cutting carbon dioxide emissions is primarily a concern of the wealthy, and that we should do nothing about it now?**

## Vocabulary

**1 Before listening to Martin Beniston, a climate scientist, talking about environmental policy and climate change, match up the words and expressions on the left with the definitions on the right.**

**1** albeit
**2** at threat
**3** decouple
**4** desertification
**5** hindrance
**6** inertia
**7** iterative
**8** on a par with
**9** political will
**10** reticence
**11** timeframe

**A** although it is
**B** at the same level as something else
**C** likely to become endangered in the future
**D** repetitive or recurring
**E** something which makes it more difficult for something to happen
**F** strong government intentions
**G** the period during which something is projected to take place
**H** the physical force that keeps something moving in the same direction
**I** the process by which land becomes dry and vegetation is destroyed
**J** to disconnect or separate
**K** unwillingness to do something

| | | | | | | | | | | | |
|---|---|---|---|---|---|---|---|---|---|---|---|
| 1 | A | 2 | C | 3 | J | 4 | I | 5 | E | 6 | H |
| 7 | D | 8 | B | 9 | F | 10 | K | 11 | G | | |

Reproduced by kind permission of *Private Eye* magazine

**2 Which of the following words mean:**

**a** to become smaller in size or amount, or fewer in number
**b** to become greater in size or amount, or more in number?

augment decline decrease diminish drop dwindle
expand extend fall grow increase inflate
multiply recede rise shrink shrivel swell

## Listening 1: A big step forward ▶ 2.25

Martin Beniston

**Martin Beniston is Professor of Climatology at the University of Geneva. Listen to him talking about climate change and answer the questions.**

1 What examples does Martin Beniston give of 'moving forward in the right direction'?
2 What is Beniston's reservation about the G8 Declaration?
3 How does he describe China and India?
4 What is the situation regarding these countries?

## Listening 2: Emerging technologies ▶ 2.26

**Listen to Martin Beniston talking about emerging technologies.**

1 Fill in the gaps.

Well, I think if we look at all the emerging technologies related to sort of [1] __green__ __energy__ and other [2] __environment__ __friendly__ technologies, it's certainly more of an opportunity than a [3] __hindrance__. I think much of the [4] __reticence__ of politicians up till now, and the general public to some extent, related to the climate change issue was that one had the impression that, you know, to try and become [5] __carbon__ __neutral__, or to try and revert ... reverse the, you know, global warming, would mean going back to the Stone Age or to the Middle Ages or something, you know, this is not really the case, I mean it's not at all the case. And certainly there are huge [6] __opportunities__ out there for, you know, transform the economy, and transformations of technology, and so on, so I would say ... in fact if you look at some of the more progressive countries towards environmentally friendly technologies you do see that [7] __GDP__ has actually grown in places like Denmark, while at the same time carbon [8] __emissions__ have not progressed at all and have even [9] __reversed / dwindled__ to some extent, the same for Sweden even if the Swedish case is less spectacular, so it does show that you can [10] __decouple__ carbon emissions from economic growth, so why not take that route?

2 What does *carbon neutral* mean?
3 Explain in your own words the false impression that Martin Beniston talks about.

## Listening 3: Can we ignore the problem for now? 2.27

**Listen to Martin Beniston reacting to Christian Gollier's argument (above) about letting future generations deal with global warming, and answer the questions.**

1 To what extent does he agree?
2 What are the reasons for starting to act now?
3 What does he say about the future economic situation of the countries of the south?
4 What examples of negative impacts of climate change does he give?

### Discussion

- **To what extent is your country threatened by global warming (rising sea levels, desertification, diminishing water resources, forest fires, extreme weather events, and so on)?**
- **To what extent is your country developing clean or green energies (wind power, solar power, etc.)? Do you think it is doing enough?**
- **Could your country increase economic growth while reducing carbon emissions? How?**
- **If reducing carbon emissions *did* also reduce economic growth, would you find this acceptable?**

## Role play: Recommending an energy policy

**The government of a developing country has invited economists to present their proposals for future energy policy. Your teacher will give you a role. Prepare it in pairs or small groups: what would you say at the meeting?**

### Writing

**Write a brief (150 word) summary of the proposals agreed upon by the meeting.**

# Role cards

## List of role cards

# Unit 5 Role play: A job interview

## Assistant Brand Manager

After a short training period, you will be involved in the development of the marketing plan. As part of a multi-functional team you will develop and execute a promotion and media plan, and work with the retail customers, relaunching an existing brand or introducing a new product.

We are looking for:

- A good university degree and a passion for marketing
- Evidence of achievements in academic and/or non-academic activities
- Self-starting capabilities, collaboration skills, creativity, and strategic analysis
- A desire to succeed in a world-class organization
- A good command of English
- Short work experience, internships and studies abroad are considered as a plus.

## Assistant Supply Chain Manager

After a short training period, you will be responsible for the physical distribution of our products and their delivery to our customers, collaborating closely with our manufacturing plants, distribution centres and external logistics. You will analyse and optimize our work processes and transport, to balance the challenge of reducing distribution costs while maintaining and improving service levels to our customers. You may also be responsible for leading a small team of people. We are looking for:

- A good university degree in any discipline
- Good communication skills in English, both verbally and in writing
- Goal orientation, organizational skills and the desire to get things done
- Leadership, problem-solving and decision-making skills
- A passion for achieving results through people.

## Executive Assistant to the Chief Financial Officer

You will support the CFO in the analysis of financial data, producing presentations to the Global Corporate team. Working alongside other members of the Finance team, you will be involved in management accounting as well as specific project work.

This opportunity will give you excellent grounding in accounting and finance, and exposure to a number of different areas of finance. You will get intensive training. We are looking for:

- Strong academic results
- Strong numerical and analytical skills
- Excellent collaboration skills and the ability to work within diverse teams
- A good command of the English language
- A genuine interest in finance
- Ambition, self-motivation and the ability to work in a fast-changing environment.

## Unit 5 Role play: A job interview

### Interviewer

You can ask questions such as the following.

*Small talk to begin:*

Did you have any trouble finding us?
I hope you didn't try to find a parking space around here?
How are you enjoying this hot weather / snow / etc.?

*Standard interview questions:*

Tell us something about yourself.
What university do/did you attend and why did you choose it?
Why did you choose to study business / economics / engineering / etc.?
What do you know about our company?
Why would you like to work here?
Who would you consider to be our main competitors?
What attracted you to this particular position?
What do you see as your strengths?
How do your skills and experience match the job requirements?
What skills did you develop / have you developed at university / in your current job?
What languages can you speak?
What do you like doing in your spare time?

*More difficult questions:*

What do/did you dislike about university / your current job?
How would you describe the way you work?
Would you describe yourself as an ambitious person?
What are your weaknesses?
What skills do you think you need to improve?
Where do you see yourself in five years' time?
Tell me about a time when you experienced pressure, at university or at work.
Tell me about a time you had to make a difficult decision.
Tell me about a time when you played an important role in a team.

## Unit 6 Role play: Do we need more women managers?

### CEO

You chair the meeting, and explain the situation – that you think the company does not have enough women managers and directors. Explain why you think this is a problem, and that you want constructive suggestions to solve it. You choose who will speak first. You will not select Director D to begin, as you suspect that he (probably not she) has very negative views on this matter. At the end of the meeting, you can briefly summarize the directors' suggestions, and inform them which ideas you think are the best and most practical.

## Unit 10 Role play: A hotel chain in trouble

### CEO

You have to explain the situation to your colleagues: your room occupancy rate has been going down for three years, and many of your hotels are no longer profitable. This seems to be a long-term trend and not just a temporary problem due to the current economic situation. There is a lot of competition in the mid-range hotel market, and your brand is continuing to lose customers, which makes it impossible to increase prices. Something radical has to be done, but you don't know what. You chair the meeting, decide who will speak first, prevent people interrupting each other, and so on. At the end of the meeting, you would like to vote on a definite proposal.

## Unit 14 Role play: Microfinance

### Director A

You chair the meeting. Let Director B speak first and explain his/her ideas, and then ask for your colleagues' opinions. Make sure that people remain polite and do not interrupt each other.

At the end of the meeting you can try to formulate a specific proposal to present to the full board of directors, if you think there is any agreement among the people at this meeting.

## Unit 18 Role play: Financial instruments

**Questions (1)**

1 What income do investors expect from bonds?
2 In what ways can companies and investors guarantee future prices?
3 In what way can investors protect their investments in tracker funds?

## **Unit 21 Role play:** Is this company restricting competition?

### Investigator for the competition authority

You begin the meeting by explaining the situation: you are investigating the company because of their large market share and high profits.

You can make the following points, not necessarily all at once, and any others that you think are relevant.

- The company's market share is already very large and increasing.
- The company's profits are unnaturally high (much higher than the industry average).
- The company has regularly bought smaller, more efficient rivals, which restricts competition.
- It is true that the company has not merged with any large rivals, for the simple reason that there aren't any!
- When new competitors enter the market, the company offers temporary discounts (reduces its prices), which can drive smaller rivals out of business.

You can end the meeting when you think you have heard enough from the company. You can inform them whether you were convinced by their arguments, or whether you are going to launch an official investigation into their conduct.

## **Unit 24 Role play:** Problems at a clothes manufacturer

### CEO

You chair the meeting and begin by explaining the production/sales problem. Your sales have fallen by 20% in the past three months, during a recession which is expected to continue for many more months. Furthermore, your sales are cyclical, increasing in the spring and summer, and you are now entering the winter season. Consequently, your inventory is much too large, and you need to reduce production immediately.

You employ almost 200 sewing staff who get paid according to the number of pieces they sew. They are very efficient and productive, having been trained (at considerable expense) by the company. Each of them makes about 150 pieces a day. You need to reduce this number to about 100 pieces a day. You can either retain all your staff but only for about five hours a day, or you can lay off about 60–70 of your sewers.

After explaining this situation, you ask your Chief Scientist to explain a second problem, concerning pollution. After that, you decide who can speak, and see if your colleagues can come to an agreement as to what the company should do. If not, as the CEO you have the deciding vote.

## Unit 25 Role play: Reorganizing the postal service

### CEO

You chair the meeting, and begin by explaining your plan, as outlined in the Reading section, but add some further arguments:

- Your current sorting offices are inefficient for several reasons, including the following:
  - they are mostly situated in city centres, which make road access for trucks difficult
  - they do not allow efficient working methods, e.g. in one large sorting office, three million letters a day have to be moved from one floor of the building to another
- The new sorting offices would have new automated machines that can scan and read addresses and sort mail. The current machines process 25,000 letters an hour; the new ones would be able to process 40,000. Manual sorting only processes about 1,600 letters an hour
- The new machines would also allow automatic sequencing: sorting the mail according to the route taken by each postman or mail carrier, which represents a gain of two hours per mail carrier per day
- A further stage of new technology would involve robots automatically moving containers of mail around the sorting centres.

After explaining the plan, and giving your reasons for supporting it, you invite your colleagues to speak, first the Financial Director (who you know agrees with you) and then the Human Resources Director. Finally you invite the Trade Union Representative to speak.

At the end of the meeting, you have to decide what to recommend at the next board meeting.

## Unit 6 Role play: Do we need more women managers?

### Director A

You think the problem is simple: it lies in the job advertisements prepared by the HR department. They often contain a picture of a man in a suit, carrying a briefcase, with a text containing words like *aggression*, *competitiveness* and *dynamism*. They also often have a paragraph with the heading 'The Perfect Candidate' that begins 'He will be ...'. The company needs to rethink its job advertising. If it wants to attract more women, it could use pictures of women, and words like *collaboration*, *innovation* and *enthusiasm*. Such advertisements might also attract a different kind of man to apply for jobs. The company could also reconsider its selection processes: you could insist, for example, that at least one of three candidates interviewed for each management job is a woman.

## Unit 10 Role play: A hotel chain in trouble

### Financial Director

You think the solution is simple, at least in the short term: you have to instruct all the hotel managers to add extra charges, and/or reduce their costs by 5–10%, by whatever means they think appropriate. For example, they could increase the price of breakfast (not included in the room price), telephone calls, internet access, car parking, drinks at the bar, etc. Or they could change the sheets and towels of long-stay customers less often, not vacuum the corridors every day, turn off the hot water at night, not have cable TV, etc. You expect that your colleagues at the meeting can come up with various similar suggestions.

Another possibility would be to close the unprofitable hotels and sell them, or convert the buildings into offices or apartments. All your hotels are in good city centre sites, and would be easy to sell at a profit, or rent out as either office space or accommodation.

## **Unit 14 Role play:** Microfinance

### Director B

According to the World Bank, 2.8 billion people – almost 40% of the world's population – are affected by poverty and live on less than US$2 a day. But 500 million of these people are economically active, trying to improve their income as 'microentrepreneurs'. They need small loans as start-up capital, and other financial services, so that they can run small businesses.

Microcredits allow people to work more efficiently as vegetable growers, animal breeders, small shopkeepers, manufacturers, roadside cooks, street vendors, market traders, hairdressers, clothes makers, etc.

Statistics from Bangladesh, for example, show that 97% of borrowers from microfinance institutions pay interest and repay their loans. The majority of borrowers are women, who have better repayment rates than men. Even if borrowers have no collateral, microcredit banks can grant group loans, or count on group pressure acting as a social control that encourages people to repay.

You think your bank should lend some money to microfinance institutions in Asia, Africa and Latin America, and publicize this fact: this would help restore the bank's image.

You will speak before your colleagues C, D and E.

## **Unit 18 Role play:** Financial instruments

**Questions (2)**

1. What income do investors expect from shares?
2. What factors determine the amount of interest paid by bonds?
3. What might change the *yield* an investor receives from a bond?
4. In what ways can companies and investors try to protect themselves against changes in interest rates or exchange rates?

## **Unit 21 Role play:** Is this company restricting competition?

### Company manager A

You defend your company. You can make the following points, and any others that you think are relevant. You do not have to make these points all at once, and can invite your colleague to join in.

- You were the first company to succeed in this field; you introduced new products or services and techniques and opened up new markets, and it is only natural that you make big profits.
- Your company grew naturally, because you provided a better product or more efficient service than your competitors.
- You are also being rewarded for developing successful and persuasive marketing strategies and advertising campaigns.
- As you grew, you naturally benefited from economies of scale in every area (production, distribution, R&D, capital financing, etc.).
- You are innovative, and have regularly improved and differentiated your products or services.
- You are a public company, and always at risk of being taken over by a larger company based in another country.

## Unit 24 Role play: Problems at a clothes manufacturer

### Chief Scientist

You have received an advance copy of an article that will soon be published in a major scientific journal. It has been discovered that an anti-bacterial chemical you use in many of your fabrics is potentially harmful to the environment. You know that small quantities of the chemical are released into waste water during manufacturing, and very small amounts might wash off garments each time they are cleaned, and get through waste water treatment plants to finish in rivers and waterways. Even if your suppliers succeed in filtering the chemical out of the waste water produced during manufacturing – which would be very expensive – you will not be able to prevent the chemical from being released when your customers wash their clothes. You think you have no alternative but to stop using this chemical in your products. Even though the quantity released when your customers wash your garments is small, and within existing legal limits, you think the company has a clear ethical duty not to pollute the environment.

## Unit 6 Role play: Do we need more women managers?

### Director B

You think the problem lies with the traditional career paths in companies. Many women who have children do so in their 30s, and are not able to devote all their time to their job. Unfortunately, this is often the age (typically between about 28 and 35) when companies identify and promote people they think have a high potential for future leadership. If the company also tried to identify leaders at younger and older ages, it might find more potential women leaders, including women who have come back from a career break of a few years. This would also encourage women who take a break to return to the company.

## Unit 25 Role play: Reorganizing the postal service

### Financial Director

You are wholly in favour of the plan. When invited to do so, you will present the costs and savings, as follows:

- The cost of building the three new centres would be (the equivalent of) about €1 billion, but at least half of this would be recovered by selling the existing buildings, which are in expensive city-centre locations
- New equipment (machines, trucks and railway wagons) would cost another €50 million
- A redundancy package and training programmes for the staff laid off would cost €100 million
- The restructuring would save €200 million a year in salaries, and in eliminating the unnecessary costs involved in transporting mail between different sorting offices. In other words, you would start making a large profit within four years.

## Unit 10 Role play: A hotel chain in trouble

### Marketing Manager

You think that reducing the quality of service or increasing prices would be disastrous, and lead to a further loss of your existing customers. You think increasing the quality of service would be difficult as the hotels (which all look the same) have small rooms, and no facilities for converting the breakfast rooms into full restaurants. The only solution is to re-brand the hotels, and attract a different kind of customer: 'back-packers'. This will involve turning the hotels into low-cost hostels for young travellers, e.g. installing bunk beds and having four people per room. You travelled extensively and used hostels like this a lot when you were younger. You know there's a market for them.

## Unit 14 Role play: Microfinance

### Director C

You listen carefully to your colleague's arguments, but you are totally opposed to getting involved in microfinance in poor countries. You have several arguments:

- Setting up partnerships with microfinance institutions in developing countries would involve a lot of work, and your staff all have plenty of other things to do.
- Your bank has no expertise in this kind of venture.
- Some of your depositors might not like their money being used in this new way.
- Even if you find reliable local partners, there are huge fixed costs involved in microfinancing. The lender has to assess potential borrowers' security and repayment prospects, administer the loans, and find ways of collecting from borrowers who don't repay, which all costs money. The expenditure involved in making a small loan (e.g. $1,000) is the same as making a very large one (e.g. $1,000,000), so small loans need very high interest rates to cover their costs and make a profit.

## Unit 18 Role play: Financial instruments

**Questions (3)**

1 Give *three* ways investors can make capital gains from shares.
2 In what way can institutions make money from fluctuating share prices?
3 In what additional ways can hedge funds make capital gains from shares?

## Unit 21 Role play: Is this company restricting competition?

### Company manager B

You will not speak for the first time until you are invited to by the investigator or your colleague. You will defend your company. You can make the following points, and any others that you think are relevant. You do not have to make these points all at once, and perhaps you only need to make them in response to accusations from the other side.

- The fact that you make big profits is an incentive to entrepreneurs and competitors to discover and implement better low-cost technologies; that's how markets work. There will never be a monopoly of brilliant technical or business ideas, and lots of people are trying to find ways to compete with your company.
- You welcome competition, which is essential to keeping your business efficient and innovative. If you had no competition you would have no incentive to be efficient or find ways to reduce costs.
- Furthermore, your competitors help expand the markets you operate in. They find new uses and users for your products or services, which is an advantage to all the companies in the industry.
- Although you have occasionally reduced your prices to attack new competitors, this is a normal and acceptable part of rivalry and competition. What is illegal, on the contrary, is fixing prices with competitors, which you have never done.
- You have bought a few small companies in your field, but a) you have to do something with your profits, and b) buying other successful and innovative firms is often less risky, more efficient, and quicker than innovating and developing new products/services yourselves.

## Unit 24 Role play: Problems at a clothes manufacturer

### Marketing Manager

You are concerned about what the Chief Scientist says. You are worried about damage to the company's image if it continues to use chemicals that could be harmful to the environment. Your garments are expensive and of a high quality, and you think that your customers (of outdoor sports clothing) are the kind of people who are very concerned about environmental issues. But this is more than a question of image: if – or when – your customers discover that your products are harmful, they will probably stop buying them. On the other hand, to stop using this chemical, or another one that had the same effect, would also be a disaster, as your 'odour-eating' fabrics are one of your chief selling points. You suggest trying to find a similar but non-toxic chemical, by using the 'wikinomics' principle: you put a challenge to develop such a chemical on a website such as www.innocentive.com, and offer an award to anyone who submits a solution to the challenge. Meanwhile you should continue using the existing chemical.

## Unit 25 Role play: Reorganizing the postal service

### Human Resources Director

While you understand the need for efficiency and profitability, you are not convinced that this plan is a good idea, as it will result in 4,500 people becoming unemployed. You will quote a well-known saying from the management theorist Peter Drucker: 'Efficiency is doing things right; effectiveness is doing the right things.'

- You do not think that efficiency should be the only criterion for the organization. You do not think destroying so many jobs is the right thing to do.
- You think the post office should try to find other jobs in the organization for the people who lose their jobs in the sorting offices, for example behind the counters in post offices, or in technical and maintenance jobs.
- You are in favour of a revised plan, in which the post office builds several secondary sorting offices around the country, as well as the three main ones.

## Unit 6 Role play: Do we need more women managers?

### Director C

You think that if the company wants to attract and retain women with strong management and leadership potential, it needs to offer childcare. The company could set up a nursery for pre-school-age children, near the company's headquarters. This would allow mothers to be near their children while they are at work, and might encourage them not to take a career break when their children are young. This day care would not be free, but managers with high salaries would be able to pay for it, so it wouldn't necessarily cost the company anything. All this would give the company a big competitive advantage over its rivals.

## Unit 10 Role play: A hotel chain in trouble

### Operations Manager

You think the only way to go is upmarket, into the more profitable luxury hotel market. If the three-star market is overcrowded, you have to be ambitious. Your hotels are all newly built, or in recently modernized buildings, in good locations. You could convert some or all of them into four-star hotels, getting a major bank to finance the project. This would involve closing hotels for several months, knocking down walls, making the rooms bigger and installing better facilities. The redesigned hotels could be re-launched under a new name, with higher prices and a higher profit margin.

## Unit 14 Role play: Microfinance

### Director D

You are absolutely in favour of encouraging entrepreneurial activity, but you think that your bank should do this in its local market. There are lots of small and medium-sized enterprises that need capital in your own country. Your bank has expertise in lending to this type of customer. Your depositors might prefer to know their money is being spent in this way. Your bank's branches would probably get a better response from their local communities if they invested locally. You could have a special advertising campaign explaining your support for local businesses.

## Unit 24 Role play: Problems at a clothes manufacturer

### Human Resources Manager

You are worried about both solutions to the production problem suggested by the CEO. If your workers start working part-time, they may no longer have enough money to live on. If you lay off highly trained workers, there is no guarantee that you will be able to rehire them when sales increase in the future, if they have found another job. You wonder if there are any other possibilities, e.g. retaining all the staff and giving them extra training until sales improve, maybe paying them the same amount as before. This would probably lead to increased motivation, loyalty and productivity in the future.

## Unit 25 Role play: Reorganizing the postal service

### Trade Union Representative

You are wholly against the plan, as it will abolish thousands of your members' jobs.

- Although the management say that only 4,500 jobs will go, it is clear that many other current employees will not be able to work in the new sorting offices, as this would involve too much travelling time.
- Many of the post office's employees are women who work part time; they clearly could not travel two hours each way to work in a new centre.
- Furthermore, people who have always worked during the day would not all be able to take on night jobs, and your union is against unnecessary night-work as it is known to be bad for health.
- Promising to offer staff different jobs in the organization is unrealistic: for example, sorting office staff are not trained for technical jobs, and offering them cleaning and maintenance jobs would be a demotion.
- Moreover, the post office clearly couldn't find anything like 4,500 jobs in this manner. The same promise was made to the staff of post offices that closed, but new jobs were not found for most of them.
- Offering training programmes would not necessarily help staff in towns and small cities where there is not very much alternative employment.
- You believe that the post office should remain a public service, and sacrifice some profits in order to preserve as many jobs as possible.
- Besides, you believe that staff morale will fall drastically if the plan goes ahead, which will not help productivity.
- You believe that the post office should build at least eight smaller new centres, spread all over the country.

## Unit 6 Role play: Do we need more women managers?

### Director D

You are not convinced that there is a problem. The company is successful, and has a lot of hard-working, full-time managers. You are very much against the idea of encouraging career breaks. People coming back from a career break for childcare are often not aware of the latest developments in the company, in the industry, or in the business world in general. Furthermore, if you offer career breaks to women, some men will start demanding them too, or other things like increased flexibility, or part-time positions, and the company will become inefficient and very difficult to run. You also think – even though you are a bit worried about saying this – that mothers should not work, but should stay at home looking after their children.

## Unit 14 Role play: Microfinance

### Director E

You agree with your colleague Director B that working with microfinance institutions in developing countries would be very good for the bank's image. You also think it would be a very good thing to do even without considering the bank's reputation. Microcredits encourage the entrepreneurial spirit and help reduce poverty in developing countries.

But you also see another opportunity. Instead of lending your current funds, you could launch a Microcredit Fund as an opportunity for socially motivated investors. They could invest money (starting at $1,000 or €1,000) in a special fund. The money would then be administered by established microfinance institutions. Investors would receive a variable return, depending on how profitable the microfinance operations were. This would give you an attractive new investment product to offer your customers.

## Unit 24 Role play: Problems at a clothes manufacturer

### Financial Manager

After listening to the CEO talking about laying off some staff you think the time is right to make a much more radical suggestion: move all your production to a country where labour is much cheaper. *Very* few clothing companies manufacture their products in your country because production costs are too high. You could relocate production to a country where wages are lower and working conditions not so advantageous. Furthermore, environmental standards and legislation in such countries would be less strict, so you could continue to use your bacteria-destroying chemical.

You are obviously opposed to any solutions to the current problem that would cost the company money.

## Unit 28 Role play: Recommending an energy policy

### Chairperson

You chair the meeting, explain the situation, decide who can speak, prevent interruptions, and listen to the opposing positions of the three economists.

You have to try to get some agreement, e.g. a list of *three* policy proposals, in order of priority, which you can present to the government.

You personally believe that your country must play its part in combating global warming.

### Economist A

You believe that your country should start producing all its electricity from renewable sources. At the moment, you import some of your electricity, and use oil-burning power stations for most of the rest. Investing in natural energy production would stop you having to rely on other countries for your electricity. You are also in favour of encouraging hybrid electric vehicles, with subsidies to consumers who buy them. You think that the trend towards hybrid cars is unstoppable, because oil production is expected to decline within your lifetime.

### Economist B

You believe that your country has far greater priorities than reducing carbon dioxide emissions. You disagree with any proposals that would limit economic growth in the short term. You think you should only invest in non-polluting energy if that would be cheaper than importing electricity or generating it from imported oil. Given the initial cost of setting up clean energy installations, you think this is extremely unlikely. You think the government should do everything in its power to increase growth. All the rich industrial countries pursued policies that increased growth for decades or even centuries; it is now up to *them* to deal with global warming.

### Economist C

You think that climate change is an extremely serious global problem, and that your country has to play its part in reducing its consumption of non-renewable carbon-based fuels. You agree that your country should start producing electricity from renewable sources, and are also in favour of a $CO_2$ tax on industry and individual consumers. Taxing oil more would encourage people to use their cars less and use public transport instead. Taxing industrial $CO_2$ emissions would encourage companies to use newer technology and cleaner industrial processes.

# Audio scripts

▶ CD1 Track 2

## Unit 1 Management

### Listening: What makes a good manager?

CARLO DE STEFANIS

... so managers should pursue the company goal, maximize value for shareholders, and so on, but on the other hand they should accomplish also the personal goals and objective of the people they manage, for instance helping young professionals to develop, and understanding the expectation of everybody in their team, and trying to match goals of the company and even helping people to develop in their team.

▶ CD1 Track 3

## Unit 1 Management

### Listening: What makes a good manager?

OLGA BABAKINA

I believe that good managers actually don't manage anybody, and good managers basically they are good executors of strategies, because the companies today, those ones who are successful, are not those who have lots of business plans and strategies somewhere in the reports and files, but those companies who have managers, executors of plans, so basically in order to be a good manager you have to know how to lead people, how to motivate people, and how to make sure that you are meeting your targets ...

▶ CD1 Track 4

## Unit 2 Work and motivation

### Listening 1: Managers and motivation

KRISHNA SRINIVASAN

I would say that coming from an auditing world where the pays are typically really low, especially when compared to the banking guys, one of the core things that was a driver in retaining our staff was, I would say, problems. The more you give them challenging problems, and the more you make them excited about solving the problem, the monetary aspect just goes out of the picture, and I have seen staff who have been almost telling every day that they want to quit the firm, but have never quit the firm for the last seven years, just because they've had so many challenging problems, that they just enjoyed solving, and you ask them, 'Why didn't you move, given that you would have had such a high pay increase in another place?' They'd say, 'Well, the pay would be great, but I don't think I'll face as many challenging puzzles or whatever problems I solved here over there.' So I think the motivation of the mind or the ultimate passion that you have is still a core driver, no matter how many hygiene factors or whatever that you learn in motivation.

CARLO DE STEFANIS

Managers can make the difference from this point of view. I think it is hard to engage people just setting up or devising a set of rules or a set of incentives to motivate people. Statistics in a way say that when people leave a company they leave their boss first. So really, it's about a balance of being a manager and being leader, having a vision, inspiring other people, helping them to develop that can get them engaged, I think.

SAKTIANDI SUPAAT

Something just came up about motivation, if I may raise the point ... Talking about managers that can motivate somebody, another additional point that I thought useful to bring up is a manager which is influential, and knows how to be an intermediary between the senior management and his staff, can motivate the staff, because he knows what the organization wants, and he's influential enough to convince the organization to do things that the staff wants. So having a manager that is influential and able to actually influence the organization is I think a great motivator, I mean from my perspective.

CD1 Track 5

## Unit 2 Work and motivation

### Listening 2: Out-of-work activities

JANINE GEORGE

I had a few team members in my operational team who were working in their jobs for about 40 years. It was a detergent factory, they came in every single day for 12-hour shifts, and can you imagine working in that role for 40 years? I came in and people were really bored, right, and what I did is, we set up small group meetings for each of the shifts, right, to find out what sports they were interested in, right, and what things they were doing outside of work. I found that there were many entrepreneurs, and also other people interested in things like driving HIV/Aids activities – in South Africa that's quite a big problem at the moment. And I just mean outside of work. I mean, if it's reading a book, if it's kicking a soccer ball, perhaps they want to organize a staff soccer team, right, perhaps they want to start a book club inside work, and I'm not just talking about, and I'm talking about things outside of things related to the bottom line, and I feel that those things could make people more passionate, just about coming into work, getting up in the morning and coming to their jobs. People then wanted to be trained, and what we found is they were even willing to come in on the off-shifts, and even not get paid for these types of things. So I think the one thing you need to learn about motivation is how do you ensure that you mobilize people by finding out what they really enjoy doing and you need to be extremely creative about these things. And I think it relates in some ways very much to jobs that secretaries do. People think that they're OK with just sitting behind a desk, and organizing your inbox, and sending out meeting requests. They're *not*, so I think it's really up to these managers and leaders to become creative, understand their people, and really think about things – and I don't want to use this word – outside of the box, to try and motivate their staff.

CD1 Track 6

## Unit 3 Company structure

### Listening: Big and small companies

KRISHNA SRINIVASAN

I guess given the way we are, or the way I am, it actually doesn't matter whether I'm in a big or a small company. What matters is, who am I going to work with? So if I have five people who are probably extremely different, or extremely similar, at the end of the day, as long as I enjoy working with them, and the basic security of supporting your family is assured, it doesn't matter which company I'm in. Problems, nice people – it doesn't matter anything else.

CARLO DE STEFANIS

I dare say it's, big company or a small company, it depends at what stage even you are in your career. For instance, should I give an advice I dare say for somebody who has just left university, working for a while in a big company can be a very good opportunity because they will form you, you will learn what are the best practices in the sector. But probably after a few years – I don't know, four or five years – everybody has to find his own way, because they think that they … in my opinion, big companies and small and medium enterprises are quite different in their mentality. In big companies, probably, politics can be more important, because you are actually a number within, you know, a large pool of people, it's hard to differentiate. In a smaller company maybe it's more a hands-on approach where you have more, it's required more an entrepreneurial style, so I think that everybody has to find his own way according to his liking basically.

OLGA BABAKINA

For me the size of the company doesn't really matter. Most important is the culture, so even if you are a small company or a big company, if you don't have the shared values with your colleagues, or if nobody understands what is the company's culture, nobody has a common vision, then it doesn't really matter. So the most important is the culture, and that everyone in the organization understands what the company is trying to achieve over the short term, over the long term, and everyone shares the same corporate values. Of course, small companies have more challenges in proving themselves as successful businesses. Big corporations, of course, on the other hand, are not that flexible, so it's more difficult for them to adopt new changes, and maybe to incorporate some creativity and innovation, so a balance in between all those issues, I think, is the key.

▶ CD1 Track 7

## Unit 4 Managing across cultures

### Listening 1: Managers and authority

KRISHNA SRINIVASAN

What I noticed in – I worked in both in Switzerland and in Malaysia – and the context of a manager is very different in these two countries. In Singapore the emphasis on hierarchy and the superiority of the manager is very important. No matter you put a group in a team, once the manager says something it's kind of accepted by everyone else, no one challenges it, whereas in Switzerland and UK what you observe is once the manager says something, people can challenge him. So manager in the western context is more a guider, who encourages people by his persuasion, either his vocal talent or his technical attitude [astute], whereas in the Asian region I still feel that the emphasis on superiority, power, is still very prevalent, so the manager has to have the commanding power.

CARLO DE STEFANIS

My theory in Italy we've still got, authority is important, as is seniority, in respect – if I make a comparison especially with the Anglo-Saxon world, in Italy seniority, the years you have spent in a certain position, in a certain company, give you formal authority, in a way. On the other hand I think that it is accepted, largely accepted in Italy, to make your point with your boss, absolutely, so to discuss about a position and problems in an open way.

▶ CD1 Track 8

## Unit 4 Managing across cultures

### Listening 2: Managers and cultural diversity

LAKSHMI JAYA

I mean I think here diversity in, say, management schools plays a very important role, because take for example Judge Business School, we have people from forty-six different nationalities, so you're working with these group of people at various points through your programme, and it kind of like gives that diverse experience to you, to be able to like work with cross, people from cross-cultural backgrounds. So I think management education does help a lot, and your ability to be, work with like, cross-cultural people.

JANINE GEORGE

I think the difference nowadays is also the fact that there's a lot more awareness about these issues. The fact that there are so many business schools, so many courses running with regards to culture, the differences in aspects regarding the US versus China, and so forth, people are just more aware. And I think with this, an American now going into China, has a completely different attitude, or at least I hope so! That people are now more aware of these situations and sort of aspects of emotional intelligence allow people to use those self-awareness aspects, to be able to be a bit more effective in their management styles …

CARLO DE STEFANIS

I read somewhere that now there are a lot of international corporations that are giving up their passport. This was an article, I mean, about a more general context, but it's true that companies like IBM, or General Electric, that are moving a lot of executives, and even middle management across the countries, contribute to create a mutual understanding of different cultures and to smooth, in a way, to round the corners, I think.

JANINE GEORGE

There's a saying that says 'When in Rome, do as the Romans do.' I went on a Japanese course where it said, 'When in Rome, learn what the Romans do, so you can become a better Japanese.' So I think that in a way sums it up perfectly, in that culture will never disappear, right, but I think in a way we're just going to become a lot more profound in what we do, and learn a lot more what everybody else in the rest of the world is doing.

▶ CD1 Track 9

## Unit 5 Recruitment

### Listening 1: Classifying the interviewee

JOHN ANTONAKIS

There is a saying in English that 'One does not get a second chance to make a first impression.' This statement is very important because what it suggests is that when individuals judge a target individual, they make a decision about that target based on, on very small slithers [slivers] of information. So it is very important that the person who is in an interview setting comes very well prepared, in terms of job knowledge, or knowledge about the post, or what background expertise and competences they have for the post, but also in their appearance, because every little slither of information, every little cue that the observer has on the target individual will influence how they categorize the target, and what is interesting is that research has shown that it only takes a few seconds for an interviewer to classify the target individual as being someone who is appropriate or not for a particular job.

▶ CD1 Track 10

## Unit 5 Recruitment

### Listening 2: Confirming first impressions

JOHN ANTONAKIS

Now the reason why observers make these rapid decisions about others in such situations is because they do not have full information on the target person. In a short interview that lasts half an hour or an hour, the interviewer cannot possibly know the target individual in terms of their personality, in terms of their intelligence. They're going to use small cues, and from these small cues they're going to make large inferences, so it's very important that the signals or the cues that the interviewee gives out are very concordant or close to what the interviewer expects. In psychology, we call this phenomenon 'confirmation bias'. So what happens is that the individual who's observing has some kind of stereotype or some kind of prototype in their heads about what a competent person should look like or what a good person for that particular post should look like. Now if you resemble that individual, they will try to confirm that initial impression by creating conditions in the interview that will make you succeed. If they don't like you, or if the initial impression is negative, the conditions that they will create in the interview will be such so that one fails. In other words, what we have observed in actual interview situations, or simulated situations where experimentally we, we have manipulated certain factors, is that interviewers don't change their minds very much from their initial impressions, so if someone is misclassified or classified badly in the beginning, it's very hard to recover that bad initial classification, again because of this confirmation bias, which is why it is so important to make a very good first impression.

CD1 Track 11

## Unit 5 Recruitment

### Listing 3: Preparing for an interview

JOHN ANTONAKIS

So in highly competitive situations where one really has to distinguish oneself, it's very very important in the interview situation to look natural, and by natural I mean that it doesn't seem like you are putting on an act. Of course it's a cat and mouse game in the interview setting so if one truly is natural one is natural because one is like that, or because one has practised to be like that. So again, the importance in preparation, I just cannot, one cannot underestimate. So, for example, if you've never had an interview before, it's very good to perhaps ask a peer, a friend, or someone who has more experience, or someone who already works, to give you a few practice runs, so that you can prepare yourself better, act in more natural ways, show a bit of, you know, positive body language, and confident body language, I mean small things like, you know, sitting up straight, smiling a little bit from time to time, maintaining good eye contact, using body gestures that are positive, those little things are like interest in the bank, they will add up, and they will really pay out in the long run. The reason why I say that is in the interview setting, the interviewer will probably pay as much, perhaps if not more attention, to things like appearance and non-verbal behaviour than actually what you say, so, you know, being natural and you know, sort of oozing positive body language and confident body language, I think is another important factor.

CD1 Track 12

## Unit 6 Women in business

### Listening 1: Women in business – a strategic issue (1)

ALISON MAITLAND

Well, there are several key reasons why women mean business, and why this issue is now really a strategic business issue – it's not a women's issue – and why it's time for CEOs to get serious about sex, as we say in the book.

One of these is the talent side of the equation, and that is that these days women actually account for the majority of university graduates. Six out of ten university graduates in North America, and in Europe, are women, so that's the talent pool, that's more than half of the world's, the developed world's, intellectual potential.

Another aspect is the market and the importance of women as consumers, and in the United States, eight out of ten consumer spending decisions are made by women these days, and that's not something peculiar to the US, it's a trend that's being followed by other countries, like Britain and France, Scandinavia, and we're going to see more of that. So women as earners earning money independently, spending, making big spending decisions, even in Japan two-thirds of car purchases are either made by or influenced by women.

CD1 Track 13

## Unit 6 Women in business

### Listening 2: Women in business – a strategic issue (2)

ALISON MAITLAND

There's another reason which is very important in terms of profitability, and that is that now there are three big research studies that have shown a link between companies that have the most women in their senior management or on the board, and greater profitability. So those companies that have particularly a critical mass of women – that's to say about 30% plus of women on the board or in senior management – are outperforming those that have no women or very few women in their senior teams, to the extent of, in one study there was an 83% higher return on equity amongst those companies that had the most women in their leadership ranks.

CD1 Track 14

## Unit 7 The different sectors of the economy

### Listening: The business news

**1** World oil prices have continued to fall today, with US sweet light crude dropping more than $3 to $63.20. Several members of OPEC, the 13-nation producers' group, which is responsible for producing about 40% of the world's total supply, want to cut output by at least one million barrels a day to increase prices.

**2** US software giant Microsoft has posted profits and sales figures well above analysts' expectations. The company made a $4.37 billion profit during the first three months of its financial year, up from $4.29 billion a year ago, while turnover rose 9% to $15.06 billion.

**3** In South Korea, Hyundai Motor Company has reported a 38% fall in third-quarter net profit, which was slightly better than expected, in a difficult year. Hyundai say that although global auto demand is shrinking, demand for smaller cars is rising. German car maker Daimler has reported a €213 million profit for the quarter, a dramatic turnaround from the €1.5 billion loss it made in the same period a year ago.

**4** Although the service sector represents three-quarters of the British economy, a report published today by an American consulting company suggests that British manufacturers are still doing well. The UK is currently the world's sixth-largest manufacturer, but the country appears set to remain in the top ten for the next 15 years. Even though it is expected to slip to ninth place by then, its share of global manufacturing value added is forecast to dip by just one percentage point.

**5** Mixed news from the airline sector today. While figures from the Association of European Airlines show that airline traffic has fallen for the first time in 25 years, because of the economic slowdown, Airbus has published its latest Global Market Forecast, which foresees a demand for some 24,300 new passenger and freight aircraft valued at US$ 2.8 trillion between now and 2026. This will create an average annual delivery of some 1,215 aircraft. The current decrease in traffic is expected to be temporary, and the long-term forecast for passenger traffic is that it is expected to grow at an average rate of 4.9% per year.

**6** In another study published today, it is predicted that the rapidly growing biofuel market, involving cereals, sugar, oilseeds and vegetable oils, will keep farm commodity prices high over the next decade. The study, co-written by the Organization for Economic Cooperation and Development and the UN Food and Agriculture Organization, predicts prices will rise by between 20% and 50% in the next ten years.

CD1 Track 15

## Unit 8 Production

### Listening 1: Purchasing

ALAN GOODFELLOW

Obviously one of the main goals of any company is to drive down the cost of raw materials and components that are used in manufacture, and Leica uses a number of techniques to achieve that. Firstly as part of the Danaher group they have the leverage of global buying power, that helps, that helps enormously because we can share suppliers with other companies within the Danaher group, and we also use techniques like, for example the reverse auction, which is a technique where we allow suppliers to bid for our business. It's rather like eBay in reverse in that they post on an internet site the lowest price with which they would do business with us and compete against each other in that way. Of course this has to be very carefully managed and there are a number of strategies in its use because price is not everything, we also have to guarantee quality, and we have to guarantee that the company can supply with reliability to that given price, so it's just one tool and even once the price has been determined we may not in fact choose the lowest price because we may deem another supplier to have an advantage with quality and delivery, but it's a useful tool used in that area.

▸ CD1 Track 16

## Unit 8 Production

### Listening 2: Low-cost manufacturing

ALAN GOODFELLOW

Well, the products are very high-tech, but Leica has always used low cost region. I wouldn't describe it as outsourcing because they are factories owned by Leica. For example, we've had a factory in Singapore for 35 years and in China for 12 years, which is a very long time in this industry, so they're wholly owned by Leica, not outsourced, but they provide low-cost manufacturing and we are able to maintain quality because they are wholly owned by Leica.

Yes, when we first set up the company in China there were a great many problems, mainly to do with training local staff, but particularly staff retention, because the economy was booming so much, we found that after training staff, bringing them up to the standards we expected, they were very attractive to other companies and could easily move and take their skills elsewhere, so there was a constant process of training and retraining, it was very hard to retain staff.

▸ CD1 Track 17

## Unit 9 Logistics

### Listening 1: Inventory, Kanban and MRP

ALAN GOODFELLOW

Yes, nowadays companies do not want to hold inventory. Inventory is capital tied up that could otherwise be used to grow the business, so there are always pressures to keep inventory as low as possible. Now throughout the business of course we need inventory, we need equipment that we demonstrate to the customer, and we need certain stocks of materials used in manufacture, but always the strategy is to have the suppliers deliver when it's needed in the production process, and that can keep us agile, it enables us to react to sales and market demands without stocking large amounts of inventory which, as I said, has a large cost implication. So we move the responsibility to the suppliers to deliver to our factories when the demand is there.

The manufacturing processes in Leica tended to be based on MRP, which is Material Requirements Planning, quite a sophisticated IT-based forecasting of the parts needed for production, but under Danaher we've changed that to a Kanban system which is a pull system. When a part is used it's immediately replaced by another in that bin and it pulls all the way through to the manufacture, so it's not Just-In-Time as such, but it is a direct link between the demands of the customer on finished products and the supply of the components from our individual suppliers.

▸ CD1 Track 18

## Unit 9 Logistics

### Listening 2: Leica's supply chain

ALAN GOODFELLOW

As you can imagine for a global company of our size it's quite a complex supply chain. We have at the moment nineteen selling units selling in different countries around the world, and nine business units manufacturing the products that are sold, and often we need to consolidate products together to ship to the customer at one time, so the supply chain therefore becomes complicated. You'll have a business unit in one country, for example Singapore, that will manufacture parts themselves, most particularly the optics, which are the key parts of these systems, but also take sub-assemblies from suppliers, produce a unit which will then in some cases be shipped to Europe for consolidation with other parts before sending on to the end customer.

And then following all of this trail of course are the financial transactions and documents that allow you to invoice the customer in the local language of that customer and the local currency. The main goal is that the customer always deals with a local party in his own language, his own currency, and where he can get local service, and all of this supply chain is transparent to him. Big challenge for the company of course is delivering on time, when you're dealing with this global operation, and that's how we have to balance local stock which is always very expensive, we try and drive down inventory, we do not want inventory, but we have to balance the needs of local customers and the fast turnover of stock with the cost of keeping that inventory.

▶ CD1 Track 19

## Unit 10 Quality

### Listening 1: Hotel customers and quality

DENIS FRUCOT

If your guests have been satisfied with what they had and they think that the service you've offered is of quality they'll come back. If you are no quality or very little quality to the customers' perception they won't come back, it's as simple as that, so the more you can offer, the better the service you can offer, the more comprehensive it can be, the more, the more you'll be successful and the more you'll have a customer base, it's as, pretty much that. After that, especially with what we do, the notion of quality is very subjective, it tends to come with the customers' perception of it.

For instance, a bed and breakfast, you have a pre-conceived idea of what the service is going to be like, your notion of quality will be, will revolve round the fact that they exceed these expectation[s] or they went below. If you find out that you have an en suite bathroom in a bed and breakfast and you've got some form of turndown service you'll be 'I'm coming back tomorrow, I'm staying a week!' Same opposite, if you find a dead cockroach in the middle of your bathroom, well certainly you have second thoughts about even spending one night, so it's pretty much like that.

▶ CD1 Track 20

## Unit 10 Quality

### Listening 2: Customer care

DENIS FRUCOT

Obviously, we're not a five-star hotel – Hotel du Vin as a group has always looked for, we aim at about three, four, but if we were to look and behave as a star rating system, but for that quality, for that level of conception, we tend to give a lot more. The service provided is usually of a higher standard. The service we offer, the notions we offer, revolves around the actual service that we provide. In order to give people the idea and that notion of quality which is very, as I said, very subjective, we have to emphasis[e] the customer care, we define what we call a guest's journey which revolves around, from the first impression they get from seeing it on a website to the last impression they get when they walk out the door of the hotel. You have to have friendly reception staff that know about the area, that know about Cambridge as if they were born there, although they are not, clearly, but they have to be able to get you a taxi whenever you need one, hairdressers, restaurants, it goes through a vast amount, array of things that people will not necessarily expect you to have but will be very, very impressed if you do, and really we try to embed that into absolutely every single member[s] of staff.

▶ CD1 Track 21

## Unit 10 Quality

### Listening 3: Selecting and training staff

DENIS FRUCOT

We have a very strong programme of progression for each member[s] of staff. All of my heads of department have come with me from a different hotel – I've opened four so far, I tend to hop around the country and I do that – but I've got a nucleon of people that I will, whenever I open a new one elsewhere I will call them or I'll go round the whole group and just select people that already have the philosophy of what we're trying to achieve, and then after that from the top down they train a smaller amount of people, reception for instance, all the girls in reception I was very adamant that I wanted local people, people that know Cambridge, because after that we have, I have at least two people, two persons in reception – head receptionist and her assistant, are both from within the company, so they know the brand – after that I take four people that know Cambridge very well, you've got at least a base to work on and they can exchange, it's interactive for both of them, as well with the idea of evolution within the company, whether it's here, whether it's elsewhere, but we open at a rate of about three hotel[s] a year at the moment so it's a lot of growing opportunity.

▶ CD1 Track 22

## Unit 11 Products

### Listening 1: Not just a juice bar

MELISSA GLASS

We launched a bar called Zeste Juice Bars. We sell a product that is a smoothie. We have two lines of products, we have smoothie which is a mixture of juice with frozen fruits, with either sorbet or yoghurt and ice, that's quite a thick drink, and the other thing we sell is freshly squeezed juice which is carrots juice, apple juice, there's orange juices and mixers of that to make different cocktails. We have a small side product of food as well, to complement the juice, so that people who come at lunchtime, they don't have to go to two places, they can buy something at ours and eat and drink at the same place, but in general our whole concept is based around a slogan of 'Zeste4Life', so it's about the image that we create, the whole, the energy behind it, the youth, the colours, the package, essentially. We're not, we don't consider ourselves just a juice bar.

▶ CD1 Track 23

## Unit 11 Products

### Listening 2: The origin of smoothies

MELISSA GLASS

OK, so the concept came, originally started in California, and that was about 20 years ago, at which point the concept was based just around juice. It progressed to be more based around smoothies. That concept then was taken to Australia in '99. I saw the concept in Australia grow in '99 through to 2001, where it became very popular, and you eventually saw bars like this all over the place. My husband and I decided that, we thought it was a product, a line of product or a concept that really wasn't existent in Switzerland, and we thought that it was a population, the Swiss are a population that would consume that sort of product and that there was a niche in the market. So we decided that we would launch Zeste Juice Bars, and we did that in 2004.

▶ CD1 Track 24

## Unit 11 Products

### Listening 3: Launching the product

MELISSA GLASS

Launching a new product from scratch is quite difficult. First off we had to ... we had the idea, we had to then do market research here obviously to work out, if the product would be, would be accepted and consumed here.

We had to do research into pricing, we had to do research into colours, what locations where it was going to be the most successful. We knew that obviously we needed high-frequency passage. The problem with that in Switzerland is the locations, the places with high passage are extremely expensive, so it's always a balance between getting somewhere that's got enough passage but not too, too expensive, because when you're selling a product that has a cost price of five francs you have to sell a lot of juices and smoothies to cover the base, the base cost. Apart from that we had to do obviously questionnaire friends, take surveys, we had to do, we also did trialling, sampling, we did a couple of parties at our place to try the different products, and to choose the different smoothies that we were going to start with.

We then had to come up with names as well, we had the big difficulty of deciding which language we were going to do it in, and we decided to take English for our names because that sort of followed where the concept came from, the base of the product, the origin, the origin of the product, and then we, we decided to launch in Lausanne because that was our home town. We knew the town very well, we knew the passage, we knew the frequence, we knew basically where the town works, the heart of the town, and we needed to test the product first off and then do our adaptations from that, and then launch in bigger towns like Geneva or Zurich or places like that, but it's important, it was important we decided to trial one store. We decided that one store, we would trial for one year and then after that we would consider expanding.

▶ CD1 Track 25

## Unit 12 Marketing

### Listening 1: Promoting a juice bar

MELISSA GLASS

After the launching of Zeste in Lausanne, in the beginning, as I said, it was quite difficult, we looked at different ways of attracting customers, we looked into different forms of marketing. The first, the first tactic on Lausanne was just sampling, we did sampling on the street, we, I sent out one of my staff members with little sample goblets, and people, little cups, and people then got to try our product, and I knew that if they tried our product they'd be happy – our product sells itself as far as taste. That was quite successful, but at the time we launched in October, so we were going into winter, again as I said before, the foot traffic was less, so then we decided what we were going to do was some sort of advertising campaign, something visual to get, to touch the people that, that hopefully they would come. This unfortunately was a very expensive experience. We went through a design agency, we designed posters to go into the buses, because the bus actually passed directly in front of our store. We saw the people in the bus, they didn't know who we were, what we did, and we, I felt we needed to touch these people. So we did a two-week campaign, which was rather expensive, to pay the time in the bus, also the production of the design of the, the flyer, and also the printing of the flyers. We went with the concept of having a fit woman with boxing gloves, with the theme of 'Get a, get a kick out of your vitamins and come to Zeste.' Unfortunately, what we realized wasn't on the pamphlet was enough information about the product, because the Swiss didn't know at that stage what a smoothie was. For them, this word didn't exist, so it wasn't a very effective campaign.

▶ CD1 Track 26

## Unit 12 Marketing

### Listening 2: The most effective form of promotion

MELISSA GLASS

The most effective thing we've found is publicity in the papers, and in general free publicity, so my partner spends a lot of time contacting the journals, papers like the, the free ones in the morning, and trying to get free articles when we have a new product or something hip, or something changes. They're often keen to have new things, or new bits of information. That then hits the target straight away that day and people tend to take … the effect is immediate. Those articles don't have an effect a week later in general, but it has the effect that day or the next day and the idea is behind this for us is that we then convince that person by the product and the taste of the product, and that they will come back because of that.

▶ CD1 Track 27

## Unit 13 Advertising

### Listening: Radio commercials

1

Espresso.

Espress – oh.

Bliss in a cup. Steamed milk on top.

You warm my tongue and my soul.

Mocha. Latte.

Whipped cream and one extra shot.

Wake up my senses, for less expenses.

High-taste escape, from the rat race.

Hand made in front of my eyes.

Cappuccino. Americano.

Fast, fresh and steamy; man that was easy.

Hey Jane, take me to that groovy place called

Sheetz.

Life is a trip, every day.

CD1 Track 28

## Unit 13 Advertising

### Listening: Radio commercials

2

Typingmaster Pro asks the question, What if you talked like you typed?

What if every time you open-ned your mooth words tumbled out like a le brunch of brokened crockery? How much timme would you wurst back spacking and sprel checking? Would anybody hire youpe? Probably nit. And life would be increbidly fustrating, no doubt. Meybe you should tink five colon backspace comma aboot Typingmaster Pro Typing Tutor for PC and lean how to touch type qickly and measily. Typingmaster Pro hash personalized exercises to target the keys where ou ned more parctice, constantitly monitoring your porgress and adjusting your trainnig. Just lik a good tutor shide, should. So, if you would lik to learn to type as effortgelelessly as you talk, visit us at Typingmaster.com detay option hat symbol seven question mark semi-colon. Typingmaster Pro Typing tutor for PC. Let the typing flop backspace flos backspace flow.

Here is a corrected version of the tapescript:

Typingmaster Pro asks the question, What if you talked like you typed? What if every time you opened your mouth words tumbled out like a bunch of broken crockery? How much time would you waste back spacing and spellchecking? Would anybody hire you? Probably not. And life would be incredibly frustrating, no doubt. Maybe you should think (five colon backspace comma) about Typingmaster Pro Typing Tutor for PC and learn how to touch type quickly and easily. Typingmaster Pro has personalized exercises to target the keys where you need more practice, constantly monitoring your progress and adjusting your training. Just like a good tutor should. So, if you would like to learn to type as effortlessly as you talk, visit us at Typingmaster.com today. Typingmaster Pro Typing Tutor for PC. Let the typing flow.

CD1 Track 29

## Unit 13 Advertising

### Listening: Radio commercials

3

Man: I get up, I take a bath, I get dressed, I eat breakfast.

I get up, I take a bath, I get dressed,

Woman: I give him breakfast.

Man: I get up, I take a bath,

Woman: I get him dressed, I give him breakfast.

Man: I get up,

Woman: I give him a bath, I get him dressed, I give him breakfast.

I get him up, I give him a bath, I get him dressed, I give him breakfast.

Narrator: Your life changes quickly. Muscular Dystrophy Association.

CD1 Track 30

## Unit 14 Banking

### Listening 1: Commercial banking

TONY RAMOS

I think there is a real kind of perception around kind of the world of investment banking and kind of what it offers. I think also as well I think commercial banking, and I guess I would say this as a previous commercial manager, I think is a kind of a best kept secret. I think if you actually and when you do talk to students, when I talk to students and I talk them to about what the commercial banking role is and I talk to them about the fact that you're kind of working in a local marketplace, you're working you know with, like, local entrepreneurs, kind of what the day-to-day job consists of, actually going to see people with their businesses, helping start up those businesses, seeing those businesses grow and the kind of excitement and the job satisfaction that provides to you, you actually do see their eyes kind of light up and open up, because they kind of think, oh, I actually I didn't think it was about that, I actually thought it was kind of sitting in front of a computer looking at spreadsheets, I think it was doing a lot of analysis, it seemed quite dull and stuffy to me ...

CD1 Track 31

## Unit 14 Banking

### Listening 2: Microfinance

ANNA-KIM HYUN-SEUNG

Microfinance schemes started with several NGOs and social enterprises, for example Grameen Bank in Bangladesh. They distribute very small loans to poor people, often without financial collateral. But they use some kind of different collateral, sometimes it can be social collateral, so they create a group of people and within the group people help each other to repay the loan, but it's usually a very small amount of money, and from the bank's point of view it actually provides a unique risk-management tool. Of course, distributing loans to poor people sounds very risky, but because we are talking about a large number of people, with a very small amount of money, it actually creates a very nice portfolio in which the risk can be diversified.

NGOs and social enterprises proved that these kinds of schemes can be scalable, and the poor people are actually repaying the loans, so now the conventional banks like Citibank and Barclays are taking part in these schemes, not for the purpose of doing good only, they are actually doing it as part of their business. They are developing their microfinancing and microcredit products in developing countries. It seems that microfinance is doing really well particularly in Bangladesh and part of India, and there are some positive cases in Latin America and Africa too.

CD1 Track 32

## Unit 15 Venture capital

### Listening 1: Background experience

CHRIS SMART

Acacia Capital Partners invests in ICT, Information and Communication Technologies, and that is very broadly based in what is called the technology field, but it doesn't include things like chemistry-based products or materials, or any of those biomedical products, it's purely technology as in IT.

... So most of the players in the funds have backgrounds in the industries in which they're investing and I mean, I, by hard experience, have, in ... run a multi-disciplinary fund, so I did a bit of bio, and a bit of ICT, and I learned very early on that I needed to get somebody into the fund who had the depth of experience in the bio, because I wasn't a bio-scientist. I didn't lose money, but I didn't make the decisions necessary to drive the growth that we wanted, and, you know, you need to have the depth of experience and knowledge in those fields to do it well.

CD1 Track 33

## Unit 15 Venture capital

### Listening 2: Investing for ten years

CHRIS SMART

OK, so the first thing to recognize is that venture capital is a business in its own right, and venture capitalists are professional in that ... and what professional means is they're not investing their own money, they're investing other people's money, so they equally have to raise that money from a market outside, and that in the most general terms is the insurance, it's the insurance industry, so pension funds and insurance companies provide institutional funding to venture capitalists. It is actually a very small percentage, so they will put one to three per cent of their asset base, and no more, into venture capital.

They raise those on a ten-year cycle, so they have to invest their, the money from a single fund that's been raised on a ten-year cycle, and realize it within the ten years. So on the whole you could say they've got five years to invest, and they've got five years to reap, but obviously what actually happens is some investments are made in the first couple of years and then might be realized within five years, but other investments, generally after five years there's very little investing happening and most of it is re-investing in the existing portfolio companies and helping them get to a point where they can be sold or listed on a stock market, so you can realize the money.

▶ CD1 Track 34

## Unit 15 Venture capital

### Listening 3: Managing new companies

CHRIS SMART

Yes, so one of the things about, certainly the sector we're in which is high-growth, early-stage tech companies, is on the whole the management teams are less experienced, I mean you try and bring in experienced people, but on the whole what you find is that emerging tech areas, the real knowledge is, you know, is vested in people who are still, are coming up, involved in new areas, but in management terms they're inexperienced. So the venture industry as a whole has one major benefit and that is it deals with a lot of these businesses and as a result knows what the challenges are for them, and establishes networks of people that are able to help these businesses. Now that does work well, and it works phenomenally well in the best cases. Equally, I think you'll find very disappointed management in lots of tech companies who say that venture capitalists held out, how much they can contribute and actually they receive very little, so in the end, the management have to deliver, and it is worthwhile if you're on the company side, looking for people that actually have the skills that you want and, you know, might have knowledge in sectors and real experience in comparable companies, and seek them out rather than just simply expect that they can necessarily deliver.

▶ CD1 Track 35

## Unit 15 Venture capital

### Listening 4: Successes and failures

CHRIS SMART

This is, this is the interesting characteristic, I guess, of venture capital in particular, as opposed to private equity, that companies investing in technology have to be failure-tolerant, you have to take some risks in order to get the higher rewards, and on the whole a venture capitalist will set out to achieve, well not to achieve but to expect, a third complete failure of his portfolio, a third will return his money back, and a bit more maybe, and the other third will produce good returns. And from that third that produces good returns, together with the money that you recover from the other third you have to produce a relatively good return on the overall fund, but that's the sort of failure percentage that a normal venture capitalist, an early-stage venture capitalist, will expect, is a third complete failure of their portfolio.

I think if one looks at the industry statistics, the good returns across the industry are driven by few, very spectacular returns, so, you know, obviously Sequoia with Google has made phenomenal returns, and the Ciscos of the world when they were, you know, succeeded, they made phenomenal returns, the Skypes of the world made phenomenal returns for the likes of Index, so, you know, you have few examples that have made spectacular returns and they actually drive the industry returns ...

▶ CD2 Track 2

## Unit 16 Bonds

### Listening: Bonds and subprime mortgages

TERESA LA THANGUE

Bonds are a very interesting way of raising money. A firm, a listed firm has two routes to raising capital. One is through debt and one's through equity. Equity is when they sell off shares in the market, and then you have debt where they'll go to a large, usually a large bank and say 'We'd like to raise X billion dollars,' and they will be sold a bond by that organization. Now most bonds are rated by the credit rating agencies. The governments do it as well and their bonds tend to be Triple A [AAA] rated, they are the 'gold standard' of bonds. And most firms that issue bonds in London they'll be Triple A [AAA] rated or Triple B [BBB] rated by the various credit rating agencies.

Now what happened in America with mortgage-backed securities, which as I said before were a very good bond, and they were considered to be a very safe investment because mortgages are long term and they tend to be solid. What happened in the States was a number of organizations had mortgages from subprime lenders who are considered to be more risky – they have bad credit history, or they have large mortgages against properties which they couldn't really afford, and what was happening in the US was that bonds were being packaged that were partly good debt, good safe secure debt, and partly this very bad debt. But the credit rating agencies didn't look too closely, it would appear, at what was happening, and had given all of these bonds Triple A [AAA] ratings.

What happens with a bond, it's then securitized, where the person, the firm that holds the bond then chops it up into small pieces and sells those small pieces on, so basically they're selling on the debt, and it's a huge market and it usually works extremely well. The problem with securitizing, of the mortgage-backed securities in the US, is that each little bit of security got a little bit of the good debt, but also a little bit of the bad debt, and these were sold off, and the bad debt is going bad, and nobody is quite sure if the bits of securities they've bought are going to go bad, or if they have gone bad, or if they've got lots of bad, and this is the problem at the moment, that nobody really trusts each other's balance sheet, so they're not, so the banks aren't lending to each other.

▸ CD2 Track 3

## Unit 17 Stocks and shares

### Listening: A financial news report

NEWSREADER

Here in New York, the Dow-Jones is down –58.86 points at 7,123.22, a drop of –0.82%, and the S&P 500 has drifted a little more to 742.55, that's down –0.37%. But the NASDAQ Composite is slightly firmer at 1,397.04, that's up 0.4%. Things weren't much better in Europe today, with the DAX in Frankfurt tumbling 2.61%, and the CAC-40 in Paris continuing its slide, finishing –1.83% lower. In London the Footsie 100 kissed goodbye to 2.5%.

It wasn't all doom and gloom in Asia though, with the Nikkei 225 in Tokyo climbing to 7,568.42, that's a gain of 1.48%. In Australia, the S&P/ASX 200 is virtually unchanged at 3,344.50.

Over on the currency markets, the dollar's lost 0.0048 cents against the euro this morning, and 0.0015 against the pound, now trading at a dollar 43, while it's steady against the yen, adding a tiny 0.00001 cents – I've never even seen one of those! – trading at $0.0102.

Over on commodities, gold is back where it started this morning, at $942, while oil's been yo-yoing, but right now it's on 43.60, that's a dollar 46 more than this time yesterday.

▸ CD2 Track 4

## Unit 18 Derivatives

### Listening: Hedge funds and structured products

TERESA LA THANGUE

Now hedge funds, it's a very, it's a term that covers a number of organ- ... ways of trading. They tend to be things that only firms, or very wealthy organizations, can invest in. In the UK, there is no retail access to hedge funds because we believe that at the moment, hedge funds don't do enough to ensure that retail investors would be aware of the risks, what they were getting involved with.

Hedge funds used to be, many, many years ago when they first became popular, just a way of hedging your bets, so if you had a derivative you would buy another product, a smaller product, to go against the risk involved with the derivative. But now they are seen as an investment tool in their own right, and they can invest in anything, and they do, they invest in, some of them are just straight equity investors, where they invest in the price of a share going up, some of them are short-sellers, some of them are very involved in spread-betting, some involved very much in the derivatives market, some will invest in bonds, so it's basically just a bit of a cover-all term now.

A structured product is pretty much similar to a hedge fund, though I understand that if you are making available to the retail community a structured product, it must have a very consistent risk profile across it, so you don't find that you're investing in a bond, a Triple A bond, but also a very risky derivative at the other end, so you must have a very consistent risk profile so that you, the ... the structured product that you buy, is consistent with your understanding of risk.

CD2 Track 5

## Unit 19 Accounting and financial statements

### Listening: Valuing assets

RICHARD BARKER

So, a company's balance sheet, in principle, is intended to give you the value of the company's business, but in practice, some assets are very easy to value, and some are very difficult to value. So if you hold some shares in another company or something, or you hold some money in a bank account, this is very easy to value. On the other hand, if your assets comprise research and development, or people for that matter, then it's in principle very difficult to put a value on those things. And when you measure the profit of a company, what you're trying to do is measure a change in value, so the difference between what a company is worth at the beginning of a year, and what it is worth at the end of a year, is the profit that it makes, or the loss that it makes. And if it's difficult to measure the value of assets in the first place, it's also difficult to measure whether a company's making profit or not.

So an example might be ... take an airport, and a runway on an airport. Well, what's a runway worth? would be one question. You could estimate that maybe, you could estimate how long you think the airport will operate for, how many planes will land on it, what the value of one airport will be, what the value of Heathrow would be in comparison with the value of Gatwick, for example. But it's actually quite a subjective thing to measure. And then you've got to figure out, well, how long is this thing going to last, because every year you want to take the depreciation on that runway and charge it against profit – you want to take a reduction in the value of the runway, and if you think the runway will last 25 years, then you will depreciate it four times as quickly as if you think it will last 100 years. So there's lots of estimation and judgement in accounting because the value of an asset depends upon the future uncertain events, and those uncertain events, by their very nature, can't be estimated very easily.

CD2 Track 6

## Unit 20 Market structure and competition

### Listening 1: Early stage companies

CHARLES COTTON

It's interesting to look at almost any industry from the perspective of an early stage company, and early stage companies get into an industry because they look at its structure and say, 'We can bring something to this industry which can potentially be highly disruptive and therefore change the landscape and give us as a company an opportunity to become fabulously successful,' and clearly there are examples of companies who've done that: Cisco going back 20 years had that sort of perspective, more recently companies like eBay invented a whole new approach, a whole new paradigm, and most recently of all you've got Google, that, you know, has evolved from a search company to compete with, you know, the biggest software companies on the planet, including the Microsofts who are now, you know, very concerned about that. So looking at all of these industries, some of them are defined by the new entrants, and I think eBay and Google are good examples of that, to an extent Cisco as well.

CD2 Track 7

## Unit 20 Market structure and competition

### Listening 2: Sine waves and bell curves

CHARLES COTTON

And even now, Google is losing people, because Google has got itself into the situation where it's no longer that brash, young, successful, sexy start-up, and it's people like Facebook and so on who are now attracting the youngest and brightest away from the Googles of this world, and attracted to something yet again new, which again is disrupting the way in which, particularly young people communicate and converse with each other.

I think that we go through sort of sine waves or bell curves in industry where, you know, a disrupter moves in to being a dominant player, potentially with other strong players, but over time their position is, becomes more vulnerable, and they are, they find themselves being competed against by younger, newer, fresher, more exciting new ideas.

So, entrepreneurs, new ideas, disrupt, address, tackle, compete with existing, well-established industries and structures, but it's an evolution.

▶ CD2 Track 8

## Unit 20 Market structure and competition

### Listening 3: Clustering

CHARLES COTTON

Clustering is perhaps the, one of the most exciting areas for governments as well as for companies to address. And everybody looks at the well-established examples. In America, it used to be around one, Route 128, around Boston area which really lost its crown to Silicon Valley, out in northern California. And today there are many examples of clusters. Each of these clusters has a number of factors associated with them, no one of which is sufficient on its own to define a cluster, but these factors in total, perhaps eight out of ten of them, you know, are to be found in every cluster. If you look at the traditional ones like Route 128, like Silicon Valley, and in Europe places like Tel Aviv, like Cambridge, like Oxford, like London, they've all evolved around a university campus, and what you've got there then are very bright people pushing the boundaries of science and technology, and seeing then the opportunities for the development of companies, and for those companies then to be successful.

What happens as a result of that is that people move from a university environment into a, into a business environment and need to learn new skills, and so what you have around those people that make that step are people, older people who've been in industry before, or people who are focusing on supporting products and services and so on, and you get this sort of virtuous circle taking place where you have a nucleus which is the individual or individuals who break away from university, then massing up as they talk to each other to gain experience, talk to other people to gain experience, and build around them this, this cluster.

So some of the other factors that make clusters successful are all of the supporting services like the lawyers, the accountants, the patent attorneys, the headhunters, the recruiters, the people who provide catering services for the companies that come along, the landlords and so on, so you get this vast circle of activity around, around a cluster, which then builds into something more than what starts as a technology cluster into a, into an economic cluster itself ...

▶ CD2 Track 9

## Unit 20 Market structure and competition

### Listening 4: Software-based clusters

CHARLES COTTON

... so it becomes a question of saying, well, what is it about your culture, the background, the technologies, the history of your industries that can provide the essence of what your cluster can be grouped around? You may not have a world-class university which these other ones have, but you may have some fabulous software programmers, and certainly if you look at places in eastern Europe and Russia, because they couldn't afford the latest computers and so on back in the 90s, and two, and sort of, you know, the 1980s and 1990s, their software programmers were outstanding, they were the most creative people on the planet, and they've continued to evolve in that way and today it's certainly the case that software developers in Bulgaria, in Hungary, in Czechoslovakia, in parts of Ukraine and so on, are in great demand for two reasons. First of all, they have this ability to do a great deal with very small levels of resource, and secondly they don't charge as much as programmers in the western world or even India these days, because India started as sort of a crèche, almost, of software developers, but has now become a much more expensive place to have that software done, so there are always opportunities creating, and around, being created, and around those opportunities can coalesce many of the other factors that can lead to a cluster formation, and so today I'm most particularly aware of the software-based clusters for development purposes in eastern Europe and the former parts of the Soviet Union.

▶ CD2 Track 10

## Unit 20 Market structure and competition

### Listening 5: Clusters of the future

CHARLES COTTON

But as we look forward I think we're going to see, you know, new powerhouses economically evolve, which will inevitably mean that there will be new clusters created. The ones that most people tend to talk around are round China and India, but I also propose that we'll see similar things happening in places like Brazil, and Brazil is a resource-rich country with, you know, an increasingly well-educated population, and I think education is at the core of any of these clusters, which is why China and India are going to become so successful, because particularly in their cases, a lot of their young people have gone off to be educated in, principally in the US but also in Europe, and then have gone back because they've seen the business opportunities in their own country. In a way we're going to see similar sorts of things happening with, with places like Brazil which has got a very large population, which is resource-rich as I mentioned, and where a lot of the population has experience of being in university in North America, and again seeing opportunities in their homeland to create something special, and along the way, you know, being a capitalist-dominated world, you know, seeing the opportunity for personal gain for, you know, the exercise of their knowledge and their skills.

▶ CD2 Track 11

## Unit 21 Takeovers

### Listening 1: The role of the Competition Commission

RORY TAYLOR

We're a competition investigation authority; it's what the Americans might call an antitrust authority. Our role is, when cases are referred to us, to look at mergers that might have the effect of damaging competition in a particular market, or indeed in certain cases we can look at the markets in general, and again see whether competition is working effectively, and benefiting the consumer.

We do have a free market attitude in this country, but markets left unchecked can develop features that are damaging to competition and, by definition, towards consumers. If you can imagine a situation, hypothetically, in which one company just became more and more successful there would be the danger that they could just buy over every single other company in that market, and ultimately that wouldn't be good for anyone in the economy, including the company itself.

We always say round here that good, efficient companies have nothing to fear from the competition authorities, and we've had plenty of companies come through here and tell us that competition is essential to keeping their business efficient and innovative, so it's, it's an essential part of the system, and I think if you look at any developed economy there's, there's always a competition regime there. How it works differs from country to country, but I think there's a general acceptance that it's a necessary, a necessary check and balance as long as it's not over-interventionist.

▶ CD2 Track 12

## Unit 21 Takeovers

### Listening 2: Market investigations

RORY TAYLOR

You won't generally come across too many markets where there's one dominant player outside the, sort of, natural monopolies and the utilities. We used to do, under the previous legislation, what were called monopoly investigations, but now they're known as market investigations, as to some extent that reflects that you're not usually looking at one player dominating one particular market but maybe a small handful. That's not necessarily a bad thing, it all depends on the structure of that market and to what degree they're competing with each other. We've just been looking at the groceries market, that's ... I would say using,

using the term advisedly, dominated by big four supermarkets, certainly got the lion's share of the ... people's shopping, but at the same time they're competing very vigorously with each other, so that's not necessarily anything we'd, we'd look to intervene in.

▶ CD2 Track 13

## Unit 21 Takeovers

### Listening 3: Breaking the law and abusing a dominant position

RORY TAYLOR

We look at the structure of markets and whether markets are working competitively. Now even if they're not working competitively that can be a range of factors, that doesn't mean the company is doing anything wrong, it just means they're acting logically, to whatever business and competitive pressures there are. On the other side of the coin, there are offences, breaches of competition law. Those actually get looked at by the Office of Fair Trading, and that's where companies have actively, are actively, in simple terms, doing something wrong. There's two offences. One is abuse of a dominant position. The, probably the highest-profile example of that in recent times is the Microsoft case, with the European Competition Commission, and the other one is cartels, or price fixing as it's also known, which is something that our sister body the Office of Fair Trading are being, are taking a great interest at the moment, and yeah, that is something that's looked [at] extremely seriously by the authorities and you can be fined as much as 10% of your annual turnover, so you can be facing big fines if you are, if you are found guilty of that thing.

▶ CD2 Track 14

## Unit 22 Government and taxation

### Listening: Government intervention

MICHAEL KITSON

... The second effect is whether we think unfettered free markets alone can ensure the long-term optimal allocation of resources and long-term economic growth. Markets are very important, I'm not denying that, but so is the role of government to actually help markets work better. Often economists talk about notions of market failure or the fact that markets are not working properly.

Let's just think of some of the areas where governments should want to intervene. They may want to spend, spend money on education, it's very important, educated workforce. People may not invest enough in their education if they have to pay for it themselves, and many people wouldn't be able to access the resources, wouldn't be able to get the credit, OK, so it's the importance of education. Similar things apply to health, we may not actually buy enough health if we are left to buy it ourselves.

Let's think about developing new products and technologies. Developing new products and technologies is highly risky and highly expensive, and highly uncertain outcomes, but possibly very big outcomes for the economy as a whole. So it makes ... it's understandable that firms do not invest in very early-stage technologies, OK, and ... because it may be very expensive for them, there's a good chance they won't succeed, and if they do succeed, somebody else will be able to copy and replicate and benefit from their effects.

These are positive externality effects of government intervention. If government helps to commercialize science, develop new ideas, those products can then at a later stage be developed and employed by the market, and by businesses.

I think there are many areas. This is about government in terms of economic growth. I think it's mainly in terms of the areas of education, particularly, again in the areas of transport and networks and infrastructure, and increasingly in helping develop science, and helping commercialize science, and bringing those ideas, which you know, ideas ultimately drive long-term economic growth, and encouraging those ideas from a science base to become new products, new services, better ways of doing things, will make economic growth happen in the future.

▶ CD2 Track 15

## Unit 23 The business cycle

### Listening 1: Consumption and the business cycle

MICHAEL KITSON

... Perhaps a year ago that question would have been considered redundant by many economists. The business cycle has ended, we now have nice economic growth, you know, consistent economic growth and the business cycle has ended, and inflation's ended. Actually the reality is that inflation is still on the horizon, and the potential of a downturn in the economy. I tend to think about the major components of aggregate demand, and how that drives economic growth. Booms [are] particularly driven by consumption, and consumption is particularly driven when people have positive expectations, their assets are increasing, particularly housing, encourages people to spend, OK. Depressions are actually that process goes into reverse, particularly when credit becomes no longer available, assets tend to decline in value, people tend to start saving more and consume less. I think consumption, particularly for the advanced countries, is the major driver of the business cycle, and the major driver of consumption is the availability of credit and the value of assets, of which houses are the most crucial one. So I tend to think it's very ... people spending or not spending.

▶ CD2 Track 16

## Unit 23 The business cycle

### Listening 2: Keynesianism

MICHAEL KITSON

... we still have the business cycle, OK, we can still have the possible problems of a downturn, which makes the argument for what I think is standard Keynesianism, the way you manipulate budget balances or budget deficits depending on whether the economy's booming or is in recession. OK, and the government's golden rule in the UK is consistent with that, in general. If the economy's turning down it may make sense for governments to have budget deficits, and to keep expenditure in the economy. That's the Keynesianism argument about ironing out the business cycle, which I think is important because recessions can have very long-term harmful effects.

▶ CD2 Track 17

## Unit 24 Corporate social responsibility

### Listening 1: Socially responsible investment

ANNA-KIM HYUN-SEUNG

I see socially responsible investment as a very effective response to Milton Friedman's famous argument, because when Milton Friedman says 'The business of business is business,' it assumes that most shareholders want to maximize their profit, maximize their return on investment, and that is the goal of the shareholders. But what we can observe now is the rise of socially responsible investment, so it shows that at least some investors do care about social and environmental standards as well as their right to a return on investment. So if that's the case, if shareholders actually do care about these criteria, then Milton Friedman's argument is ... is facing the serious problem of his assumptions, because it assumes that shareholders only care about the profit, and therefore corporations have to maximize the profit for their shareholders. But what if shareholders want something different for their corporations? It is true that socially responsible investment is still a fraction of the total investment at the moment, but is very very rapidly increasing, and it will be very interesting to see how the trend develops.

▶ CD2 Track 18

## Unit 24 Corporate social responsibility

### Listening 2: Different stakeholder groups

ANNA-KIM HYUN-SEUNG

I think it is very important to respond to different stakeholder groups, because obviously companies tend to be more responsive to the shareholders rather than other stakeholders, but I think when a company really considers different stakeholder groups seriously, including their community, including their own employees, then they are likely to have more genuine corporate social responsibility policies and practices.

For example, there are companies which are probably doing very good things for the community, for the external society, so that they can really improve their reputation with their external stakeholders, but for example, if they are not very nice to their own employees, if there is something going wrong within their supply chain management, with regard to human rights, low-cost child labour, working hours, then probably they don't really have a good response from their own employees, who are their own internal stakeholders, so I think it is very important to listen to all different stakeholders, internal and external, to develop a holistic approach to corporate social responsibility.

▶ CD2 Track 19

## Unit 25 Efficiency and employment

### Listening 1: Efficiency and the number of employees

ANNA-KIM HYUN-SEUNG

Increasing business efficiency doesn't necessarily conflict with the interests of employees, although that is often the case. In most cases companies probably just want to lower the number of employees when they increase their efficiency. But I know of a few companies which managed to increase their efficiency but they actually, instead of going for lay-offs, instead of reducing the number of employees, they actually decided to reduce the average number of working hours per employee, so that the employees can invest their time in training, development, education, arguably even leading to a better quality of life, and work and life balance, especially at the factory level, at the shop-floor level. So, there are cases that actually achieve both increasing efficiency and maintaining the benefits for employees. But of course that's probably only a few examples.

▶ CD2 Track 20

## Unit 25 Efficiency and employment

### Listening 2: Efficiency, training and productivity

ANNA-KIM HYUN-SEUNG

I have one example which is a Korean company. It's called Yuhan-Kimberly and it's a form of joint venture between Yuhan, a local company, and Kimberly Clark in the United States. So Yuhan-Kimberly is itself a local player, they are the market leader in their industry, they make toilet paper, tissues, and sanitary items. Within South Korea they are probably one of the most respected companies because of their very consistent corporate social responsibility policies and practice. For example, in 1984, they launched the very first nationwide environmental campaigning, which was about developing forests. The company really tried to commit themselves in social and responsible causes.

I don't exactly remember the year, but at some point the company had problems and they had the situation that they needed to cut down the total number of working hours, and what they chose was instead of cutting down the number of employees they cut down the number of average working hours, so they actually changed their shift system. Before the change it was three teams, three shifts, but they changed it into four teams, two shifts, and I think each worker worked consecutively four days, 48 hours, 12 hours each day, and they took off four days, and one of the four days was committed to a training programme operated by the company. It was part of their lifelong learning programme as well, so I think the employees responded in very good ways because for them it was obviously a much better choice than losing their job, and it was also a training opportunity. Also after this change there was a big increase in productivity because obviously the workers could have the proper rest for three or four days.

▶ CD2 Track 21

## Unit 26 Exchange rates

### Listening 1: Currency flows and the Tobin Tax

MICHAEL KITSON

... it's very difficult of course to intervene, to regulate exchange rates, because now they're changing very very quickly. Money is flowing instantaneously backwards and forwards, it's what many people call 'hot money'. Money flowing in another country quickly, and in and out of a country quickly, and it has been, arguably, helped to deepen financial crises, such as the south-east Asian crisis in the end of the 1990s, when money flew out of these economies, and money can flow very quickly and destabilize, and we should add that then leads to real effects, real effects I mean people lose jobs, unemployment goes up, and output falls. So we've got this problem of these, of money flowing in and out of countries. Can we regulate it? Well, it's very difficult, but there are arguments that perhaps we can, or certainly arguments to consider.

Now one, for instance, is something called the Tobin Tax. Now the Tobin Tax is an argument you tax, at a very small rate, 0.01, or 0.1, very small tax on currency purchase and currency selling. OK. Now, what that would do is should dampen down currency speculation, because remember what people are doing in terms of currency flows is they're ... they're buying and selling currencies with very small differences, OK, you spend, you buy and sell currencies, a big volume of currency, on a small difference to make you money. Sometimes it's called 'highly leveraged' – you borrow a lot of money – to buy a currency or sell a currency. If you make a small tax, you may discourage people from buying and selling so rapidly, and just dampen down those currency fluctuations.

I may add, a Tobin Tax will not prevent a major crisis, but may dampen down the currency speculation over time. Now the Tobin Tax, which was suggested by a Nobel Prize winner, James Tobin, who I think thought it was a theoretical issue and perhaps wasn't ... wouldn't be practical. Many have argued it just wouldn't be possible to implement this Tobin Tax, but what's interesting as the world economy's developed, as exchange rates have suffered from crises, increasingly people are thinking it's back on the agenda. OK, we need to reconsider, perhaps the Tobin Tax would be possible in certain circumstances, and perhaps with ICT – information technology – we could coordinate it at a global level.

One country cannot introduce a Tobin Tax because then other, all the trading would take place elsewhere. It has to take place globally ... but now we say that actually we can have a global system of regulation, the ICT may actually now facilitate it, and we can actually implement this sort of policy.

▶ CD2 Track 22

## Unit 26 Exchange rates

### Listening 2: Developing Africa

MICHAEL KITSON

And the other argument of course is, it's a very small tax but it will raise a significant amount of revenue.

What would you do with that? Again, another issue. One of the arguments, you could use that revenue to go to the parts of the world where the world economy does not invest. OK, it doesn't make sense for individual investors in most cases to put lots of money into, say, Africa, to build up infrastructure, roads and education, which will help to develop that region of the world. But you could use the resources generated from a Tobin Tax, which would generate significant, significant social benefits for Africa, and significant economic benefits for the region and the world economy as a whole. It would be a world tax and a world expenditure, and you'd spend it where the world economy and the depressed regions would benefit most. I mean, I don't think you can criticize individual firms for not investing in Africa, because they won't get what they call a private rate of return, they will not make profit from it, but there's a significant social rate of return – better education, better economic growth, better standards of living, people living longer. OK, we need to think about how we're going to get those resources into Africa, I think it's one of the great challenges.

▶ CD2 Track 23

## Unit 27 International trade

### Listening 1: Free trade

MICHAEL KITSON

I think I would argue that many economists favour free trade, and some governments see the problems with free trade, under certain circumstances. We all know that economics is based on simplified models. And sometimes those simplified models are not useful in explaining the way the real world works, or sometimes there are exceptions to those models.

Let's take into account the standard argument for free trade – OK, that everybody gets better off, more efficiency, we can consume more goods and services. Well, that may be the case, but there may be some people who lose out. Take the very simple argument, we often have two economies with two goods, OK, we simplify and then we extend. So say we've got two economies with two goods. We've got a developed country producing computers and cloth, and we have an underdeveloped country that's trying to produce computers and cloth. OK, and then we say, well actually with free trade you should specialize in what you're best at, or least worst at. OK, so under that situation we say, right, to the developed country, you produce computers, and sell some computers to the developing country, and the developing country, you focus on cloth, and buy the computers from the developed country, and so on. That's our standard model, OK. And we can see that there's efficiency gains, ultimately we should be able to get, consume more computers and cloth through that process.

But let's think what happens there. I'm working in a cloth factory in a developed country. We move from going from no trade to free trade. My country specializes just in computers. What's going to happen, I'm going to lose my job. OK. Now that may be a big concern, governments may be concerned about workers losing jobs in certain sectors. Now we could argue in theory I just need to reallocate my job and become working in computing. It may be very difficult for me to do that. I may be in the wrong part of the country, I may not have the right skills and so on.

Basically what happens with free trade is that many many people gain and a few people may lose and they may lose big time, and if we're concerned about those people we may want to have some transition process, we may be concerned about unfettered free trade.

▶ CD2 Track 24

## Unit 27 International trade

### Listening 2: Exceptions to free trade

MICHAEL KITSON

OK, so that's case number one. OK, that some people may lose out and we may be concerned about protecting them. Let's go back to our free trade example. Now we've got our one country specializing in computers and another country specializing in cloth. Now that cloth-producing country may say OK, that's our comparative advantage, cloth, but we don't want to remain cloth producers for the rest of our ... in the future, we want our country to develop and grow. We want to produce a wider range of goods and services, or goods and services that are higher value added. And it would generate higher wages and economic growth. We want to move out of cloth into something else. We want to move out of cloth into automobiles and perhaps into computing in the longer term. How are we going to do that with our comparative advantage just being cloth? We may need to protect certain sectors of our economy to let them grow.

There's a very good argument in economics called the infant industry argument. OK, we establish these industries, and they're new and young, they cannot compete with the bigger more established industries in the advanced countries. We need to leave them time to develop and grow, and then they can compete with other countries. So we need to protect those sectors, so they can grow and we can have a new comparative advantage in the future. So I think under those circumstances we can have arguments where you may want to not have unfettered free trade.

Now let's think about advanced countries. Advanced countries, arguably, mainly focus on free trade and the advantages of free trade, but even here we can have arguments about why you want to, why you want to support or protect certain sectors. This is sometimes called strategic trade theory. OK, we can identify strategic sectors of the economy. Those sectors may benefit other parts of the economy. It's what economists call externalities. Externalities basically means, a positive externality, something in one part of the economy may have positive benefits elsewhere. OK, or those sectors may generate economies of scale, so as you protect them they become bigger and more competitive. Say, for instance, we say aerospace, it's crucial to have an aerospace industry. Why? Because the knowledge generated in aerospace will ... will go elsewhere, be porous. The ideas generated in aerospace will go into automotive, will go into electrical engineering, go into other sectors, so if we have a strong aerospace sector, it will benefit the rest of the economy. That may be an argument for protecting that sector, under certain circumstances.

▶ CD2 Track 25

## 28 Economics and ecology

## Listening 1: A big step forward

MARTIN BENISTON

Well, as a climate scientist I feel we are moving forward in the right direction, albeit too slowly in terms of some of the urgent issues that need to be addressed in terms of climate change. But certainly, compared to 10 or 15 years ago, climate change is now on the agenda of policy, it's on the agenda of large companies, who are thinking ahead in terms of remaining competitive while at the same time addressing energy and climate issues, so I think there has been a big step forward. On the other hand, one still sees many declarations, like the G8 Declaration, which looked very promising, but whether anybody is actually going to put that into effect within the proposed timeframe is another matter. And it's not just a matter of political will, it's also ... is the technology there to help us along, and so on and so forth. What's going to happen with the emerging economic giants like China and India, who are sort of not too keen on going ahead with this, and China's almost on a par with the United States now in terms of its global carbon emissions, so it's a huge actor in the game, and if China doesn't come in, and India doesn't come in, then we're going to be in trouble.

▶ CD2 Track 26

## 28 Economics and ecology

## Listening 2: Emerging technologies

MARTIN BENISTON

Well, I think if we look at all the emerging technologies related to sort of green energy and other environmentally friendly technologies, it's certainly more of an opportunity than a hindrance. I think much of the reticence of politicians up till now, and the general public to some extent, related to the climate change issue was that one had the impression that, you know, to try and become carbon neutral, or to try and revert ... reverse the, you know, global warming, would mean going back to the Stone Age or to the Middle Ages or something, you know, this is not really the case, I mean it's not at all the case. And certainly there are huge opportunities out there for, you know, transform the economy, and transformations of technology, and so on, so I would say ... in fact if you look at some of the more progressive countries towards environmentally-friendly technologies you do see that GDP has actually grown in places like Denmark, while at the same time carbon emissions have not progressed at all and have even dwindled to some extent, the same for Sweden even if the Swedish case is less spectacular, so it does show that you can decouple carbon emissions from economic growth, so why not take that route?

▶ CD2 Track 27

## 28 Economics and ecology

## Listening 3: Can we ignore the problem for now?

MARTIN BENISTON

I think in some instances the comment can be legitimate, in the sense that one cannot take all actions immediately to counteract climate change, and it's more sort of iterative process, you know, you see climate change kicking in in various regions of the world, then you can start adjusting whatever sector is, needs to be adjusted. On the other hand, you do also have at the same time reasons to act now because of the inertia of the climate system. So the thing is, even if you are rich and you can possibly adjust to that in the future, to some of the negative impacts of climate change in the future, we still need to start acting now to reduce greenhouse gas emissions, because, you know, the more we accumulate GHGs in the atmosphere, the stronger will be warming, and the more negative will be the impact. And many of the impacts are going to affect countries that are still extremely poor, so the sort of countries of the south, basically, which even if they might be richer in tomorrow's world than they are today, will still be poor countries in the next 50 to 100 years, and may not have the economic strength to counteract some of the very negative impacts of climate change like sea level rise or desertification, changes in water resources, and so on.

# Appendix 1: How to give a good presentation

## A checklist

**A good presentation**:
- is well-planned, with a clear, logical structure
- has clear and explicit links between the parts
- has information that is relevant to the audience
- has a memorable introduction and finish.

**In preparation the speaker:**
- **plans** the presentation thoroughly. What is the purpose of the presentation – to inform, to persuade, to review? What information needs to be communicated? How will this information be structured?
- thinks about the **audience**. Who are they: colleagues, business partners, customers? How formal or informal does the presentation have to be? How much does the audience know about the subject? How long will they be able to concentrate? What is their first language?
- thinks about how **visual aids** can help the audience understand what is being said.

**During the presentation the speaker:**
- speaks loudly enough to be heard by everybody
- doesn't speak too fast or too slowly
- does *not* read a prepared text, but improvises from notes or visual aids
- pauses for emphasis when necessary
- looks relaxed, positive and confident
- seems competent, organized and enthusiastic
- makes eye contact with the audience
- uses appropriate body language and gestures to convey meaning.

The **introduction** to a presentation should contain:
- a welcome to the audience — Good morning/afternoon, ladies and gentlemen.
- (perhaps) a thank you to the audience — Thank you all for coming today.
- your name and position (if necessary) — My name is ... and I'm the ...
- the subject or title of your presentation
  The subject of my talk is ...
  This morning I'm going to talk about ...
  The theme of my presentation today is ...
- a statement of the purpose of your presentation
  ... because this is something we will all have to think about in the future.
  ... because you will be responsible for carrying out these new procedures.
- (perhaps) a statement of the length of time you will take
  I'm going to talk for about 15 minutes.
  My presentation will take about 20 minutes.

- an outline of the structure of your presentation (a list of the main points to be covered)
  My presentation will be in four parts.
  I've divided my talk into three parts.
  First ... Second ... Third ...
  In the first part ...
  Then ... After that ... Next ...
  Finally ...
- (perhaps) a statement of when the audience may ask questions
  If there's anything you don't understand, please don't hesitate to interrupt.
  Please feel free to ask questions at any time.
  I'd appreciate it if you would save any questions until the end.

The **main part** of a presentation is the most difficult. Beginnings and ends of talks often contain similar phrases, but in the main part you give your audience the information they have come to hear. If you have said in your introduction that you are going to divide your presentation into several parts, you should clearly signal the beginning and end of each of these parts as they occur.

That completes the first part, so now we come to ...
So, to move on to the second part of my talk ...
That concludes the second part, so let's move on to ...
That's all I want to say about ... so unless you have any questions let's turn to ...

The **ending** should:

- include a clear signal that you have finished or are about to finish the last point
  That ends the third part of my talk, so ...
  That's all I'm going to say about ...
- briefly summarize the main information*
  So, to sum up ...
  I'll end by emphasizing the main points.
  So now I'll just summarize my three main points again.
- perhaps draw some logical conclusions from what has been said
  So what we need to do now is ...
  This shows that we have to ...
  So, to conclude, I have two recommendations.
- perhaps include a thanks for listening
  Thank you for your attention ...
  Thanks for listening ...
- include an invitation to ask questions.
  ... and now I'd like to invite your comments.
  Now I'd be interested to hear your comments.
  Right, does anyone have any questions or comments?
  Now we have 20 minutes for discussion.

* This means that speakers often make their most important points three times: in the introduction, they tell the audience what they are going to tell them; in the main part of the talk, they say it; and in the summary and conclusion, they tell the audience what they have just told them. This should make certain that everyone hears the key points at least once! They won't necessarily all hear them three times, because they won't all be concentrating all the time.

**Answering questions** can be difficult because you can't prepare for it. (You might even think: 'I explained everything perfectly, so why are they asking questions?') But you should:

- welcome questions and listen carefully (and look at the questioner)
- not interrupt the speaker
- clarify the exact meaning of the question if you are not sure
  Sorry, I didn't catch that.
  Could you repeat that, please?
  Sorry, I'm not sure if I've understood exactly ...
  If I've understood you correctly, you want to know ... Is that right?
- take time to think – briefly – before you answer, if necessary
- be as brief and direct as possible
- be polite
- check that your questioner is satisfied with your answer
  Is that OK?
  Does that answer your question?

Sometimes, it is impossible to answer a question, because:

- it is not relevant to your presentation
  I'm afraid that doesn't really relate to my talk. Perhaps you could discuss that with ---.
- for some reason you don't want to give this information
  I'm afraid I'm not in a position to comment on that.
  I'm not really the right person to ask about that. Perhaps --- could help?
- you simply don't know the answer
  I'm afraid I don't have that information with me, but I will try and find out, and get back to you.
  That's a difficult question to answer in a few words. Could we talk about that later?

- At the end, thank your audience (again).

## Listening, seeing and doing

In a presentation, it's important to think about your audience and how they are going to understand your message. Different people have different learning styles, which affect how they take in information.

Some people learn by listening, and remember things they have heard. These people are clearly at an advantage at presentations.

Some people learn by doing, remember things they have done, and don't like sitting still for a long time. Such people are obviously at a disadvantage when they have to sit still during a presentation.

Some people learn by watching, remember things they have seen, find graphs, charts and diagrams very useful, and need to write things down to remember them.

Speakers can help people who learn best by watching – and probably everyone else too – by using **visual aids** as well as talking, so that the audience are using at least two senses.

## Visual aids

PowerPoint slides (or whatever you use) should be:

- large and clear, not too detailed, and visible to the whole of your audience
- displayed for long enough for the audience to read them (you should not use more than one a minute)
- possibly laid out in bullet points like this, rather than long sentences or paragraphs.

You can refer to visual aids with expressions like:

As you can see from this slide ...
I'd like you to have/take a (closer) look at this ...
I'd like to draw your attention to ...

## Equipment

You should check the equipment before starting. For example:

- Does the data projector work?
- Can you connect your laptop to the projector?
- Can everyone see you and the screen, or do you need to move the chairs?
- Is there any light reflecting on the screen? Do you need to close the blinds or dim the lights?

## Presenting across cultures

A good presenter who has to talk to an international audience will research the style of presentation that is appropriate to that particular audience. Some audiences, for example, may want to participate actively during the presentation while others will want to sit quietly and listen without interruption to what is being said. As part of the planning and preparation process, it is essential to find out what is appropriate.

# **Appendix 2:** Writing emails, letters and reports

## Writing professional emails

Various writing activities in this book involve in-company emails. While emails to colleagues can be quite informal, emails to senior managers are generally more formal. The first contact between a company and a business partner, client or customer is also generally written in a very polite, formal style, whether it is a letter or an email. Subsequent correspondence between people who know and like each other often becomes less formal (at least in most English-speaking countries).

Things you **should** do when writing professional emails:

- Clearly summarize the contents of your messages in the subject line (so recipients can find them again later in their inbox). For example, write 'Recommendation of candidate for Chief Operating Officer' rather than just 'Recommendation'.
- If you normally address a person as Ms/Mrs/Mr ---, do the same in a first email; if you normally call them by their first name, then do that. In most English-speaking countries people often switch to first names after a couple of emails.
- Try to keep messages short so that readers (especially those using cellphones and mobile devices) don't have to scroll.
- Reply to messages, keeping the 'thread' by leaving the original messages (unless the thread is extremely long), rather than starting new emails.
- When writing informal emails to friends and colleagues, many people use **short forms** of common words, such as yr (your), pls (please), thx or thnx (thanks), rgds (regards), and **acronyms** (the first letters of words), such as FYI (for your information), asap (as soon as possible), BTW (by the way), TIA (thanks in advance), BR (best regards) and BW (best wishes). These are probably best avoided in professional emails (and certainly when writing to non-native users of English who may not recognize them).
- Send copies (Cc) to people who also need the information. When writing to large groups of people who don't necessarily need to know each other's names or email addresses (e.g. a whole list of customers) you can use blind copies (Bcc). But sending blind copies so that a person doesn't know that other colleagues have also received the email is generally best avoided.
- Use the spell check and reread your message one last time before you send emails to business partners, customers or important colleagues.

Things you **shouldn't** do when writing emails:

- Write in capital letters, as they are more difficult to read.
- Write anything you wouldn't say to a person's face or say in public or write on the back of a postcard. Remember that there is no such thing as a private email: the system administrator can probably read all emails, and people can easily forward your emails (sometimes accidentally).

# Writing letters

Most organizations have models or templates of standard letters for all common situations: texts giving standard information, with spaces or blanks to be filled in depending on the details. This saves time, allows the organization to control the quality of what goes out to customers and business partners, and helps ensure that they comply with laws and regulations.

When you need to write a letter without a template you should:

- Establish a clear purpose: *why* are you writing? (to inform, persuade, request, etc.)
- Know your audience: *who* are you writing for? The audience will determine the style and language you use.
- Plan a logical sequence, and organize your ideas into paragraphs.
- Be brief and precise (or if you prefer an acronym: KISS – Keep It Short and Simple).
- Use plain language: avoid jargon, complex words and abbreviations your reader might not understand.
- Use a formal (or at least neutral) business tone.
- Always be courteous and polite.
- When you've finished writing, check everything: the content, the format, the language (grammar, punctuation and spelling) and the style. For very important letters, you might want to get someone else with perfect English to check for you.

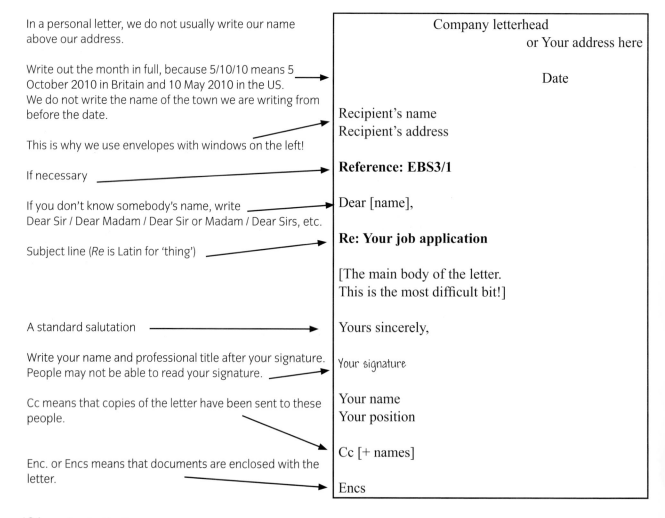

| | |
|---|---|
| In a personal letter, we do not usually write our name above our address. | Company letterhead<br>or Your address here |
| Write out the month in full, because 5/10/10 means 5 October 2010 in Britain and 10 May 2010 in the US.<br>We do not write the name of the town we are writing from before the date. | Date |
| This is why we use envelopes with windows on the left! | Recipient's name<br>Recipient's address |
| If necessary | **Reference: EBS3/1** |
| If you don't know somebody's name, write Dear Sir / Dear Madam / Dear Sir or Madam / Dear Sirs, etc. | Dear [name], |
| Subject line (*Re* is Latin for 'thing') | **Re: Your job application** |
| | [The main body of the letter.<br>This is the most difficult bit!] |
| A standard salutation | Yours sincerely, |
| Write your name and professional title after your signature. People may not be able to read your signature. | Your signature |
| | Your name<br>Your position |
| Cc means that copies of the letter have been sent to these people. | Cc [+ names] |
| Enc. or Encs means that documents are enclosed with the letter. | Encs |

# Writing reports

The **standard structure** of a report is as follows:

1 The **introduction**, which states the report's aims or objectives, or its terms of reference: why it was written and who it was written for
2 The **main part** of the report, which gives and discusses the facts and findings, and perhaps considers alternative courses of action
3 **Conclusions**, based on the facts and alternatives
4 **Recommendations**, the action the writer thinks should be taken based on the facts, discussion and conclusions.

Genuine reports are of course usually much longer than the short (100–150 word) reports practised in this book. Longer reports might also have:

- a **title page**, giving the subject, the writer's name, the date and (if necessary) a reference number
- a **contents list** (after the title page), including headings and sub-headings with page numbers
- a **summary** (before the introduction), giving the main points, such as important conclusions
- an **appendix** or **appendices** (at the end), with tables, figures, etc.

Here are some example sentences and paragraphs.

**An introductory sentence** (See Unit 9)

This report was written by ---, Retail and Logistics Director, at the request of the Chief Executive Officer, to attempt to identify the potential supply chain risks for our fruit and vegetable department.

**Conclusions** (See Unit 11)

Our conclusion is therefore that we should open a well-equipped, up-to-date gym and fitness centre right at the heart of the financial district, preferably in a large office building that has shops and restaurants on the lower floors. We would attempt to compete on quality, and convenience of location, rather than price.

**Recommendations** (See Unit 24)

I believe that we should immediately issue a press release stating that we will stop using this chemical as soon as possible (but without giving a date). For the moment, however, we need to continue using this chemical. At the same time, I strongly recommend putting out a challenge to develop an alternative anti-bacterial chemical agent on www.innocentive.com.

Apart from the verbs in this paragraph – *should* [+ *infinitive*], *need to* [+ *infinitive*], *strongly recommend* [+ *-ing*] – other common verbs for stating recommendations include *ought to*, *must* and *is/would be advisable to* [+ *infinitive*].

### Writing minutes and summaries

Other common documents are the minutes of meetings – written records of what was said or decided ('action points') – and summaries or confirmations of what has been agreed in a phone conversation. These can be sent as documents or as emails.

For example:

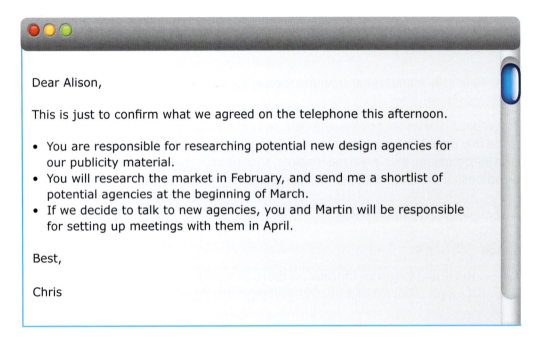

> Dear Alison,
>
> This is just to confirm what we agreed on the telephone this afternoon.
>
> - You are responsible for researching potential new design agencies for our publicity material.
> - You will research the market in February, and send me a shortlist of potential agencies at the beginning of March.
> - If we decide to talk to new agencies, you and Martin will be responsible for setting up meetings with them in April.
>
> Best,
>
> Chris

# Acknowledgements

**The author and publishers acknowledge the following sources of copyright material and are grateful for the permissions granted. While every effort has been made, it has not always been possible to identify the sources of all the material used, or to trace all copyright holders. If any omissions are brought to our notice, we will be happy to include the appropriate acknowledgements on reprinting.**

Diagram on p27 © Richard D. Lewis; Text on p39 by Yvonne Roberts © Copyright Guardian News & Media Ltd 2008; Text on p43 from *Nice Work* by David Lodge, published by Secker & Warburg. Reprinted by permission of The Random House Group Ltd and Curtis Brown Group Ltd, London on behalf of David Lodge. Copyright © David Lodge 1988; Excerpts on pp49 and 53 from *The World is Flat: A Brief History of the Twenty-first Century* by Thomas L. Friedman. Copyright © 2005, 2006, 2007 by Thomas L. Friedman. Reprinted by permission of Farrar, Straus and Giroux, LLC.; Text on p56 taken from *Quality is Free: The Art of Making Quality Certain* by Philip B. Crosby © The McGraw-Hill Companies, Inc.; Text on p67 taken from Marketing is Everything, *Harvard Business Review* © Regis McKenna; Text on p84 titled 'Rush to buy government bonds' by Julia Kollewe © Copyright Guardian News & Media Ltd 2009; Text on p84 titled 'Corporate bonds: the only "hot" story in town' by Julian Knight © *The Independent*, 11 January 2009; Text on p84 titled 'Why high-yield bonds are only for the brave' by Rob Griffin © *The Independent*, 28 March 2009; Text on pp89–90 taken from *Cityboy* by Geraint Anderson reproduced by permission of Headline Publishing Group Limited; Text on p93 titled 'Things to know about spread-betting' © NI Syndication, 2009; Text on p110 taken from chapter 3 'The Anatomy of Crisis' from *Free to Choose: A Personal Statement*, copyright © 1979 by Milton Friedman and Rose D. Friedman, reproduced by permission of Houghton Mifflin Harcourt Publishing Company (which was first published on October 29, 1979 in the issue of *The Journal of Portfolio Management*, Volume, No. 1 (pp15–21); Text on p110 taken from chapter 4 'Cradle to Grave' in *Free to Choose: A Personal Statement*, copyright © 1980 by Milton Friedman and Rose D. Friedman, reproduced by permission of Houghton Mifflin Harcourt Publishing Company; Text on p133 reprinted by the kind permission of Ha-Joon Chang; Text on pp136–7 reprinted by kind permission of Christian Gollier.

**Photographs**

The publishers are grateful to the following for permission to reproduce copyright photographs and material:

Key: l = left, c = centre, r = right, t = top, b = bottom

Alamy/©Profimedia International s.r.o. for p29(blb), /©Phil McElhinney for p29(bcr), /©Robert Harding Picture Library Ltd for p42(t), /©Illustration Works for p49, /©Chad Ehlers for p51, /©Jeremy Pardoe for p56(tr), /©Mark Sykes for p56(cr), /©imagebroker for p63(bl), /©Elizabeth Whiting & Associates for p63(cl), /©VStock for p63(cr), /©Maria Grazia Casella for p63(tr), /©David Robertson for p66(tr), /©The Print Collector for p67(t), /©J G Photography for p69(t), /©Mopic for p80(tr), /©Webstream for p80(br), /©Peter Carroll for p81, /©Joern Sackermann for p98(b), /©vario images GmbH & Co KG for p126; Andrew Lamb for p38(t); Atlantic Books for p21; Aviation Images/©Mark Wagner for p101; Cartoonbank.com, all rights reserved /©The New Yorker Collection 2004 Sam Gross for p10, /©The New Yorker Collection 2002 Tom Cheney for p15, /©The New Yorker Collection 2005 Robert Mankoff for p19, /©The New Yorker Collection 2003 Jack Ziegler for p25, /©The New Yorker Collection 1992 Tom Cheney for p30, /©2009 Robert Mankoff for p33, /©The New Yorker Collection 2004 Matthew Diffee for p39, /©The New Yorker

Collection 2006 David Sipress for p47, /©The New Yorker Collection 2006 Leo Cullum for p64, /©The New Yorker Collection 1997 Robert Mankoff for p66, /©The New Yorker Collection 2002 Alex Gregory for p70, /©The New Yorker Collection 2006 Tom Cheney for p88(r), /©The New Yorker Collection 1992 Leo Cullum for p95, /©The New Yorker Collection 2006 Bruce Eric Kaplan for p100, /©The New Yorker Collection 1997 Leo Cullum for p106, /©The New Yorker Collection 2004 Charles Barsotti for p109, /©The New Yorker Collection 2004 Michael Shaw for p112, /©The New Yorker Collection 2009 David Sipress for p115, /©2009 Robert Mankoff for p124; Charles Cotton for p102; Christian Gollier for p136(b); Competition Commission for p107(t); Corbis/©Sygma/Bob Daemmrich for p10(cr), /©Peer Grimm/dpa for p10(b), /©Jiang Yi/Xinhua Press for p55(t), /©Gideon Mendel for p55(tcr), /©Everett Kennedy Brown/EPA for p57, /©Kieran Doherty for p75(b), /©Kendra Luck/San Francisco Chronicle for p80(bl), /©John Gress/Reuters for p91, /©Image Source for p107(b), /©Hulton-Deutsch Collection for p117; Dell Inc. for p50; Education Photos/©Xin Pang for p44(tl), /©John Walmsley for p44(cr), 80(tl); Getty/AFP for p11(tl), /©Christian Lagereek for p29(br), /©Ian Murphy for p44(tc), /©Retrofile for p72, /©AFP for p130(b), /©Altrendo Travel for p132(t); istockphoto/©Thomas Stange for p29(bcl), /©Leonid Nyshko for p56(br), /©Rafa Gabowski for p56(bl), /©Matthew Dixon for p66(tr), /©Joel Johndro for p80(tc), /©Ilya Genkin for p128; Ian MacKenzie for p68(t), p139; John Antonakis for p36; Leica Microsystems for p48(b), p52(b); Mary Evans Picture Library for p67(b); Masterfile for p62(br); Melissa Glass for p62, 68(b); PA Photos/©AP for p10(cl), 12, /©Bullit Marquez/AP for p134; Pete Kyle for p83(t), p92; Photolibrary/©Creatas for p44(tr), /©Daryl Pederson for p55(bl), /©bambooSIL for p123; Pictures Colour Library/©Peter Treenor for p44(cl); Rex Features/©Sipa Press for p11(tr), /©Invicta Kent Media for p42(b), /©Sipa Press for p55(br); Richard Lewis Communications for p26(b); Science Photo Library/©NASA/Goddard Space Flight Center Scientific Visualization Studio for p136(t); Shutterstock/©Royik Yevgen for p44(bl), /©David Benton for p56(cl); Will Capel for pp11(c), 11(b), 18(t, c, b), 19(t), 24(l), 26(tl), 29(tl, cl, cr), 48(t), 52(t), 58, 76, 77, 98(t), 111, 116, 122, 125, 130(t), 132(b); www.cartoonstock.com for p83, p88(l).

Front cover of *Why Women Mean Business: Understanding the Emergence of our Next Economic Revolution* by Alison Maitland & Avivah Wittenberg-Cox on p38(b) reprinted by permission of Wiley Blackwell.

Front cover of *Nice Work* by David Lodge on p43 and *Free to Choose* by Milton and Rose Friedman on p109(b) reprinted by permission of Penguin Books Ltd.

Front cover of *Cityboy: Beer and Loathing in the Square Mile* on p89 reprinted by permission of Headline.

We have been unable to trace the copyright holder of the photograph on p69(b) and would welcome any information enabling us to do so.

**Illustrations**

p86 Sean Sims; pp119, 123 Ed McLachlan